Foreword

by the Chairmen of the Joint Policy Committee
of the East Anglia Consultative Committee and
the East Anglia Economic Planning Council

We welcome and commend this Report presented by Mr R. A. Bird on behalf of the Regional Strategy Team.

The preparation of a Regional Strategy had its inception in work undertaken both by the Economic Planning Council, in preparing 'East Anglia: A Study', published in 1968, and by the East Anglia Consultative Committee, which had prepared 'A Regional Survey' in 1967, 'A Regional Appraisal' in 1968 and a 'Regional Strategy Preparatory Report' in 1971. To ensure co-ordination and co-operation, a single project was undertaken jointly, and the Department of the Environment, which had by then adopted a policy of Regional Strategies for all regions, agreed to take part.

A team of professional officers, seconded from the staff of the local planning authorities and of the Department of the Environment, was created, with Mr Bird as Director. The Consultative Committee and the Economic Planning Council set up a Joint Policy Committee to supervise the work; this Committee, which consisted of three members from each of the two constituent bodies has met the Director, and officials from the local authorities and the Department, at quarterly intervals throughout the currency of the project. The Team began work in 1972, and has completed its work within the two-year period allocated for this stage.

The Director has also had meetings with the Consultative Committee and its Panels, and with the Council and its Committees, at which each stage of his work was explained and discussed. He has also consulted widely with interested bodies throughout the region.

Both the Council and the Consultative Committee have been closely associated with the project, and have been able to make their views known as the work developed. The Report is, of course, the sole responsibility of Mr Bird, but the close relationship which has developed between him and the Committee and Council, has ensured that his Report takes full account of the views of the two bodies and that the broad strategy proposed is in general acceptable to them.

When the Report has been considered publicly, we hope to be able to produce a joint document, setting out the views of the two bodies on the Report for submission to the Secretary of State for the Environment.

We should like to conclude by congratulating the Regional Strategy Team on completing the Report within the time allotted, to express our satisfaction with the Report itself, and in particular, our appreciation of Mr Bird's patience and co-operation in explaining his work as it proceeded, and in listening to our views.

J. R. D. Huckle
Walston

Preface

What does the future hold for East Anglia? In this report, we attempt to find some of the answers to this question. To do this, we have to look at a number of other questions on the way. What kind of change is likely? Where will it occur? Who will benefit and who will lose from it? Will the region continue to be a pleasant place to live and work in? Is it possible to influence what will happen? What is the best way to use this influence?

Each of these questions is important to the people who live in East Anglia. In practice, the answers to them will be determined by the foresight, enterprise and imagination that is shown in decisions about the future of the region. The opportunities brought by change will need to be seized. Critical to this will be the willingness of many people and agencies to work together constructively to achieve common goals. The reorganisation of local government, and the possibility of changes in the structure of regional bodies, may produce a better framework for this to happen. But the obstacles are large and very real. It will always be easier to define questions and the solutions to them very narrowly, without regard to their wider implications. Our experience of the people we have met in East Anglia makes us optimistic that these obstacles can be overcome.

Fortunately, our task has been much simpler. We have only to chart, to the best of our ability, the directions which decisions about the future of East Anglia could take. Even so, we are conscious of the inadequacy of the skills we bring to this task. We cannot claim perfect vision of an uncertain future. We do not pretend that the value judgments which we have had to make are necessarily the best. These limitations have made us aware of the need to draw on the experience of others as our work has taken shape, and we are indebted for the patience and sympathy they have shown to us. The same limitations also mean that a task such as this is never complete—others must follow and try to improve on what we have done.

This is not the point at which to set out our conclusions. We have done this at the end of the report as a short summary and a formal statement of our conclusions. We hope this will assist those who find the form we have adopted for the main body of the report difficult to follow. In this way, we trust we are able to convey the importance we attach to the questions we have tried to answer, and the modest contribution we hope to have made to their practical resolution.

East Anglia Regional Strategy Team
April, 1974, Cambridge

Contents

Figures

Maps

Section A   The Approach

The first section establishes the foundations upon which the remainder of the report is built. It is concerned with the approach we have adopted in the light of what we know about the region and our ability to affect the future.

Chapter one identifies some of the issues that seem to us to represent different aspects of concern facing East Anglia in the future. This enables us to focus upon the particular characteristics of the region, whilst at the same time allowing us to range over a wide spectrum of current and potential problems. In the second chapter, we turn to look at the various aspirations that appear to lie behind these issues. They can be formalised into a set of objectives for the future of the region, setting the longer term direction that change should follow. In order to allow for the maximum range of choice both now and in the future, the objectives must also be seen to be comprehensive. In this way, the objectives provide the width, whilst the issues give the focus, to the content of this report. With this background, in chapter three we describe the stages of work that have been followed. These have been set out to assist an understanding of both the structure of the report, and the way in which each stage has implications for those following, and, in certain cases, for those coming before.

Chapter 1

The Regional Issues

1.1 Introduction

1.1.1 The initial focus for the work set out in this report was achieved by defining a set of regional issues. In this way, it has been possible to draw most effectively on the valuable work of our predecessors and to bring in the experience and advice of many people directly involved with decisions affecting the future of the region. To put these issues into perspective, we begin this chapter with a brief description of the historical development of East Anglia. Particular emphasis is placed on recent, post-war changes when the momentum of growth in the region gathered pace. This helps to establish a continuity from the past for the issues which have to be considered for the future.

1.2 The Historical Background

1.2.1 The locational advantages of East Anglia within the national economy, which have again become evident, were most marked in the mediaeval period through to the seventeenth century. During this time, the region, particularly Norfolk and Suffolk, was not only the most densely populated area in England, but also a major contributor to national wealth. Cereal and stock farming formed the basis for exports of barley and woollen goods to the Continent from many local ports. The development of the textile industry, particularly in the fifteenth and sixteenth centuries, was stimulated by the influx of Flemish and French weavers, by the economic growth of the Low Countries, and later by the growth of London. Most of the present settlement pattern owes its origin and charm to the prosperity of this period. The shift of emphasis in the national economy towards the coalfields and the ports of the west coast, along with the growth of population in the cities, and the onset of water, and later, steam power, progressively eroded East Anglia's importance nationally.

1.2.2 Throughout the nineteenth century, the region's share of the population of England and Wales declined, particularly after 1851. Industry was confined to those activities with a strong craft tradition, small production units, and local markets. The small market towns at first shared in these developments, but later, concentration around the main towns became increasingly evident. The railway network was extended into the region, but with the exception of Peterborough, the lines served more to strengthen links with London than to develop the region. At the end of the century, therefore, there had been a net decline in the population of many small towns and villages, and with the agricultural depression the labour force employed in agriculture both declined and suffered considerable poverty. From a position of importance and prosperity the region had been transformed into a relatively isolated backwater, with its primary industry in a state of neglect and depression.

1.2.3 This state of affairs continued until the early nineteen-thirties, and was characterised by migration both to the towns, and to other parts of the country. The state of the national economy generally, however, ensured that a large proportion of the population remained dependent on agriculture. The revival of the national economy and the increased attention paid to agriculture in the thirties, led to an upturn in the region's prospects. The Second World War, which brought a large influx of defence establishments because of the proximity of the region to the Continent, continued this process.

1.2.4 During the post-war period, East Anglia has been drawn increasingly into the national context. Already by 1946, a third of the establishments in the region, employing 55% of workers in manufacturing, were controlled by interests outside the region. During the fifties, the region was growing faster than the country as a whole and some changes occurred in the internal distribution of the population. The development of personal transport encouraged the relative growth of the four main towns, and the continued stagnation or decline of many small towns and villages. These trends meant that while the larger towns, and the agricultural industry, faced a prosperous future, the more isolated parts of the region were adversely affected by the reduction in the numbers of agricultural workers and by the changes in the service functions of the smaller towns and villages.

1.2.5 It was in this context that the first town expansion schemes were agreed with the London County Council in the late 1950's and early 1960's, bringing prospects of new jobs and a larger population to selected towns, particularly in West Suffolk and Huntingdonshire. The more general prosperity of the 1960's continued to favour the growth of the main towns, and proximity to the South East became more important. Both people and jobs moved into the region in greater numbers than they had before, with planned migration becoming a major component of total population change in the decade. The region increased its share of national population, and became the most rapidly growing part of the country. The designation of Peterborough as a new town has been the peak of this phase in the region's recent history.

1.2.6 East Anglia is clearly in the later stages of

evolving from an agricultural to an urban society with an economy linked closely to national and international circumstances. The most apparent sign of this is its rapid population growth, of which the major component is net inward migration. The fast regional rate of growth obscures, however, the underlying pattern of wide differentials within the region. The towns experiencing planned migration are growing much faster than the region as a whole. At the same time, rural areas still experiencing some reduction in agricultural employment may be stagnating or declining; in terms of employment opportunities and services, if not always in terms of population. The rapid rate of growth from both planned and voluntary migration means that sensitive policies are required if change is to be absorbed without undue strain. Care has to be taken to ensure that the physical development of housing, the provision of jobs, and other private and public services, are kept in step with each other. Similarly, those areas not experiencing growth to the same degree also need attention to ensure that the standards of services they enjoy are reasonably equivalent to those in more favoured areas. The nature of much of the growth also reflects the dependence of East Anglia on external forces; not just on planned migration, but also on retirement migration, attracted by a pleasant environment, and by the relatively low house prices in much of the region compared with the neighbouring South East. Concern with such external pressures, and their potentially unbalancing effects on different parts of East Anglia, is clearly apparent in the regional issues.

1.3 The Sources for the Issues

1.3.1 Several sources can be drawn upon in seeking to define the issues in detail. Both the Economic Planning Council (EAEPC) and the Consultative Committee (EACC) have commissioned separately and jointly a number of studies. In October 1968, the EAEPC published 'East Anglia: A Study', which identified several issues for further consideration. The EAEPC also suggested the need for city-region studies around the four main centres: that for Cambridge was specially commissioned in association with the local authorities, and published in March 1974. The problem of the rural areas and small market towns has been the subject of a joint EAEPC and EACC project and the conclusions have been published as the 'Small Towns Study', (December 1972). This gives advice on the feasibility of helping rural areas through the selection and building-up of a few small scale growth points.

1.3.2 The EACC has produced three regional reports: a 'Regional Survey' in 1968, a 'Regional Appraisal' in 1969, and a 'Preparatory Report' for this Strategy in December 1971. This work has provided a source of ideas and essential background for the preparation of the report. Other background work helping in the definition of issues has included evidence presented to the Hunt Committee on the Intermediate Areas; this evidence was specifically concerned with the problems of rural areas. Much helpful information has also been made available, in the form of preparatory reports, by the structure plan teams in Norfolk and Suffolk, and by the local planning authorities themselves.

1.4 The Issues Defined

1.4.1 There is dissatisfaction with several aspects of life in this largely rural region. At the same time there is a concern to retain its more pleasant qualities. There is no easy or convenient solution to this. To gain some of the advantages enjoyed in more urbanised regions, people may have to surrender some of the qualities they would in ideal circumstances wish to retain. Alternatively, they may wish to retain these qualities and forego some of the other things that people in urban areas require to compensate for their less attractive environment. The answer probably lies in some middle course: the problem is to find it. The following list of issues, therefore, contains a mixture of views about the existing problems of the region; assumptions regarding the nature and extent of change that may occur; the effects of policies in encouraging or modifying this change; the type of future that people want; and the aspirations they may have about that future.

1.4.2 There is concern for the **employment structure** in parts of the region. There is a relatively heavy dependence on agricultural employment, which is contracting. Generally, there are fewer women in employment, local concentrations of male unemployment, and lower than average wage rates. For school leavers, there is a narrow range of employment opportunities, with few openings in professional and managerial jobs. This results, over time, in the out-migration of the younger, more energetic, person seeking better opportunities elsewhere. Growth in manufacturing and service employment is concentrated in the major centres and in the town expansion schemes, which offer larger pools of labour and of general skills. Jobs in the public sector, and in service employment, are likely to become increasingly important.

1.4.3 There is a high proportion of **small, isolated, rural communities** in parts of the region. The degree to which these combine low household incomes, relatively poor housing, employment opportunities restricted largely to agriculture, with long journeys to work to other employment, poor access to social, health and education facilities, and the out-migration of younger age groups, needs to be considered. The provision of public services (gas, sewerage, electricity, water, etc.) to these communities is likely to involve higher costs.

1.4.4 There is concern over the quality of **housing and public buildings in rural areas.** The stock of public and community buildings in the more remote areas appears to be old and in need of replacement. The economics of such replacement leads to concentration into larger units at a few centres. Similarly, the rural housing stock may be less adequate than the urban stock, though this receives little expression. New housing may need to be concentrated into a number of selected settlements.

1.4.5 The original service functions of many of the region's **small market towns** are being eroded by improvements in transport, increases in personal mobility, and changes in distribution methods. These towns, and their buildings, are an important part of the character of the region. Any attempt to retain their service functions, or to increase other forms of employment, raises difficult questions about means to these ends, and those of ensuring that their essential qualities are maintained. The 'Small Towns Study', referred to above, has explored many of these questions, and has made a number of proposals for improvement.

1.4.6 The **medium sized towns** in the region, King's Lynn, Great Yarmouth, Lowestoft, Bury St. Edmunds, and perhaps Thetford, have different characteristics and problems. The coastal towns have difficulties in maintaining their economic base in the face of competition from larger centres, combined with remoteness and poor communications. The holiday industry and tourism produce problems of seasonal unemployment. The towns away from the coast have looked towards town development to secure their future, and major questions are concerned with the effects of this policy, and its possible continuation.

1.4.7 The four **major urban centres** in the region (Norwich, Cambridge, Ipswich and Peterborough) are growing. For Norwich and Cambridge, the impact of further growth on the historic cores of the towns is a continuing cause for concern. The size, form, and location of this growth is an issue allied to the question of how it may be implemented. There are also questions about the impact of growth on the surrounding areas and the possibility of diverting some of it to more remote parts of the region.

1.4.8 There is a more general concern with the **effects of rapid population growth.** Unrestrained growth could create severe problems for parts of the region in the future. Growth is unevenly distributed throughout the region, and those areas now under pressure are likely to face pressures for further growth. The provision of facilities may not keep pace with demand: there is the less tangible problem of absorbing newcomers into the social and economic structure of local communities. Any imbalance in the provision of jobs and housing can lead to dislocations of production, and considerable hardship for those involved.

1.4.9 There is a strong feeling that the region could lose some of its character and traditions through **external pressures.** The increasing influence of London, the removal of control of major firms and divisions to centres outside East Anglia, and the apparent insensitivity of some national policies to regional and local questions, are all aspects of this feeling, and of the effects of accelerated change. Particular concern has been expressed about the increasing tendency for certain resources to be exploited to the advantage of other parts of the country without subsequent benefit accruing to the region. This applies to water resources and reservoirs in a climatically dry region; sand and gravel as a reserve for the London area; brickclay, offshore gas and oil, and some possibility of inland exploration of reserves.

1.4.10 Allied to the insecurity induced by change is the question of the **absorption of people migrating** into the region. There are two major streams. One, of younger working age families, is directed towards the new and expanding towns, leading to the rapid population growth cited above. This stream will be influenced by variations to the planned migration programme. The second stream of more elderly migrants, retiring, or anticipating retirement, is attracted by the coast, the more picturesque villages, and even towards very remote rural areas if relatively inexpensive housing is available.

1.4.11 A further external influence which has aroused considerable interest is the effect of Britain's entry into the **European Economic Community.** The main immediate effects are foreseen on agriculture and on the ports. There may well be other equally significant effects, particularly as the Community develops its regional, economic and social policies. The regulations on subsidies and grants to freight and passenger transport services are one such area.

1.4.12 **The region's ports** are well placed to benefit from increased trade with Europe. They are planned to grow very quickly over the next few years. Their trade is not based on major industrial centres in the immediate hinterland, and their transport connections to the north and west are across tortuous cross-country routes. These links require capital investment if they are to carry the traffic loads that port expansion is now creating. At present the heavy freight traffic has detrimental effects, not only on other road users, but also on the environment of those towns through which it has to pass.

1.4.13 No other issue occasions so much discussion, or has presented more difficulties for definition than that of **communications,** and the transport using the route systems. It is a series of related questions which can be treated under the headings of roads, railways, public transport using these physical structures, and air transport.

(a) Roads

Car ownership rates in the region are high and increasing more rapidly than in the rest of the country, reflecting the increasing dependence of the population on private forms of transport. East-west links with other regions, particularly the North and Midlands, are especially difficult, with the Fens still providing something of a barrier. Frustration and delays arise from heavy port and industrial traffic, seasonal holiday trips, and slow moving agricultural vehicles on narrow roads. Improvements are concerned largely with the progressive dualling of major routes, and with providing bypasses to the towns, rather than with the provision of new routes. As yet, the national motorway system does not extend into the region, and there seems little prospect that it will do so for a considerable time. Consequently, the dramatic reductions in journey times in other parts of the country have left East Anglia in a relatively more isolated position. Furthermore, the development of giant industrial and container traffic in conjunction with the motorway system has led to increasing numbers of these vehicles travelling across the region along roads which were not designed to accommodate them and which do not have a suitable alignment. There must also be doubt as to whether the emphasis given to journey-to-work difficulties in national criteria for road improvements is wholly applicable to a region with low population density and a high seasonal incidence of recreational traffic. It would, therefore, seem that attention must be given to questions about the size and length of industrial and port vehicles in relation to the nature of the roads they are using, and also about the size and peaking of recreational traffic.

(b) Rail
Rail closures in the region have been widespread in the past, with no direct benefits accruing from the national electrification programme. Almost all the existing passenger services are operating at a loss, and there could be further reductions in services, and in the number of lines and stations open. Changes in freight services could also be significant in terms of the movement of goods by road and rail to the ports in the region.

(c) Public Transport/Bus Services
Rural bus services have suffered a severe decline, and may well be further curtailed. As yet there does not appear to have emerged either a clear policy on the degree and nature of subsidy to these services, or an alternative form of transport orientated to the needs of those sections of the population who do not have access to private vehicles.

(d) Air Transport
There would seem to be few problems at present concerning airports and opportunities for business flights. It seems unlikely that the region will be able to support the development of a major airport. The region does possess a series of defence airfields, which represent a considerable capital investment. A change in defence requirements could conceivably lead to the release of one or more of these sites, which may provide an opportunity to upgrade civilian flying facilities at relatively low costs.

1.4.14 Allied to the question of improving communications is concern for the impacts of **recreation and tourism** upon the region. The relatively unspoilt coastline, countryside and towns of the region are increasingly attractive to a wide range of visitors. These visits take many forms—tourism, weekend, and day trips—and use a variety of accommodation—caravans, boats, second or holiday homes, guest houses and hotels. The improvements of roads to the south and west of the region will increase these pressures. There is considerable concern about the impact on towns, on coast and countryside, on wildlife, and about the long term effects on the local economy and social services.

1.4.15 There is not only concern about competing demands for the land but also about modern **agricultural methods** employed to farm it. Capital intensive farming has far-reaching effects on the region's landscape, wildlife, and environment. The removal of hedgerows and trees, land drainage, factory farming, the disposal of animal sewage, the side-effects of pesticides and fertilisers, the effects of heavy machinery on soil structure and country roads, the possibilities of damage to archaeological remains beneath cultivated land, and the changing quality of new farm buildings, are all specific instances of things causing concern. The associated decline in the agricultural labour force has been instrumental in changing the basis of the rural community and of its villages and smaller towns.

1.4.16 The issues facing East Anglia are thus only partly a legacy from the past. There is as much concern about the possible effects of those pressures for change, many of them external, that are moulding its future. This applies not only to the expanding influence of London and its metropolitan area, but also to the likely effects of policies, and changes in them, conceived by the EEC and at national level. How far is it possible to influence the ways in which these forces affect the region as a whole, and specific places and people within it? Can services be adapted to meet changing demands, and can the environment be managed to resolve competing demands upon it? Implicit in the issues, and in these questions, are the aspirations that people have for the future of the region. In the next chapter, an attempt is made to formalise these aspirations into a set of objectives for the future of the region. These objectives can act as guidelines in the search for answers to both issues and questions.

Chapter 2

Objectives for the Region

2.1 Introduction

2.1.1 The regional issues express concern about a wide range of topics, although they concentrate on questions of particular importance to East Anglia. Even so, it is no small task to cover all the questions raised, and the kind of answers that are required. What objectives do they imply? Are there other objectives at present dormant that may be important to the future of the region? To cover this second question it is useful to begin by discussing the overall purpose of this report, before identifying the objectives appropriate to the region.

2.2 The Purposes of a Regional Strategy

2.2.1 The main purpose of a strategy is to identify broad economic, social, and land use policies which can guide development and change in the region towards 'desirable' ends. The strategy should:

(i) provide a framework for major decisions on investment and development, by central and local government, public corporations, and the private sector, and

(ii) provide a context within which local planning authorities can prepare structure plans.

The strategy thus requires broad statements on the future economic potential of the region, and on the way in which it can adjust to future change. These are designed to help the region's decision makers, suggesting policies and courses of action that enable the region to develop in an ordered fashion. The strategy stresses co-operation in policies in seemingly disparate fields—such as transport, housing and recreation—to the benefit of all parties. It has to take account of existing commitments, found especially in capital investment programmes, and go beyond physical development to look at the development of attitudes, values, and expectations, as expressed in broader social priorities.

2.2.2 The strategy covers a long time span—some twenty to thirty years. This requires it to look beyond short term tactical questions, although the practical problems of putting it into operation must not be ignored. Further, a study of the total resources available, and agencies involved in putting recommendations into practice, is an essential element of the work. In sum, the purpose of the strategy is to suggest a desirable, yet at the same time, robust, path for the development of East Anglia until the end of the century. We are interpreting development in its fullest sense—the assimilation of all changes likely to affect the lives of both the existing population and future generations.

2.3 The Objectives of the Strategy

2.3.1 The main reason for identifying regional objectives is to provide some yardsticks to help in deciding between alternative courses of action. They are essential if we are to understand, and therefore plan for, what is recognised as a 'desirable' future. They must be as comprehensive as possible; they must relate to detailed policy proposals as well as to more general points; and they must state directions for the region's future, rather than inflexible targets to be achieved. The final list is in fact an amalgam of points culled from the issues, from experience gained in similar studies, and from commonsense.

2.3.2 As a first step, it is useful to state a single overriding goal for the region, encompassing the major objectives. This has as its core a concern with the use of scarce resources available to the region for the benefit of future as well as present generations, both within and outside East Anglia. This is as follows:

to use resources made available from both national and regional sources to contribute both to national welfare, and to the improvement of the quality of life in the region in the future.

2.3.3 What are the main features of this goal? First of all it is concerned with the resources available for the future development of the region. Secondly, there is a concern with the relationship between East Anglia and other parts of Great Britain. Thirdly there is a desire to improve the standard of living of the region's population. This implies that the distribution of such improvements should be fair, and have regard for the life styles of future generations. Finally, it does not state an optimum position or target to be reached, relying upon the achievement of compromise for the resolution of conflicts. In the following paragraphs we consider each of these features, or groups of objectives, in turn.

2.4 Resources

Five separate resource objectives can be identified.

2.4.1. The first objective requires the **capital costs** of development and construction to be kept as low as possible. This need partly explains the concentration of population growth in the region—why growth follows past growth. It is normally cheaper to build one large sewage works, for instance, than a series of small works of equivalent total capacity. With a fixed budget, more can be done in total when individual projects allow low unit costs to be realised.

2.4.2 The second objective is to keep the day-to-day **running costs** of services and facilities as low as possible, and in many cases is directly related to capital costs. Fewer people are required to service one large power station than many small units. The forces behind this objective are illustrated by the tendency to concentrate population and employment growth into the major centres. The relatively high costs of servicing more remote areas helps explain the falling standards noted in the issues. It can conflict with capital costs when an inexpensive solution to a current problem leads to higher running costs in later years.

2.4.3 The third objective is to make full use of the region's **labour resources.** Although there is some concern with unemployment in agricultural areas and in coastal towns, the objective does not just imply the maintenance of full employment. It is also concerned with the range and variety of work offered, and with the effectiveness of training facilities, so as to ensure that the potential skills in the workforce are used to best advantage.

2.4.4 A fourth objective is to keep the rate of take-up of undeveloped **land resources** as slow as possible, because once land is built on it is unlikely to return to its former state. It requires not only consideration of the quality of land being taken for new development, but also reassessment of the use made of land already developed.

2.4.5 A fifth objective is to conserve the region's **environmental resources,** both natural and man-made. In the case of the natural environment, demands from several sources must be carefully managed. There are demands from recreation, wildlife and ecological conservation, agriculture, building, and the exploitation of land for reservoirs, brickclay, sand and gravel. Issues of growth, and those of the impact of agriculture and recreation upon the environment, give some indication of the priority to be placed on achieving this objective. The impact of rapid growth on historic sites and settlements is of equal concern in conserving man-made resources.

2.5 The Region and the National Economy.

Three objectives concerned with East Anglia's relationship with Great Britain as a whole have been identified.

2.5.1 The first objective of this kind is concerned with East Anglia's **contribution to the national economy.** This involves producing the goods and services required by other parts of the country and for export. The priority given to improving road communications with the Haven Ports is one example demonstrating the current force of this objective. The planned migration programme is related to the service East Anglia is providing for London. The provision of homes for retirement migrants is a further example The development of tourism provides a service for visitors from other countries, as well as from the rest of Great Britain, whilst the region's universities have an important national role.

2.5.2 The second objective involves the strengthening of and **support for the regional economy.** Good communications and good public transport systems widen both labour markets and final goods markets, allowing a choice of labour for the firm, and the opportunity to manufacture at an economic scale. The achievement of the objective may rest upon a

concentration of population and employment—a certain scale of industry is required, for instance, before supporting services such as solicitors, merchant banks, education facilities, and office equipment suppliers, will set up locally.

2.5.3. The third objective seeks to **shield the region** from the impacts of changes occurring in the national economy. Many issues express this concern—fear of the effects of joining the EEC; the extension of metropolitan influences in the south and west; and the rate of migration, both planned and voluntary, that the region is now accepting. It is realised to the extent that local markets are developed, and as wide a range of industry as possible is established. It expresses a concern with the development of industries that are especially vulnerable to swings in the national economy. Achievement would be aided by the strengthening of local firms, under local management, reducing the likelihood of closure in difficult economic conditions.

2.6 The Quality of Life.

Four separate objectives highlight the major features involved in improving the 'standard of living' of the region's population.

2.6.1. The first objective is to give people the opportunity to increase their **incomes.** This involves giving people a choice of employment, so that they can realise their potential skills. It also involves training; family incomes can rise if workers develop their skills and take on more demanding and better-paid jobs. In many rural areas, the lack of opportunities for female employment depresses household incomes. Improvements to public services could help redress this situation.

2.6.2 The second objective, concerned with **public sector services,** has two main elements. It requires the achievement of recognised standards in such services and, leading directly on from this, seeks to ensure that people are aware of, and can make use of, the services to which they are entitled. Concern arises, once again, in rural areas, and smaller urban settlements. A larger number of small schools and of teachers is required in areas of low population density. The concentration of secondary and further education establishments into larger settlements brings transport problems. Particular concern over standards arises in the rapidly growing areas. Here, the new population may include a large proportion of young children, requiring the provision of facilities in step with the house-building programme.

2.6.3 The third objective is to ensure that **goods and services** produced by the private sector are available to people in the region. In urban areas, rapid growth can mean that services are inadequate, and the use of the private car has led to the concentration of services such as shopping, into a smaller number of centres. The elderly, the young, and those living in rural areas, are experiencing greater difficulties as a result.

2.6.4 The final objective looks for the most effective mix of **standards and opportunities** in those services provided by both the public and private sectors. Housing and transport are the most important of these services, though recreation and employment are also significant.

2.7 The Distribution of Improvements to the Quality of Life.

Two objectives cover the way in which the quality of life improvements are shared amongst the region's population.

2.7.1 The first objective is to share improvements in standards of living fairly between **different sectors of the population.** This means that disparities between the standards enjoyed by various sectors should certainly not increase, and where possible, should decrease. This objective is again founded on the concern that the opportunities available to the unskilled to improve their incomes, for instance, are far fewer than the opportunities available to the skilled. Such a situation is difficult to remedy. Restricted job opportunities lead to the loss of the more energetic and younger members of the workforce, a situation discouraging to a potential new employer.

2.7.2 The second objective is to share improvements in standards of living fairly between **different parts of the region.** Again, existing disparities between fast and slow growth areas should be reduced if possible, but certainly not increased. Concern with employment and services is felt in the central and northern rural parts of the region, rather than in the prosperous main centres. In the larger towns a fairly wide range of employment is available, including modern, well-paid industry and services. To the extent that new services are provided on the criterion of population growth, improved equipment and facilities come to these prosperous towns, but not to slowly growing rural areas. The issue of public transport is again important. Custom is sufficiently large in towns to support a viable service, but country services must rely on government subsidies, or on the munificence of the bus companies. Many issues suggest that existing pressures and policies are widening disparities in real income levels between different parts of the region.

2.8 The Timing of Improvements to the Quality of Life.

The two final objectives are concerned with when and how the region should accept improvements to the population's standard of living.

2.8.1 The first objective is **to continue improvements in living conditions** over time. It seeks to ensure that such conditions improve, and certainly do not decline, in the future. Issues expressing concern over the use of the region's irreplaceable resources reflect this aim. It implies careful management of the exploitation of mineral and water resources, and the need to avoid excessive building in areas of outstanding landscape and agricultural value. It is reflected in a concern for the preservation of historic towns and settlements.

2.8.2 The second objective is to **smooth development** in such a way that short term fluctuations in the standard of living are avoided. The concern expressed about the effects of rapid population growth puts a high priority on this objective. The fear is that short term dislocations can occur in, for instance, service provision when supply and demand are out of balance. There is also a concern for the effects of a rapid growth in tourism, not only in terms of the overuse of some facilities, such as in the Broads, but also in terms of the effects on routes serving tourist areas. Rapid port development without associated road improvements can also lead to poorer living conditions for those living next to these routes.

2.9 The Basis of Choice

2.9.1 Three qualities of the objectives described above should be noted. Firstly, they are sufficiently broad to be applied to other regions apart from East Anglia. Secondly, they attempt to be comprehensive. It is essential that in making choices for the future of the region no substantial factor should be overlooked. Finally there is considerable scope for conflict between the different objectives. At each stage, the priority given to individual objectives has to be carefully judged. In the following chapter, we set out the stages of work that have been used to identify choices, and to assess the degree to which these choices realise the different objectives.

10

Chapter 3   The Stages of the Analysis

3.1 Introduction

3.1.1 The issues and the objectives for the future of East Anglia provide the basis for the analysis set out in this report. In this chapter we go on to describe in a simplified form the mechanics of the process we have adopted to resolve the questions that are posed. In doing this, the hope is that the description will also act as a guide to the structure of the remainder of the report, and will allow the reader to have some appreciation of the relationships between each of the stages of the work.

3.2 The Main Questions

3.2.1 Firstly, it is useful to state the main questions which arise from the regional issues, and to which answers have to be found. We are interested in what will happen to the region as a whole—**how much** change can be expected?—and whether or not it is either possible or desirable to influence the amount and nature of change that is likely to take place. **Where** will this change occur? The intensity of the impacts of change will vary from place to place in the region. **Who** will be affected by change? For some people, the future will bring much greater opportunities, while others may suffer some reductions in the things they enjoy. **When** will change occur? It is much simpler to absorb change when it is steady, rather than when it is erratic.

3.2.2 To find answers to any of these questions, an attempt has to be made to look into the future. Each of the forecasts that result—of the growth of population, of hedgerow loss, of the demand for public transport—should be consistent with all the other forecasts. There is no assured method of achieving this. All forecasts are subject to uncertainty, and the degree of uncertainty is greater when contemplating the prospect of change in international circumstance and national policy over the lengthy timespan covered by this report. It is debatable too at what point it is worthwhile taking the most extreme contingencies into account.

3.2.3 Given these forecasts, it is then possible to consider the effects that the indicated changes will have on the region. The objectives described in chapter two provide broad guidelines for deciding the degree to which these effects are desirable. The next step is to consider whether or not the expected situation can be influenced. This implies policies to encourage, restrain, or in some other way modify, the expected outcome of these pressures in the region. In some cases it is possible to devise a number of policy options, while in others it is more appropriate to move directly to a conclusion on the mix of policies

that seems to be required. The nature of the policies may be dependent on the degree of uncertainty associated with the forecasts. Where these are reasonably firm, the policies can be more precise; where there is much more uncertainty, policies must be capable of adapting to a wide range of contingencies. In all cases, the process of arriving at conclusions is one of assessment and judgment.

3.2.4 The steps described above express the overall approach in a very simple form. The reality of the analysis is more complex. This is particularly so in the final stages, where the conclusions from the various strands are drawn together, and reconciled where there is some apparent conflict. This process of reconciliation is made easier if a logical order has been used for the analysis. Similarly, we have decided that it would be easier to understand the reasoning that lies behind the conclusions, if we adopted for the report a structure which paralleled the main stages of the analysis we have carried out. This we have done. It is shown in outline in Figure 3.1, and is described in brief in the next part of this chapter.

3.3 The Structure

3.3.1 The next stage (Section B) of the strategy looks at the future of East Anglia as a whole during the next thirty years. The region is open to external influences affecting the styles of life of its population, as well as the rate at which that population grows. In this stage, therefore, the emphasis is placed on forecasting the wide range of future changes that could have an impact on the region, many emanating from outside East Anglia itself. These external 'pressures for change' include changes in personal behaviour—particularly working and spending habits; changes in technology—such as increased use of telecommunications; growing pressure from the Midlands and South East—for housing, recreation, etc.; and the impact of EEC membership. These 'pressures for change' are then interpreted for their effects on the main features of the region's life—among others, its employment and industrial structure, its agriculture, and its attractiveness as a place to live and work. This interpretation is taken a step further for population and employment growth where the magnitude of change becomes most obvious. The results provide the opportunity to consider in terms of the objectives whether or not the expected rate of growth is too fast or too slow, and whether it can be modified to better advantage. It is also intended as the base upon which all the later stages of the analysis can draw.

3.3.2 The third stage (Section C) builds on the second. It is concerned with where population and employ-

Figure 3.1 The Stages of Work

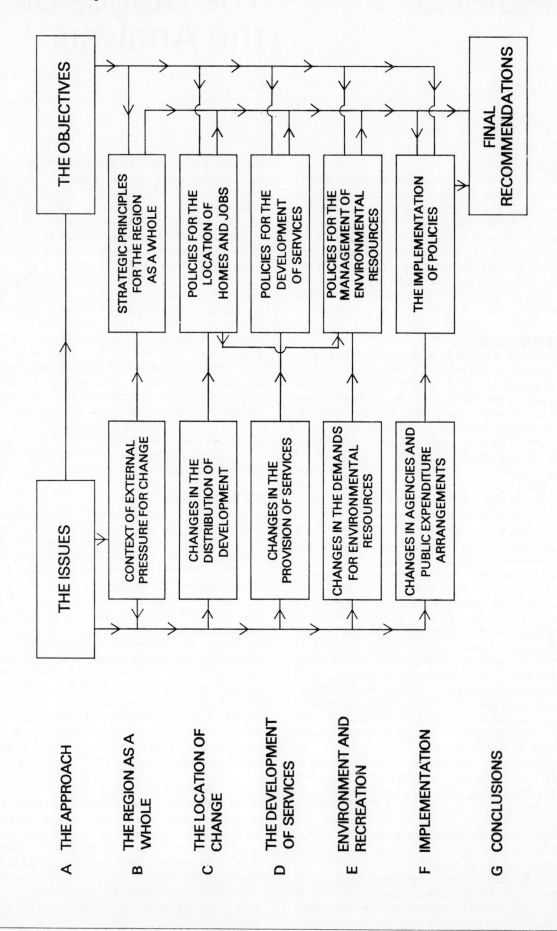

ment change will occur and with the main transport links that support and influence this pattern. Through the examination of a number of 'ideal' patterns it is possible to arrive at a set of strategic principles to be taken into account in decisions of this nature in the future. From these principles it is then reasonable to suggest a broad pattern of development for the region. This is recommended for further consideration in the preparation of structure plans, in which more detailed questions of local feasibility and advantage can be set against this regional perspective.

3.3.3 In the fourth stage (Section D), attention is transferred to those services, in both the public and private sectors, that make major contributions to the quality of life which people in the region enjoy. It builds on the context of change and overall population growth established in the second stage, and on the location of that growth considered at the third stage. At the same time, those concerned with the forward planning of each service are constantly exploring ways of improving those services, and there may also be considerable potential in more integrated forms of service provision. From these sources, an attempt has been made to indicate the broad principles which could guide service provision in the future, and the more specific recommendations that flow from those principles.

3.3.4 The fifth stage (Section E) of the work runs concurrently with the fourth stage. It is concerned with those physical features of the region that are not so easily adaptable to change, and where change, once it has occurred, is likely to be irreversible. It concentrates on the natural and man-made environmental resources of East Anglia, and the demands that are being made on these by modern agriculture, recreation and tourism, and, to a lesser extent, by population and employment growth. The approach which has been adopted goes beyond husbanding resources in response to these pressures. It seeks more positive policies by which the environmental qualities of the region can be managed in order to work with these pressures, producing an environment which is not merely conserved but enhanced.

3.3.5 The final, and sixth stage (Section F), looks at the implementation of the principles and recommendations made in the other sections. It begins with a review of the agencies which are concerned in the future development of the region. In the light of expected changes, and of the policies that are put forward as a consequence, ways are suggested in which these agencies could be strengthened separately and at the same time effect the degree of joint operation that would seem desirable. As a second step, it examines the financial resources available, particularly to the public sector, and the possibilities that exist for reallocating these along the lines indicated in the remainder of the report. Finally, it looks beyond the present report, to ways in which its conclusions can be kept up-to-date as we advance into the future. This includes both proposals for further research, where we consider improvements to the base on which it has been necessary to construct this report, and means of monitoring and reviewing the strategic principles and recommendations on a continuous basis.

3.4 The Reconciliation between Stages

3.4.1 We have previously stated that the order of study does not follow in practice as neatly as the above framework would suggest. A certain amount of feedback is necessary. A particular instance of this, which could cause confusion if the different sections of this report are read out of sequence, is the amount and location of population growth in the region. It is evident that the scale of population growth will be affected by the choice of areas where population growth is to be either encouraged or discouraged. This choice will, in turn, be influenced by considerations of service provision and the sensitivity of environmental resources. In this report, we have brought forward in broad terms these latter considerations to the third stage, but there remains the question of the interplay between the second and third stages. To illustrate this, Figure 3.2 sets out the initial estimates of population growth in East Anglia arising from the second stage, and the way in which these ranges have been narrowed, following the reconsideration made in the light of the conclusions of the third stage.

3.4.2 This demonstrates that the conclusions from each stage of the work must be compared with the conclusions of other stages, and reconciled. In some cases, conflicts may be resolved by introducing a compensating policy. As an example, it may be desirable on certain grounds to encourage population growth in an area which also has high priority for environmental conservation. The matching of these two conflicting claims may be resolved by the establishment of joint committee structures in which the operation can be managed.

3.4.3 The conclusions also combine what is likely and feasible, with what is judged to be desirable, thus incorporating value judgments which may be rooted in present experience. It is not possible to claim that such value judgments are necessarily the best, or those that will prove valid in the future. By acknowledging them, we hope that they will be carefully scrutinised, so that those that follow us will be able to work on a firmer basis. Finally, the coverage of the report and the conclusions it presents has meant many omissions in terms of detail. It is inevitable that some of these omissions will be criticised, but we hope that in overall terms we have achieved a balance between clarity, length, and depth of material necessary to justify the conclusions.

Figure 3.2 overleaf

13

Figure 3.2
Estimated population growth in East Anglia, 1971–2001 (Thousands)

Year or Period		1971	1981	(1971–1981)	1991	(1981–1991)	2001	(1991–2001)
Stage B Estimates	Total population	1680	1895–1940		2045–2250		2170–2600	
	Growth in decade			(215–260)		(150–310)		(125–350)
Revised Estimates on basis of Stage C	Total population	1680	1895–1940		2090–2220		2225–2525	
	Growth in decade			(215–260)		(195–280)		(135–305)

Source: East Anglia Regional Strategy Team

Section B

The Region as a whole

This second section takes as its starting point the premise that the region does not exist in isolation, but is part of a much wider social and economic system. The main thrusts for change within the region will come from outside sources. What does this imply for the future of the region as a whole, and for the choices that are open at this level?

Chapter four examines the major pressures for change and the impacts they are likely to have on East Anglia. This analysis is taken forward as possible population and employment growth levels. In the following chapter the focus moves to an assessment of the way in which this growth and its impacts affect the achievement of the objectives. The next stage is to establish the degree to which it is possible to promote or retard the volume and type of growth that the region will experience. This provides, in turn, a basis for defining those principles appropriate to the selection of policies best suited to achieve regional objectives. This set of principles consequently underlines those other principles and proposals put forward in the rest of the report for different areas, and for different aspects of development.

Chapter 4

The Rate and Nature of Change

4.1 Introduction

4.1.1 A broad outline of the changes that will take place in the region over the next twenty to thirty years can be quickly sketched in. The region will continue to grow at a relatively rapid rate, increasing in importance in national terms, as its towns and industries achieve greater significance. These expectations reflect not only the attraction of the region as a place to live and work, but also the ability of many modern industries to locate away from the source of their raw materials. Beyond this, however, there is much less certainty about how the region will change, other than that such change will occur, and at an accelerating rate. It would be a relatively simple task to construct a lengthy list of the changes that have occurred in the past twenty years, whose significance has not been foreseen, and which now form part of everyday life. Any attempt to construct a similar list for the next twenty years must be hazardous and there are bound to be surprises. What is more certain is that East Anglia will not be unique in the way it changes. Its social and economic life is increasingly intermingled with the wider national and international scene. In the modern world, a poor harvest in East Anglia will have little effect on what people in the region have to eat, but world food shortages, or problems of energy supply, are certain to have a major impact on everyday life, as in many other areas.

4.2 The Context of Change

4.2.1 The main changes that will affect the region in the future will come from outside. Five major sources of pressure can be identified. Firstly, in their personal patterns of behaviour and spending, people express social choices and values which can be expected to show considerable variations over time. Secondly, developments in technology, and in ways in which that technology is managed, will lift some of the restrictions—perhaps imposing others—on how people choose to live. In practice, these two forces come together within the framework of a mixed economy, where some of the choices people make are left to individual decision, whilst others are carried out through the collective action of government. There is no clearcut and final dividing line between these two types of action, and the boundary is constantly being explored and redefined in terms of the problems of the day. A current example is the scrutiny of the complementary roles of public and private transport, and it may be some time before a clear and stable consensus emerges. The two remaining forces are apparently more immediate in their nature. The recent entry into the European Economic Community, (EEC), is already having initial effects, and the development of the Community's policies in the future could well have far-reaching implications. In a different way, the proximity of both London, and its dependent areas, to East Anglia can be expected to exert an increasing influence in the future. The South East already supplies much of the region's new industry and population, and is the main source of pressure seeking to take advantage of the environmental attractions of East Anglia.

4.2.2 It is impossible to know all the forms that change from these sources will take. In order to prepare for them, however, it is important to attempt a better understanding, allied with a greater vigilance in the future. To do this, a method of exploring the future—known as the Delphi Technique—was adopted in a modified form. Panels for each of the pressures for change were drawn from members and officers of the Economic Planning Council and Board, the Consultative Committee, and selected outside experts. Members of each of the Panels were asked to complete a questionnaire, prepared from scanning the relevant literature, in terms of what was likely to happen, rather than what should happen. This method had the advantage of involving and drawing on the experience of a large number of people, knowledgeable about the region, and concerned in some of the major decisions about its future. It also lessened the degree of reliance on past trends, which can be a poor guide to the future. At the same time, some reservations have to be stated. There are many potential sources of bias and omission. These include the selection and expression of the questions, the choice of members of the Panels, and each individual's willingness to make forecasts on the basis of limited information. The timing of the exercise in relation to national circumstances could affect the degree of optimism or pessimism present in the results, and it was also noticeable that the forecasts made tended to predict change in the first 10–15 years, rather than later. The method does not lead to a nicely rounded and precise picture of East Anglia in the future, unclouded by any uncertainty. The large number of possible combinations of individual forecasts precludes such an outcome. What follows, therefore, is an interpretation of the results in terms of the likely effects of change on the future of East Anglia, rather than a clearcut catalogue of events.

4.3 The Context Study Results

4.3.1 There will be both material and less tangible changes in people's lives in the rest of the century.

In material terms, the annual rate of growth in the Gross National Product is expected to increase to an average of 4% and above by 1980. On this basis, real incomes would increase by half by the eighties and perhaps double by the end of the century. A similar scale of growth is expected in private household expenditure, probably resulting in substantial increases in leisure activities and personal mobility. A slower rate of growth of public expenditure is anticipated, compared with that of the recent past. In less tangible terms, there is expected to be increasing tension between the drive towards greater efficiency and the rise in individual and community awareness. In principle, efficiency, coupled with the application of technology, will continue to be seen as the mainspring of economic growth, leading to greater affluence and improved social welfare. In practice, the application of efficiency criteria to the conduct of both business and government, is likely to lead to increased centralisation and larger units, giving rise to decisions which are apparently remote from, and arbitrary in their effects on, individuals and communities. The demand for improved responsiveness to these more local circumstances, as channelled and highlighted through mass communications, increases the possibility that social moods will become more volatile, and that a wide and stable consensus about aims for the future will be less assured. The reconciliation of these tensions may be sought through increased experimentation with social institutions, bridging and co-ordinating the executive actions of authorities and firms over wide areas of economic and social life.

4.3.2 Many of these tensions will be felt in the economic life of the region, with the continued spread of automation in industry and offices, and in the growth of financial and industrial groups on an international scale. As a result, the ultimate control of both production units, and the employment they provide in East Anglia, is expected to become more remote. This brings the prospect of changes that are unrelated either to the performance of individual units, or to the social implications. Similarly, the growth of automation will increase the amount of shift working, with significant changes in the employment structure. There will be an overall redistribution of manpower into the service sector, a higher level of skills will be required, and the labour force will need to adapt to several changes in occupation through working life. One result will be a reduction in the number of unskilled jobs, and a rise in the number of people who are regarded as unemployable. Some compensation for these changes will arise from the expected reductions in working hours and working life. Towards the end of the century, the working week is expected to fall to four days or its hourly equivalent. Formal education may be extended to the age of 17, possibly 18, with retirement for both sexes brought forward to 55.

4.3.3 These forecasts lead to certain questions about the future growth of employment in the region. In particular they have implications for the movement of jobs into East Anglia, especially in the longer term. In the immediate future, up to 1980, the enlarged planned migration programme can be expected to increase the intake of manufacturing jobs. In the longer-

term, however, this volume could reduce as automation causes a stabilisation, and an eventual reduction, in the numbers of manufacturing jobs nationally. Similarly, the immediate prospects of a substantial increase of office jobs moving to the region are good, but the potential automation of routine, clerical tasks, could also lead to fewer moves in the longer term.

4.3.4 The possibilities indicated above are dependent to a considerable extent on economic conditions remaining largely unchanged. There are signs, however, that these conditions could be disturbed; basic resources may become exhausted or be conserved, unless it is assumed that technology will quickly develop substitutes. One clear example of this is the expected world shortage of fossil fuels, particularly petroleum. While the development of North Sea and Celtic Sea sources are expected to ensure a continuity of oil and gas supplies, it seems inescapable that the costs of energy consumption will show substantial rises. Some substitution of other sources, particularly atomic energy, can be expected, though the problem of safety margins could again have an effect on costs. The results in real terms could well be both increases in the energy costs of production and transport, and much greater attention to energy conservation in the future. This in turn could have effects on the speed with which automation is introduced, since this implies increased energy consumption, as well as the substitution of capital and machinery for labour inputs. Similarly, it could lead to greater emphasis on insulation in building construction, and for the conservation of energy in agricultural production.

4.3.5 Perhaps the most substantial effects can be expected in transport, which is at present wasteful both of basic energy resources and human effort. Increasing fuel costs may see a slowing in the growth of car ownership, and a reversal towards more use of, and investment in, public transport, particularly in urban areas. Alternative energy sources are not easily adapted to power the private vehicle, and the opportunity may be taken, in view of traffic densities and safety considerations, to switch to transport systems which are more co-ordinated. In the longer-term, this could involve automatic guidance systems, allied to the development of telecommunications to increase the responsiveness of public transport to individual and community needs. Indeed, these latter systems could reduce the need for personal travel and assist in the dispersal of office work. More immediately, however, the pressures for change having most impact on the region's route system arise from entry into the EEC and from proximity to London. At present, high quality routes extend to the southern boundaries of the region, and entry into the EEC has brought increased priority for the roads from the Midlands to the Haven Ports. The ports of East Anglia, particularly Felixstowe, are expected to handle an increasing proportion of the United Kingdom trade. The present internal road network of East Anglia, even with the improvement of selected strategic routes, is unlikely to be able to cope with the growth in industrial and port traffic without considerable environmental damage. Increases in lorry weight and size would only add to this. Consequently, the restriction of much of this traffic to those modern routes designed to carry it, is likely in the relatively near future.

4.3.6 The probable need for much greater conservation and recycling of resources is likely to have an effect on public services and public expenditure. This is evident at the present time in water supply and sewerage services, where the requirements of efficient management have led to the transfer of direct control from local to regional level. A shift in emphasis towards public transport could have equivalent results. A different question occurs in welfare services where immediate contact at the time of need is important. The potential for expanding these services seems to be great, as 'need' is progressively redefined and expanded in terms of expectations. It is not at all clear whether further developments requiring increased financial and manpower resources will occur through greater specialisation and concentration on those in greatest need, or by expanding preventive services, organised on a community basis. In housing, the expectation is that increasing costs of raw materials and labour could lead to more prefabrication, based on the development of mobile homes.

4.3.7 Some of the resource and energy conservation questions could bite on the agricultural industry in East Anglia. At present it provides about 12 to 15% of the national output and can claim to be the leading region in the country for the diffusion of new ideas and techniques in arable farming, particularly cereal cropping. Except for the Fens, its farms are large, and there is a high proportion of owner-occupation. This structure has encouraged the substitution of capital for labour and a rapid decline in the labour force. The concentration on machinery, and chemical fertilisers and pesticides—all of which require a large energy input—has enabled the industry to achieve consistently high levels of productivity and output. In general, this structure allows agriculture in East Anglia to take advantage of favourable opportunities and to withstand adverse conditions. Entry into the EEC is expected to reinforce the concentration on arable and cereal cropping, although the prospects for horticulture and livestock are less favourable. The scope for expansion of the arable area is limited perhaps to 2 or 3%, but this would mean a considerable further reduction in the residual grassland area. The labour force is expected to continue to decline, levelling off to a smaller number of highly skilled workers earning wages equivalent to those in industry.

4.3.8 Recent large rises in the price of agricultural land have created further pressures on methods of agricultural production in terms of return on the capital employed. This has been coupled with world food shortages and higher food prices. These factors have increased the possibility of substantial changes in the industry's capital structure, with a greater degree of institutional financing and ownership. This could, in turn, lead to much greater problems of reconciling short-term profit levels with good husbandry, and with good quality landscape. The risk of damage to the inherent fertility of the soil by wind blow, soil compaction, and the application of chemical fertilisers and pesticides, may be slight, but it is certain that both the appearance of the landscape and local ecology are changing rapidly, to the detriment of the traditional pattern.

4.3.9 These marked changes in the appearance of the region could lead to increased interest in conservation, ranging across the spectrum from archaeology to wildlife, with effects on recreation and tourism. The pressures for various forms of conservation could be intensified as those moving into the region come to value its attractiveness. Similarly, the demands from recreation and tourism can be expected to increase as more time becomes available for leisure. The proximity of London, and prospects of much easier access than at present, are expected to lead to more second homes, more short recreational trips, and additional holidays. Self-catering is likely to be an important feature of this new holiday growth. By the eighties, therefore, the region is expected to be under much greater recreational pressure and any decline in the attraction of its landscape will lead to increased concentration on a small number of facilities, with a consequent need to channel and spread recreation more widely.

4.4 The Parameters of Change

4.4.1 The results of the context studies presented above do not provide a direct measure of the volume of change likely to be experienced by East Anglia. The most obvious expression of this can be the expected change in population and employment, the two channels by which external pressure is transmitted to the region, not least through the demands which they generate for transport, housing, recreation, and a whole range of public and private services.

4.4.2 In **population** terms, the mid-1930's saw the close of a long period of stagnation and outward migration from the region. From this time, growth has accelerated, so that by the sixties (Figure 4.1) the region was growing at a faster rate than any other region. The most dramatic increase has been in the inward flow of migrants, which became the single most important element in the growth of the region, as Figure 4.2 demonstrates. The planned migration programme took effect in the last decade, but it was overshadowed in importance by the increase in voluntary movement. It is estimated that more than four-fifths of this migration came from the neighbouring South East. The indication in Figure 4.1 is that recently the South East has experienced a net loss of population. This movement may be a significant augury for the future relationship of the two regions.

4.4.3 The planned migration programme is expected to increase considerably in the seventies, with the continued progress of existing town development agreements, and the major building phase of Peterborough New Town. If the present targets for all the schemes are met, the rate of planned migration could reach a maximum of 8,000 people per annum compared to 3,000 per annum in the sixties. This would leave Peterborough New Town as the only scheme continuing into the eighties. There must, however, be some doubt about whether the national economy, affected by developments in regional policy and by internal issues within the South East, will be able to

Figure 4.1

Rates of growth of home population by regions* 1951–61 and 1961–71

Region	1951–1961 %	1961–1971 %
South East	7·4	5·8
South West	5·8	10·4
East Anglia	7·3	13·2
East Midlands	7·8	9·1
West Midlands	7·6	7·6
North West	2·0	3·1
Yorks and Humberside	2·4	3·9
Northern	3·8	1·5
Wales	1·8	3·4
England and Wales	5·4	5·8

*The regional boundaries for 1951–61 rates are those at 1966, and for 1961–71 are those at 1971.
Source: Abstract of Regional Statistics, 1971, 1973.

Figure 4.2

Components of home population change in East Anglia, 1951–61, 1961–71. (Thousands, average annual change)

Period	1951–61	1961–71
Population at beginning of period	1,387·6	1,484·2
Natural increase	+6·5	+8·4
Armed Forces	+1·0	−1·3
Net Migration	+2·7	+12·1
Population at end of period	1,484·2	1,686·0

Source: Abstract of Regional Statistics, 1971, 1973.

support the increase in mobile jobs which would be necessary to meet this programme. In practice, therefore, it seems more likely that not all the present schemes will be completed before the eighties.

4.4.4 The future volume of net voluntary migration could be much more volatile. The context studies produced the expectation that it will continue to accelerate, to reach over 20,000 people a year. This contrasts with official projections which foresee a continued reduction in the net flows of migrants between regions during the remainder of the century. A similar contrast exists on future levels of natural increase which could affect the rate of voluntary migration. The context studies indicated that birth rates would continue to fall. If this does happen, the population pressures in the regions of net outward migration will not be so intense, and there may be some kind of structural ceiling on the future rate of inward migration to East Anglia.

4.4.5 Against this background, we produce the notional future population levels for the region set out in Figure 4.3. These attempt to identify the degree of uncertainty which must exist about the rate of growth of the region's population. The high extreme represents the situation in which natural increase continues at about its present rate, the planned migration programme proceeds on target, and voluntary migration accelerates to its highest feasible rate. In contrast, the low extreme is based on a fall in natural increase, the stretching out of the planned migration programme into the eighties, and voluntary migration at or slightly above the present level. The official projections are of the same order as the low extreme, but presuppose a slightly higher rate of natural increase, and an even lower rate of voluntary migration. In practice, this difference seems acceptable. There appear to be rather more penalties attached to underprovision than overprovision, and it is not axiomatic that forward estimates adopted for prudent planning at the regional level should automatically aggregate to an overall national forecast.

Figure 4.3

Notional future population levels in East Anglia, 1971–2001 (in thousands)

Date	Population	Natural Increase	Net Inward Migration	Total Increase
1961	1490			
1961–71		80	110	190
1971	1680			
1971–81		70–80	145–180	215–260
1981	1900–1940			
1981–91		50–80	100–230	150–310
1991	2050–2250			
1991–01		25–80	100–270	125–350
2001	2170–2600			

Source: East Anglia Regional Strategy Team.

4.4.6 The growth of **employment** in East Anglia has paralleled that of the population. Indeed, it has been the only region in Great Britain to increase its total number of employees between 1966 and 1971.

Figure 4.4 illustrates that East Anglia has experienced relatively more growth in every major sector of employment than has the country as a whole. There are two sources for this growth in employment. An analysis of the components of the changing employment structure suggests that there has been an above average performance by companies in the region, rather than an over representation of growing industries. Secondly, about 40% of the total manufacturing growth in the sixties came from firms moving in from the South East and this was closely linked to the town development schemes. Figure 4.5 indicates the substantial number of jobs created in manufacturing firms that have moved into the region since 1945.

4.4.7 The context studies produced the expectation that the movement of firms into the region would increase, possibly by about 50% in the case of manufacturing employment, and perhaps by 200% or more

Figure 4.4

Employees in employment, East Anglia and Great Britain, 1966 and 1971 (in thousands)

Industrial Group	East Anglia			Great Britain		
	1966	1971	Percentage Change	1966	1971	Percentage Change
Extractive	62·6	47·5	—24·1	1,038·3	745·8	—28·2
Manufacturing	190·0	209·0	+10·0	8,976·4	8,431·6	— 6·1
Construction	51·9	41·5	—20·0	1,636·6	1,248·6	—23·7
Service	309·0	322·4	+ 4·3	11,649·4	11,600·4	— 0·4
Total	**613·5**	**620·0**	**+ 1·1**	**23,301·0**	**22,027·0**	**— 5·5**

Source: Department of Employment

Figure 4.5

Employment in manufacturing firms moving into East Anglia, 1945–1970 (in thousands) *

Period	Male	Total
1945–51[1]	1·7	*3·6*
1952–59[1]	2·7	*4·2*
1960–65[2]	7·6	*12·0*
1966–70[3]	6·3	*9·5*

*Employment figures are for different dates. Thus for moves up to 1959[1] employment is as at 1966; for moves 1960–65[2] employment is as at 1970; for moves 1966–70[3] employment is as at 1972. The figures do not necessarily reflect the final employment potential, especially for later dates.

Source: Department of Trade and Industry.

Figure 4.6

Notional future labour demand in East Anglia, 1971–2001 (employees in employment: thousands)

Date	Total	Growth
1971	620	
1971–81		70–100
1981	690–720	
1981–91		50–110
1991	740–830	
1991–2001		40–130
2001	780–960	

Source: East Anglia Regional Strategy Team.

in the case of office employment, though this is more open to question. To a large extent, the movement of jobs into the region will determine the progress of the planned migration programme. This dependency will be reduced as schemes progress however, and as a greater contribution to new employment opportunities is made by the growth of firms already established in the region. Much voluntary migration has been in response to job creation, and it has, in turn, led to a growth of employment serving the increased population. Future growth is likely to be increasingly in this category and in those services supplying a wider market. Thus, within the context study expectations of a rate of regional employment growth of between 0·7% and 2·0% per annum, the importance of mobile flows would begin to decline, compared with a greater contribution from indigenous sources. On these assumptions we can produce notional estimates of future demand for labour, as shown in Figure 4.6. The lower levels reflect pessimistic assumptions about both the national and regional economies, while the higher levels represent more buoyant growth prospects. In both cases, the expansion of the planned migration programme will mean a higher inflow of mobile industry in the seventies.

4.4.8 The strong interdependencies between the rate of population growth, and the rate of growth of employment opportunities, can be formalised through notional estimates of future labour force levels in the region. Nationally, male activity rates are declining,

and the context studies produced the expectation that these will continue to decline. Female activity rates, on the other hand, are expected to increase considerably, and in East Anglia could well come up to the present national average by the late seventies. At present, an extra 25,000 women at work would be required for East Anglia to match the national average, an increase of about 10%.

4.4.9 Acting against this are a number of contrary factors. The first is the increasing proportion of elderly in the population, at least up to 1981, and the possibility of a lower retirement age. The second factor is the likely increase in the numbers in full-time education, arising from changes in the school leaving age and from the general tendency to spend more time in further education. In fact, an increase in female activity rates may be insufficient, therefore, to prevent a decline in overall activity rates. Although the actual timing of changes and the actual levels reached are, of course, subject to considerable uncertainty, Figure 4.7 indicates the notional supply of labour in the region on the assumptions given above. The ranges shown in this table, and in Figure 4.6, indicate that there is no great disparity between the two notional estimates of supply and demand, based on the context study results.

4.4.10 Over the next ten to fifteen years, East Anglia can expect to experience a rate of growth in excess of anything experienced in the past. Beyond this period, the completion of the planned migration pro-

Notional future labour supply in East Anglia, 1971–2001
(population aged 15+ potentially seeking employment;
thousands)

Date	Total	Growth
1971	756	
1971–81		84–134
1981	840–890	
1981–91		45–140
1991	885–1030	
1991–2001		35–160
2001	920–1190	

Source: East Anglia Regional Strategy Team.

gramme, and uncertainties about the future rate of
voluntary migration suggest that allowance must be
made for circumstances ranging from stabilisation to
further rapid growth. In the next chapter these
changes are discussed in terms of their expected
impacts on the regional objectives.

Chapter 5

The Choices for the Region

5.1 Introduction

5.1.1 In this chapter, we look at what can be done to influence the future of the region as a whole. As a first step, the effects of change outlined in the previous chapter are considered in conjunction with the objectives for the region, so as to indicate factors that are expected to be beneficial and factors likely to bring disadvantages. This establishes a basis for considering the use of major policies which could either promote faster growth, or restrain it when change seems likely to be detrimental. The concluding part of the chapter goes on to set out the general principles appropriate to the selection of specific policies for the region.

5.2 The Assessment of Expected Change

5.2.1 Not all the objectives for the region described in chapter two are equally relevant at this stage. A full appreciation of the distributional consequences of the expected changes, or of their timing, can only follow from the depth of the analysis set out in later sections. This assessment has been restricted, therefore, to those objectives concerned with the overall **quality of life** enjoyed by people living in the region, the use of the region's **resources,** and the form of the region's **relationship with the national economy.** Even so, there are difficulties. There are problems in discerning effects in respect of individual objectives, and in deciding what emphasis each should be given. To represent people's quality of life, we have chosen to concentrate on the opportunities that change can bring for people to **increase their incomes,** and to **obtain goods and services.** In resource terms, we have placed the emphasis on **labour resources,** and **environmental resources.** In comparison, the take-up of **land resources** for urban development seems likely to be marginal, and we have deferred an attempt to assess the overall effects of change on **financial resources** until chapter fifteen. Finally, we complete the picture by considering whether or not the region's **contribution to the national economy** will increase, the degree to which the **regional economy will be supported,** and the extent to which the region will need **shielding against disruption from external forces.**

5.2.2 The assessment is carried out in two complementary ways. The main argument is set out in the text. This is supported by Figure 5.1, which attempts to express the conclusions in a more quantitative form. A scale up to a hundred has been used to indicate relative effects, though no attempt has been made to formalise the standard represented at either extreme of the scale. The direction of effect is shown as a positive or negative movement away from the level experienced at the present day, with the ranges reflecting the extent of uncertainty we associate with our assessment.

5.2.3 It is convenient to begin the assessment with the objectives concerned with the region's relationships with the national economy. In overall terms, the rapid growth of the region ensures that performance will be substantially positive. The most clearcut item is the increased importance of the region for holidays, and more spectacularly for short recreation trips from surrounding regions. Most benefits will fall to the South-East, where recreation resources are nearing capacity, and where the M11 will provide better access. The Midlands could benefit in a similar way from the construction of a link between the M1 and the A1. The contributions from the growth of employment in the region, and from the continued development of agriculture, are likely to be less obvious. The planned migration programme assures a faster rate of employment growth. Whilst there are some grounds for thinking that the resulting increase in the region's share of the GNP will add more to the national total than if the growth occurred elsewhere, it is not possible to demonstrate this conclusively. Further contributions from agriculture are limited by the amount of land that can be brought into cultivation, and by the diminishing returns that may arise from extending current practice. However, all these contributions are supported by planned improvements to the infrastructure of the region, which will bring a more efficient transport system. Connections with the expanding Haven Ports will benefit most of all.

5.2.4 The improvement in the overall contribution to the national economy seems likely to be matched by improvements to those ancillary functions which service the region's economy. The increase in activity in the region will encourage the development of more specialised financial and advisory services. At the same time, however, considerable problems are expected in terms of the third objective. Whilst the planned migration programme assures a faster rate of growth over a period of time, its progress at any one time will be dependent on the state of the national economy, particularly as evidenced by the supply of mobile industry. Sizeable irregularities in the rate of growth are likely to result. The peaking of planned migration in the late seventies can be expected to produce an increase in the proportion of the population either too young or too old to work, with a consequent bunching of the demands for

Figure 5.1
Assessment of change for the Region as a whole

Objectives	Source of Effect Direction of Effect	Labour Markets	Recreation and Tourism	Agriculture	Physical Infra-structure	All Sources
A. Resources	+				10	
	−	10–30	20–55	20–35	20	15–40
A.3. Labour Resources	+	0	5			0
	−	20	40	10–20		20
A.4. Land Resources	+			0		0
	−			10		10
A.5. Environmental Resources	+			10		
	−	30–60	35–65	40–70	20	30–60
B. Region and the National Economy	+	40	55	40	10–20	40
	−	20	5	15		15
B.1. Contribution to National Economy	+	0–40	50–75	0–40	10–20	0–40
	−					
B.2. Supporting the Regional Economy	+	5–45	20–50	0–50	20–30	5–45
	−					
B.3. Shielding the Region	+	10	15	5		10
	−	30	25	30	5–10	25
C. Quality of Life	+	0–40	20	0–25	5–10	5–25
	−		5			
C.1. Incomes	+	0–40	10–20	0–25	5–10	0–40
	−					
C.3. Private Sector Goods and Services	+		20			20
	−		15			15

Source: East Anglia Regional Strategy Team

educational, health and social facilities. In the long term, the demand for employment from second generation migrants will show a corresponding rise. The improvement of the region's road infrastructure could produce fairly sudden impacts. The completion of the M11, and the M1-A1 link, could lead to very rapid increases in traffic using the internal network, where an equivalent level of improvement is not in hand.

5.2.5 The overall performance against those objectives concerned with the use of regional resources is expected to be adverse. We expect to see a long term decline in the use of labour as an input to economic activity. Falling activity rates will result from earlier retirement, longer periods in full-time education, and the possibility of 'technological unemployment'. Standards for assessing the effects of change on the landscape are peculiarly subjective, and it could well be that the landscape which is now being produced will be more highly valued in the future than it is at present. Subject to this reservation, the continued application of modern agricultural methods, and the expected increases in recreation and tourism, will produce a considerable deterioration. This is a question which we consider at length in Section E.

5.2.6 Overall performance in terms of opportunities for people to increase their incomes is positive. This reflects the growth in the number and type of employment opportunities available, and their increasingly skilled (and hence high wage) content. Performance is tempered, however, by the recognition that these wider opportunities will not be available to all sections of the population. In particular there will be discrepancies between newcomers to the region and existing residents, many of whom may have difficulty in grasping the opportunities created. This arises largely from the technical difficulties of providing appropriate education and training for those possessing little or no industrial skill, or living in the remoter rural areas.

5.2.7 Any overall assessment is affected by the inter-relationship between objectives. The simplest case is the interplay between the growth of recreation and tourism, and the depletion of environmental resources. A reduction of environmental assets in the region may only result in a fall in the level of recreation and tourism, if other parts of the country maintain their attractions. The relationship between the economic objectives and the region's labour force is more complex. To some extent, a fast rate of growth of employment opportunities will involve a high pressure of demand for regional labour resources. Yet the fact that growth may be in new industries, leading to a restructured regional economy, could prevent a large section of the labour force from taking full advantage of the new opportunities.

5.2.8 In general, therefore, the most significant benefits will stem from improved economic performance to the advantage of both regional and national economies. These are somewhat counterbalanced by a growing dependence on the national course of events. Gains here should be related closely to improvements in the 'quality of life', but there are some problems related to those sections of the present population unable to fully benefit. Finally, whatever economic and social benefits result there are likely to be substantial costs to the natural and man-made environment of the region. In East Anglia improved economic prospects appear to be associated with a reduction in some of the qualities that make the region attractive. It may be very significant, however, that these costs do not arise so much from population and employment growth, as from other forces in modern life. This suggests that there are possibilities for improving the expected situation, without automatically foregoing many of the real benefits that change will bring for East Anglia.

5.3 The Available Choice

5.3.1 At first sight the possibility of improving the future performance of the region seems limited. Few decisions are made directly at regional level, so the search for effective policies must be focused on the area where national and local priorities coincide. It is important, therefore, to establish both the degree to which growth may be promoted or restrained, and the options available for modifying the composition of that growth in ways which seem most suited to the achievement of objectives.

5.3.2 One major area where national and local priorities come together is the planned migration programme. Under any circumstances, this will expand considerably over the next ten years, though its future beyond that time has still to be decided. The programme presupposes a substantial increase in the supply of mobile industry, not all of which may be realised because of circumstances arising outside East Anglia. There seems little scope, therefore, for any extension to the programme before the eighties, and there may indeed be advantages in smoothing the present programme over a longer period. This would reduce the risk of labour shortages or lack of jobs, and reduce the peaking of demands for public services. In the longer term, however, there are opportunities to agree new schemes or additions to existing schemes following their completion. Policies directed towards stimulating the rate of growth would probably accept the risk involved in the present programme and look for additions to existing schemes. Policies of restraint would be more inclined to smooth out the present programme over a longer

period, and seek to develop new schemes designed to suit the region's needs.

5.3.3 Policies designed to influence the level of voluntary migration are less clearcut and present major problems of principle. Any major restriction on people's ability to choose where to live must raise strong objections. It has to be recognised, however, that many policies have such effects, if only indirectly. Voluntary migration is given an impetus by planned migration. For example, the emphasis given in central and local government spending to advanced investment in new development, as against the provision of better services for the existing population, may significantly affect the overall rate of voluntary migration. Faster growth could be encouraged by forward spending on industrial promotion, serviced sites and local infrastructure. Joint schemes with private developers could assist in keeping down the loan charge burden so incurred. In contast, some restraint on the rate of growth might be effected by replacing the stock of public facilities only as and when they become obsolete, or by pursuing more active conservation policies. More specific controls over those forms of voluntary migration liable to lead to population imbalances, such as retirement migration, present major difficulties. There is likely to be an understandable reluctance to impose restrictions, through special rate levies, or the direct purchase of houses by local authorities, for example, until local problems have reached a scale where some such action has to be taken.

5.3.4 Outside the planned migration programme, the efforts of local authorities in the field of industrial promotion have had some success. Any attempt to increase the rate of growth would place more emphasis on such schemes, although there would need to be more effective co-ordination between authorities. Similarly, attempts to restrain growth would tend to confine promotional activity to those parts of the region most likely to increase opportunities for the existing labour force. Growth of employment requires a workforce with the requisite skills. The existing training programmes in the region are designed to meet these specific demands and faster growth would require their further development. An alternative is to give greater attention to the longer term demand and the need to build up the general level of skills in the population. This might involve a re-orientation of existing training programmes, less specific in the skills which they transmit, and more responsive to the needs of particular groups of workers.

5.3.5 The development of the region's communications network, can be used to support the process of change. The preparation pool for road schemes provides a short to medium term instrument for affecting the scale and type of investment in transport infrastructure, but developments in the rail network and at the ports will be less open to change. Options are available at a number of levels. The M11 and A45 improvements are already under way and represent a commitment. To achieve faster growth a continued priority to trunk, as opposed to principal or local routes, and a concentration on external links would be advantageous. Within the region, more resources would need to be given to principal routes connecting with the trunk network. The alternative would be a long term shift in emphasis towards principal and local roads serving all parts of the region so as to provide an internal network catering for recreational pressures and localised development. Between these extremes, there are clearly many combinations that could be applied to produce different mixes of effects.

5.3.6 The final areas of choice concern the use of the environment, and the pressures of recreation and tourism. The expected scale of growth in recreation and tourism is such that major efforts will be required to keep pace with it. The major opportunity is, therefore, in attempting to alter the nature of the activities that take place in the region. This can range from planning the maximum use of facilities, through encouraging off-peak holidays, to promoting formal accommodation, thereby increasing per capita expenditure. Attempts to spread demand over wider areas, by selective development related to a designated holiday route network, could be part of such a package. This leaves the question of environmental policies relating to faster or restrained growth. For faster growth, as few restrictions as possible might be placed on activities affecting the environment. This would imply a system of grants and incentives, rather than the definition of standards with strict regulatory controls. Such standards would seem more likely to restrain growth.

5.3.7 The policies considered for faster or restrained growth represent extremes, and clearly exaggerate what could be achieved in practice. Their consistent application will be subject to the exigencies of national circumstances, and these external uncertainties could be much more significant than the benefits obtained from putting the appropriate policies into effect. This is illustrated in Figure 5.2, where we attempt to formalise our assessment in comparable terms to Figure 5.1. It is clear that both options would improve on the 'expected growth' in terms of the overall performance of the region. Each produces more gains in respect of the objectives than losses, suggesting that conscious choice in the application of policies is preferable to a passive acceptance of events and trends. The choice of a mix of policies is more complex than the extremes presented here. In later sections of the report we explore many of these policy areas in greater depth. In the concluding part of this chapter, however, we produce a set of principles or presumptions to guide the selection of policies most suited to the future of East Anglia as a whole.

5.4 Principles for the Future of the Region

5.4.1 There are real choices to be made about the future of East Anglia as a whole. How much growth? What kind of growth? These questions are too important to go by default through the passive acceptance of forecasts, and require careful and continuous attention. After sifting the evidence, we can present our conclusions as principles of long term validity. We have avoided the temptation to pinpoint more specific policies at this stage, as the opportunity to do so exists in the later sections of the report, where variations within the region are considered in more depth.

5.4.2 The first principle is perhaps the most difficult to express. Anyone with knowledge of East Anglia is impressed by its character and charm, elements that are difficult to capture in words. Perhaps these elements lie in the region's variety and diversity, and in a sense of being unhurried and detached. We realise that growth, and the shrinkage of travelling time to and from East Anglia, will tend to make the region more like other places. We find it impossible to regard this with complete equanimity. While it would be far too simple to look on the region as a refuge from the stresses of modern life, we consider it essential that its continuity with the past should be maintained, and that it should be encouraged in its diversity. On this partly subjective basis, the first principle we suggest is that:

B1 policies should be designed to maintain the diversity, and the sense of continuity with the past, that make East Anglia recognisably different.

Figure 5.2

Assessment of faster and restrained growth options

Objective	Effects of Change			Direction of Effect	
	Faster Growth Policies	Expected Growth (See Fig. 5.1)	Restrained Growth Policies	Faster Growth	Restrained Growth
National Economy (B.1)	(+5)—(+45)	(0)—(+40)	(0)—(+35)	+	—
Regional Economy (B.2)	(+10)—(+50)	(+5)—(+45)	(+5)—(+40)	+	—
Shielding (B.3)	(—35)— (+5)	(—25)—(+10)	(—15)—(+15)	—	+
Labour Resources (A.3)	(—20)— (+5)	(—20)— (0)	(—10)—(+15)	+	+
Environmental Resources (A.5)	(—60)—(—35)	(—60)—(—30)	(—50)—(—20)	—	+
Incomes (C.1)	(+5)—(+40)	(0)—(+40)	(+5)—(+40)	+	+
Goods and Services (C.3)	(—10)—(+25)	(—15)—(+20)	(—5)—(+30)	+	+

Source: East Anglia Regional Strategy Team

5.4.3 The second conclusion follows from the region's rapid rate of growth. This will accelerate in the seventies as the planned migration programme reaches a peak. Even if national circumstances are such that the full extent of this growth is not realised, it seems inevitable that for the foreseeable future the region will grow at a considerably faster rate than that of the country as a whole. This poses at least two major issues. Rapid growth tends to proceed in a jerky, rather than steady, fashion. Secondly, we are uncertain as to the degree to which previous growth has taken up whatever slack existed in the region, and the extent to which greater difficulties will be experienced in absorbing further growth. In the assurance that the region will grow relatively faster than the country as a whole, it can afford to forego some of the absolute volume of growth it might achieve, in favour of greater encouragement to forms of growth which would be more balanced, both in composition and location. On this basis, the second principle is that:

B2 policies should be designed to be selective both in the composition and location of growth encouraged in East Anglia.

5.4.4 The third conclusion arises from the degree of uncertainty that must exist about the precise rate and composition of future growth in the region. Over half of the present growth of population and employment comes from outside the region, and even with the general assurance of a relatively faster rate of growth, there are many circumstances in which some, if not all, of this growth could be stimulated or curtailed. Coupled with the potential unsteadiness of whatever growth occurs, this makes advanced preparation to accommodate it subject to a large degree of risk. This is accentuated by the low population densities of the region, which make it difficult to absorb growth without exceeding the capacity of existing urban areas. To cope with this, it is considered that policies, in general, should take a more adapatable form than elsewhere, with the emphasis on small rather than large capital projects. On this basis, the third principle is that:

B3 policies should be designed to be adaptable, with emphasis on smaller units of provision, to minimise the risk associated with a large degree of uncertainty.

5.4.5 The fourth conclusion is in many senses an extension of the third. The planned migration programme, including in particular the town expansion schemes, forms the single most important policy area at the regional level. At present, this rests on a coincidence of interest between the participating authorities in the region, the Greater London Council, and central government. The area may, therefore, be vulnerable in the long term to any change of view, and is too fragile a base on which to secure a very important part of the region's future. It is considered that some buffer or reinforcement is required to prevent any large or sudden dislocations to the programme. The answer appears to lie in the development of institutions with appropriate financial powers and resources, that might take some share of the responsibility for the present programme, and take part in decisions concerning its future extension. In a similar way, such institutions could act as a shield against other disruptions to the steady process of growth and development in the region. On this basis, the fourth principle is that:

B4 regional institutions should be developed, with appropriate powers and resources, to give a firmer basis for the forward planning of capital investment, and to shield the region from major disruptions from external sources.

5.4.6 The fifth conclusion is again a related one. We have indicated that policies need to be adaptable, with institutions able to shield the region from excessive disruption from external sources. As a corollary to these, there exists some possibility of building up an internal structure in the region which is resilient in its capacity to absorb shocks. In forgoing some of the short-term volume of growth, as suggested in the second principle, it is considered that more emphasis should be placed on enhancing its longer-term potential and assets. This may be best exemplified by the transport pattern, where present tendencies are leading to a heavy reliance on the private car, and on a small number of high grade routes. On this basis, the fifth principle is that:

B5 policies should be designed to build up internal structures in the region which are likely to be resilient to change, by a greater emphasis on securing longer term potential and assets, rather than on realising the totality of short-term growth prospects.

5.4.7 These principles are clearly interdependent, and in total represent the view that neither the total pursuit of growth nor its total restraint is desirable or necessary for the future of East Anglia. The form in which we have chosen to express them clearly begs the question of what they mean in practice. We hope to provide an answer in the following sections of the report.

Section C

The Location of Change

In this third section of the report, the emphasis shifts to the broad pattern of development within the region. It is concerned with where people live and work, and their ability to move between places. It takes as its context the expectations of change described in the second section, and attempts to work out how these will affect different areas of the region.

Chapter six describes the forces that have moulded the present pattern of development in the region, and the situation that has resulted. It moves forward to consider the opportunities and constraints on future development in strategic terms. Finally, it draws these together into estimates of the ranges of future population that seem likely in different parts of the region.

The next chapter builds on this likely future pattern by examining the possibility of modifying it in accordance with the objectives for the region. It does so by establishing a number of 'ideal' themes for development, which are then assessed against the objectives. The conclusions of this process are set out in chapter eight. Within the broad principles arising from Section B for the region as a whole, it states the principles which seem appropriate to guide the future location of development. The process of making these principles specific in terms of particular places has to recognise the responsibilities and forward planning work of both county and district authorities. The opportunity has been taken in this chapter to suggest how the principles would lead to a particular pattern of development. This leaves the planning authorities free to consider the local feasibility of these proposals and the degree to which their more detailed knowledge suggests changes in this pattern.

Chapter 6

The Present Structure of Development

6.1 Introduction

6.1.1 Why is the present settlement pattern of East Anglia as it is? What are the opportunities and obstacles it contains for future development? What is the likely pattern in the future? These are the main questions to be answered in this chapter. A starting point for this is the regional issues described in chapter one. Many of these are locational in character, and can be grouped together in respect of the problems or the nature of the areas with which they are concerned.

6.1.2 The first group centres on the problems of the more lightly populated areas of the region Their relative isolation results in a lower level of opportunities and services for the people living in these areas. The numbers employed in agriculture have declined and alternative employment is restricted The private car has enabled some people to benefit from the wider opportunities available in the larger centres. This has resulted in a gradual withdrawal of local public transport and the services available in smaller towns

6 1.3 The second group of issues, in contrast, is concerned with the problem of areas experiencing rapid growth. To a large extent they are related to the intense pressure for development in areas with attractive environments, or which are unable to cope with the rate of demand for new social services, such as nursery education facilities. The difficulties of the rural areas, and those of faster growth, are opposite poles of the problem of imbalance within the region.

6.1.4 A third group of issues is concerned with the future of the four main centres and the larger towns of the region. The emphasis here is on continuing and extending the influence of these centres. For this reason there is a basic concern with employment structure, and with the progressive improvement of the main road and rail connections of these centres. There is a concern that road improvements may be unduly delayed because criteria for such investment are existing traffic loads, rather than the other potential benefits. Without such investment, growth might have detrimental effects on the historic centres of the towns. Finally, the fourth group of issues is essentially a collection of special cases reflecting particular characteristics of the region. In this category comes the question of the future of the ports, and the effects of recreation and tourism, particularly on the coasts and major tourist centres. Allied to this are the conservation issues in Cambridge and Norwich, and in other historic settlements of the region.

6.2 The Existing Situation

6.2.1 There appear to be several longstanding features of the distribution of population and employment within East Anglia, and they each contribute to the issues described above. These are:

(a) a general stability of the overall distribution of population over long periods of time, against a background of substantial changes in human activities;

(b) a tendency for population to concentrate around larger centres, reflecting the greater competitive ability of those centres;

(c) a tendency for these larger centres to extend their direct influence over increasingly wide areas;

(d) a tendency for communication improvements and population growth to support and encourage each other.

6.2.2 A number of forces have led to these features. The increase in personal mobility provided by the private car has been perhaps the most important factor affecting where development occurs. This has allowed more people to choose not only where to work, but where to live as well. A larger number of people have been able to live further away from where they work with less reliance upon public transport. There has been a reduction in the numbers employed in agriculture and in other traditional employment opportunities. More recently, other forces shaping the settlement pattern have become apparent. These include the planned migration programme, and the general extension of metropolitan influence tied in with M1 and A1(M) developments. This has encouraged voluntary migration including a growth in commuting—living within, but working outside the region. Rising affluence has also allowed more people to move on retirement to attractive areas within East Anglia.

6.2.3 These forces are clearly reflected in the existing structure of the region and this can be described in two ways. The first is in terms of the pattern of employment opportunities; the second in terms of the attractiveness of the region as a place to live. We can illustrate the distribution of employment opportunities with the help of Map 6.1. The index mapped combines the number of jobs available in different parts of the region with accessibility to them as provided by the major roads. The result is a 'surface' of employment opportunities available to people living in different parts of East Anglia, and expressed in terms of deviations from the regional average. The surface confirms the features described above, and could well represent in general terms the

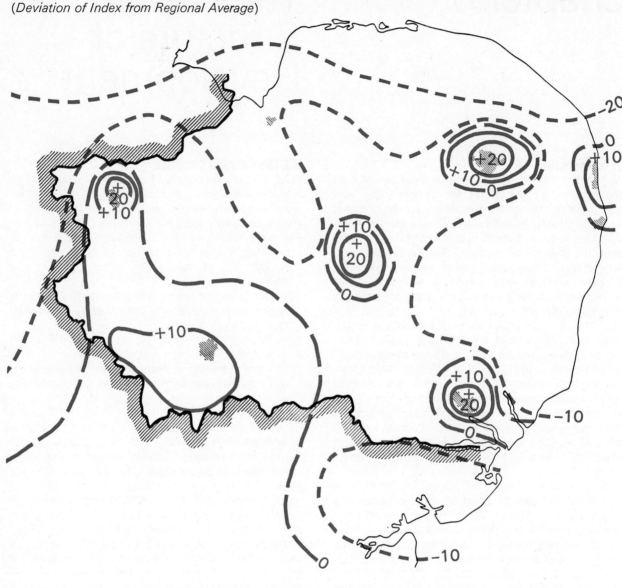

Map 6.1 Access to Employment Opportunities, 1971
(*Deviation of Index from Regional Average*)

relative potential of different areas of the region to grow in the future, provided such forces continue unabated. The second factor, the attractiveness of different parts of the region as places in which to live, can be represented using a similar method but substituting environmental and recreation attractions for the number of jobs. The 'accessibility to recreation' surface illustrated in Map 6.2 shows that compared with employment the picture is somewhat reversed, with the northern and eastern parts of the region as the more attractive areas in which to live.

6.2.4 The significance of the employment surface needs some further explanation. The general illustration in Map 6.1 conceals the problems which exist for certain groups of workers. In percentage terms, for example, unemployment is highest in the central and northern rural areas, i.e. the areas of low opportunity on the map. Perhaps of more significance is the relatively higher incidence of unemployment among the older, unskilled sections of the labour force. Some

under-employment is indicated by female activity rates. Many married women will work if there are suitable opportunities, without going to the point of registering as unemployed when no jobs are available. Figure 6.1 shows that female activity rates are higher

Figure 6.1

Female activity rates 1971

	All Females 15 and over	Married Females
	%	%
Major Centres	42·3	41·9
Other Urban Areas	40·7	37·7
Rural Districts	36·3	35·0
East Anglia	38·7	37·8
Great Britain	42·7	42·2

Source: Census 1971, Economic Activity Tables.

Map 6.2 Access to Recreational Opportunities, 1971
(*Deviation of Index from Regional Average*)

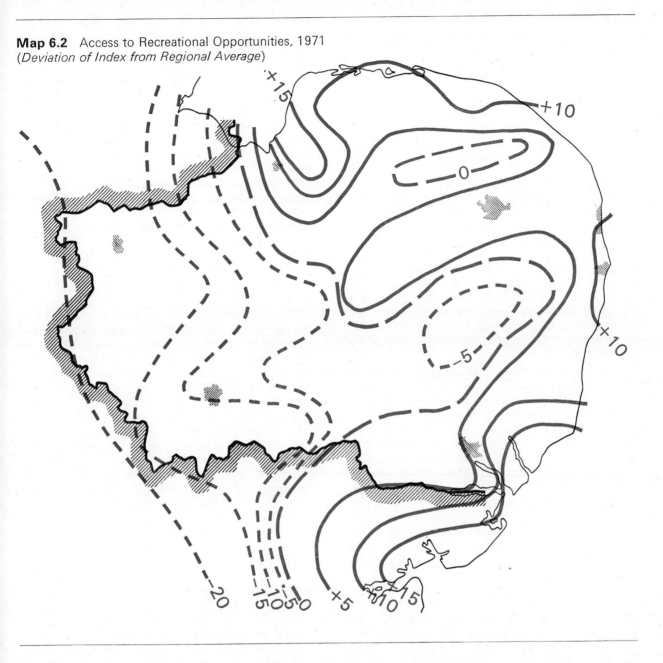

in urban than in rural areas and the difficulties of access to employment appear to be the major cause of this difference.

6.2.5 Furthermore the number of people in a household bringing home a salary or wage packet directly affects the total household income. Thus there is a direct link between areas with low female activity rates, and households with low incomes. In addition, areas with few job opportunities also provide lower than average earnings for each worker. In April 1973, the average gross weekly earnings of full-time male manual workers was £33·9 in the north-east of the region compared with £35·3 in the south-east and £35·6 in the north-west. The average for Great Britain as a whole was £37·0. The difference between East Anglia as a whole (£34·7) and Great Britain is somewhat misleading. East Anglian workers tend to work longer hours at a lower wage rate than the average and these figures conceal even greater differences between the urban and rural areas. The

precise impact of town development schemes on income levels in rural areas is uncertain, although many new firms appear to pay higher local rates, similar to those at their previous location, with some increase of wages in nearby rural areas in order to retain workers, especially in agriculture.

6.2.6 A major influence on the pattern of opportunities in the region has been the continued decline of agricultural employment in the central rural areas, still substantially dependent on employment in farming and related industries. The decline in direct farm labour is expected to continue, possibly into the mid 1980's. The planned migration schemes have helped to achieve a more dispersed pattern of employment growth in manufacturing, attracting firms new to the region (Figure 6.2). Similarly the availability of female labour has encouraged other firms to move into the rural areas. Both have been important in replacing in full or in part employment lost in agriculture.

Figure 6.2

Employment in manufacturing firms new to East Anglia by area of destination 1960–70 (thousands)

	1960–65[1]	1966–70[2]
Major Centres[3]	1·8 (15%)	1·0 (11%)
Expanding Towns	6·6 (55%)	6·3 (66%)
Rest of East Anglia	3·6 (30%)	2·2 (23%)
Total	**12·0 (100%)**	**9·5 (100%)**

(1) Employment at June 1970.
(2) Employment at June 1972.
(3) Norwich, Cambridge, Ipswich, Peterborough, Great Yarmouth/Lowestoft.
Source: Department of Trade and Industry.

6.2.7 While there has been some spread of manufacturing employment through the region, the rapid growth of the service sector in the larger centres has produced an overall concentration of employment opportunities. Since the mid 1960's there has been some slowing down of this process, but overall concentration is in keeping with the force behind managerial and productive efficiency, often equated with large production units, and hence large population centres. This has emerged in services administered by local and central government, in nationalised industries, and in retailing within the private sector. The growth of services in the town development schemes does not match as yet their growth of population and manufacturing employment and fails to counterbalance this overall concentration of opportunities.

6.2.8 Such centralisation has also been accompanied by a greater degree of separation between home and job. Long-distance commuting, mainly by private car, has enabled increasing numbers of people to live in places that are attractive, or offer lower priced housing. Attractiveness of locale has also influenced retirement migration, creating a further pressure for population growth. Together, these pressures have been greatest in the south and west of the region

6.2.9 As a result the areas of commuting dependence on the region's four main centres have grown markedly. Ipswich has the most restricted area, with retirement pressure to the west, and coastal areas to the north and south, raising house prices beyond the scope of prospective commuters. Norwich has a more extensive commuting area, overlapping in part with that of Great Yarmouth, and extending to the north and west. Cambridge's influence has spread especially towards the centre of the region—Newmarket and Ely—whereas Peterborough has looked to the north and west outside the region, and east within it. The commuting hinterlands generally extend in the direction of poor alternative employment opportunities, attractive surroundings, and relatively cheap housing. The town expansion schemes in the south and centre of the region are showing similar tendencies, compounded by low house prices and poor employment opportunities in nearby villages. Employees leaving agriculture are entering unskilled and semiskilled work, and the proportion of women seeking work rises as suitable jobs are made available.

6.2.10 The main road and rail network in the region has also encouraged recent population and employment changes. Long distance commuting is one obvious outcome which is most marked in the south and west of the region. Rail commuting is possible from Ipswich, Cambridge, Huntingdon and Peterborough to London. Within the region, the four major towns all serve at least three separate railway lines. This provides an encouragement to firms seeking improved access to other centres, and a wider labour pool. Both road and rail routes favour north/south rather than east/west movement. North/south routes are relatively direct, especially those linking London with the region, yet with the exception of part of the A45, those running east/west are poor, and a barrier to easy travel. Map 6.3 shows the existing major road and rail networks within the region. The rural areas are also poorly served, not only by major routes, but by more local connections. Poor roads, and a skeletal railway system, make access to the main towns inside the region difficult. Centres which are effectively linked to surrounding areas and settlements have a considerable advantage for the prospective employer, reinforced as rural areas decline.

6.2.11 A large number of forces, therefore, combine to influence where people live and work. New job opportunities, arising from a changing industrial structure, and from the planned migration programme, together with the opportunity to live some distance from work, have all had an impact on the distribution of population within the region. This can be illustrated with the aid of Map 6.4, and the accompanying Figure 6.3. This shows, for 13 areas, how each has fared in terms of reducing or increasing its share of the total regional population. Two post-war decades are considered, 1951 to 1961, and 1961 to 1971.

6.2.12 Map 6.5 illustrates the changes occurring between 1951 and 1961. It is immediately obvious that many parts of the region retained stable shares of the total East Anglian population over the period. Only three areas grew considerably faster than the region as a whole, and thus increased their 'share' by more than 0·3% of the total population. All three are on the region's boundary with good Midlands and/or London connections. The areas declining in these relative terms (although not losing in absolute population terms) included rural northern, central and eastern sectors of the region, well away from the four main towns which, in contrast grew at, or above, the regional average.

6.2.13 The period 1961 to 1971 is covered in Map 6.6. This is a little more difficult to explain, partly because more substantial changes have occurred during the decade. The immediate impression now is of accelerating growth in the south-west of the region, particularly in the Huntingdon area (D) which contains two town expansion schemes. Two other areas containing such schemes, Bury St Edmunds, Thetford (H) and Haverhill/Sudbury (I), also grew rapidly. It is somewhat surprising that Peterborough (C) and Ipswich (J) did not continue the fast rates of growth experienced in 1951 to 1961. It must be stressed that both areas did experience some population growth—but in an era when other parts of

Map 6.3 Strategic Transport Network, 1973

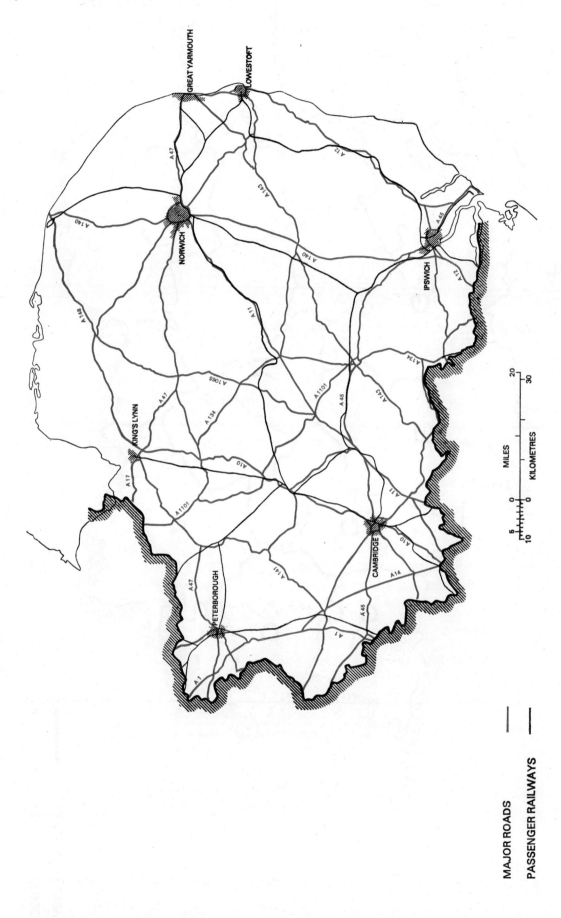

MAJOR ROADS

PASSENGER RAILWAYS

Map 6.4
Areas of the Region

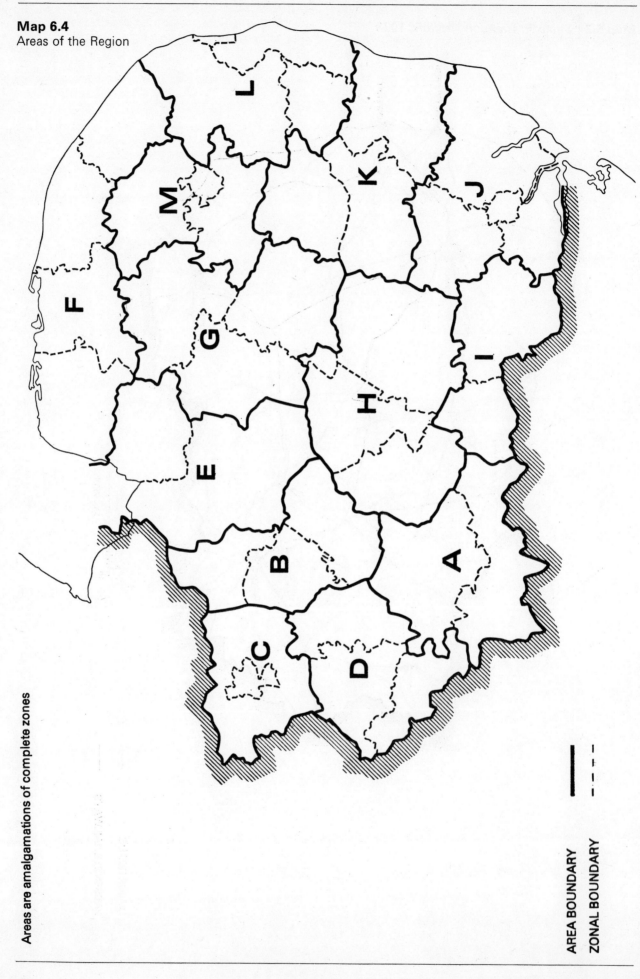

Areas are amalgamations of complete zones

AREA BOUNDARY
ZONAL BOUNDARY

the region were undergoing much faster rates of development. This seeming anomaly may be explained in part by the uncertainty that surrounded proposals for new town designation. Until these were resolved, towards the end of the decade, population growth appears to have been artificially depressed. In the case of Ipswich, no new town designation was given. It is likely that some of the potential growth in the sixties was channelled into neighbouring areas. Tight controls on development in Cambridge help explain the slow rate of absolute, as well as relative, growth in area (A) during the period. Again it is possible that some of the expected growth was diverted to the Huntingdon area (D).

6.2.14 Central Norfolk (G) improved its relative position in the second decade, partly because of the continued growth of Norwich and Thetford, to the east and south. However the Diss-Eye area (K) and the Fens (B) continued to lose ground. King's Lynn itself benefited from town expansion, but this growth has not been substantial enough to offset the forces for decline in the rest of the area (E). The most seriously declining area has been the North Norfolk coast (F). During the decade its share of the region's population fell by nearly 1% and was the only area to lose absolutely as well as relatively. This is explained only in part by a reduction in the numbers of armed forces stationed in the area. The Norwich area (M) has continued to grow at or around the regional average, maintaining its function as the main employment and service centre for surrounding areas.

6.2.15 Comparison of both decades confirms the general stability of the overall distribution of the region's population. Over the twenty-year period, only three of the thirteen areas showed an increase or decline of over 1% in their share of the region's

population. One possible explanation for this lies in the structure of growth and decline in the two ten-year periods. This indicates that at any one time only about a third of the areas have been increasing their share of the population. In the period 1951–61 five areas increased their share, with two areas growing at more than double the rate of the region as a whole. In 1961–71, when the region's population growth itself increased to over 13%, only four areas grew more rapidly and three of these grew at double the regional rate. Over the twenty-year period only three areas consistently gained in their share, whereas seven areas declined. From this it would appear that gains tend to be more concentrated and extreme than reductions, which are spread over a much wider area.

6.3 Constraints and Opportunities

6.3.1 There are relatively few physical limitations to development. The Fens and Broads are not merely unsuitable for building, but are important for agriculture and recreation respectively. The Fens will also continue to be a barrier to east-west routes. The various qualities of land, in the form of agriculture, as well as landscape and other environmental attractions, are far more important restraints on growth than the actual costs of construction. The areas of above average quality agricultural land, of high landscape quality, and towns and villages with specific historic interest, are described in chapter twelve.

6.3.2 The provision of public utilities is unlikely to affect where development occurs in the long term; capacity limitations are far more likely to affect short term decisions. For example, problems of water supply could affect major development proposals for some time in areas where the threshold of existing supply capacity has been reached, and a major new source of water needs to be developed. In most of the

Figure 6.3

Proportions of regional population* in areas of East Anglia, 1951, 1961 and 1971

	1951	1961	With planned migration	Without planned migration
			1971	1971
A. Cambridge Area	11·26	11·55	11·34	11·55
B. Fens (Wisbech-March-Ely)	5·61	5·29	4·76	4·86
C. Peterborough Area	6·65	7·27	7·48	7·59
D. Huntingdon Area	3·70	4·06	5·26	4·89
E. King's Lynn Area	5·75	5·65	5·37	5·26
F. North Norfolk Coast	7·08	6·62	5·67	5·78
G. Central Norfolk	4·22	3·86	3·75	3·83
H. Bury St Edmunds-Thetford Area	7·16	7·39	8·20	7·69
I. Haverhill-Sudbury	3·28	3·19	3·92	3·46
J. Ipswich Area	14·07	14·62	14·27	14·54
K. Diss-Eye Area	5·22	4·81	4·45	4·53
L. Great Yarmouth-Lowestoft Area	12·42	12·20	12·05	12·28
M. Norwich Area	13·57	13·48	13·47	13·73

Source: East Anglia Regional Strategy Team

Planned Migration occurred in the following areas:
C. Peterborough
D. Huntingdon, St Neots
E. King's Lynn
H. Bury St Edmunds, Thetford, Mildenhall/Brandon
I. Haverhill, Sudbury/Melford

*Census enumerated population

Map 6.5 Changes in the Share of Total Population of the Region, by Area, 1951–61

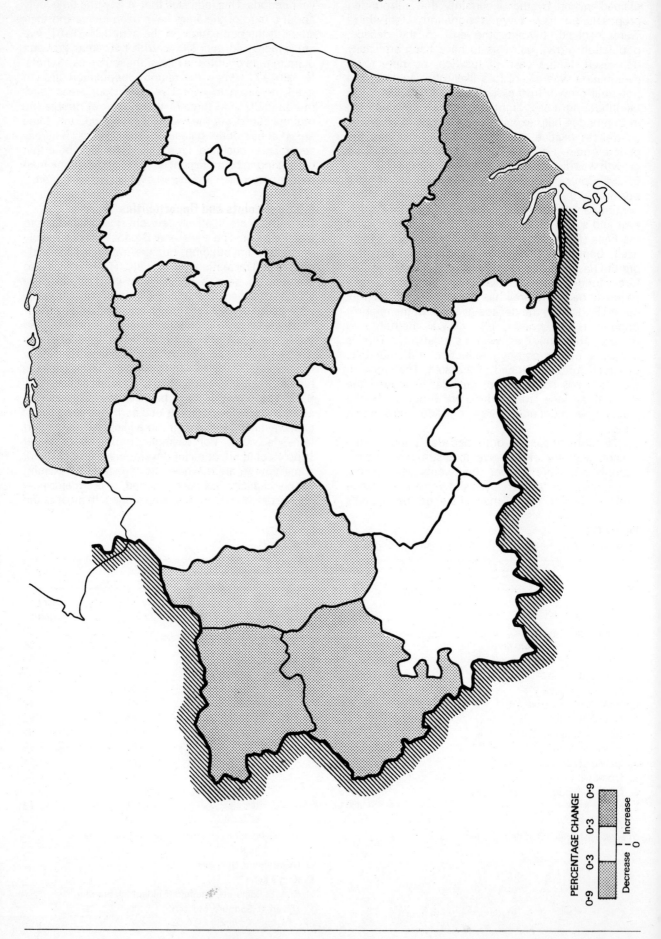

PERCENTAGE CHANGE

0·9 0·3 0·3 0·9

Decrease   Increase
         0

Map 6.6 Changes in the Share of Total Population of the Region, by Area, 1961/71

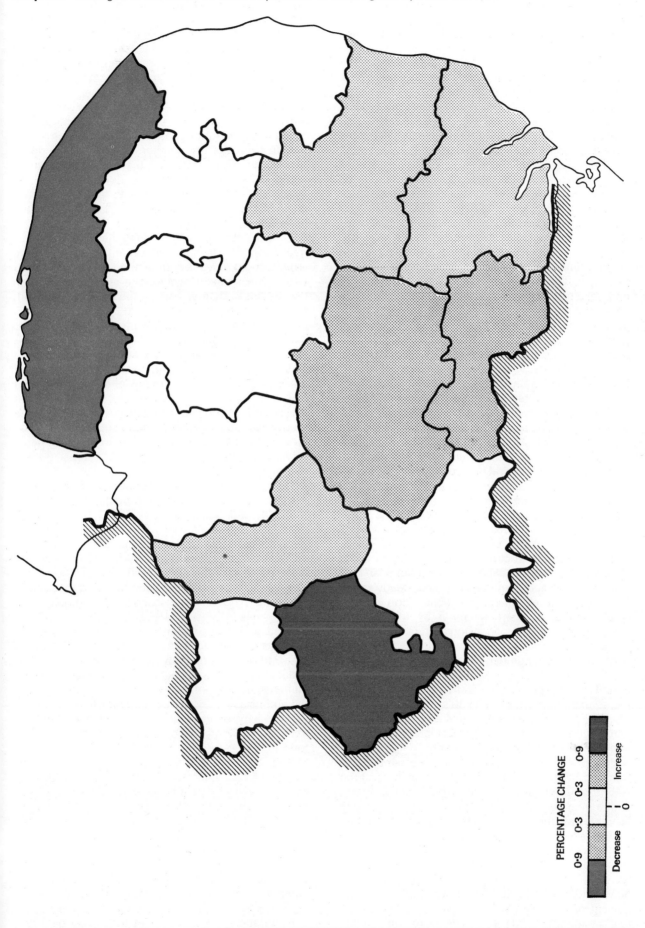

PERCENTAGE CHANGE

0·9	0·3	0	0·3	0·9
Decrease			Increase	

region, however, there is a surplus of water, and local increases in demand can normally be met through advance programmes of river regulation and new boreholes.

6.3.3 The resources available to the regional organisations concerned with the supply of water, electricity and gas, should ensure a ready response to any major demands. Under the new Regional Water Authority (RWA), a regional responsibility is held for sewage disposal, with local authorities acting as the RWA's agents for sewerage, rather than as independent bodies. Electricity is supplied to all but the most isolated farmsteads, and can service even large scale developments. Gas is supplied to virtually all small towns, and local distribution systems can be extended as these grow. However, it is unlikely to be supplied to small communities outside the present distribution system. In the longer term a question-mark lies over natural gas supplies and industrial customers may only be granted contracts on an 'interruptible supply' basis. Mains sewerage is steadily being introduced in rural areas that require it on public health grounds. The programme should be completed by the mid 1980's, but even with central government grants, the cost per house in more scattered settlements is very high. This may slow the present programme, and services may not be extended to all areas.

6.3.4 A possible constraint on development can be the availability of raw materials for construction, as well as the capacity of the construction industry itself. Shortages of sand and gravel in the South East could mean that East Anglia will export considerable amounts, though at the moment transport costs are such that sand and gravel is used generally within 30 miles of extraction. Conflict with agriculture, or with amenity considerations in river valleys, and on the coasts, may arise in the future. The region has a preponderance of small firms in its construction industry, and relies on national concerns for major developments. Major construction outside the region could absorb some of this capacity and the region can best accommodate and manage small and steady rather than 'lumpy' development. The construction industry is affected more than any other by the national economic situation, experiencing exaggerated booms and slumps.

6.3.5 There are a number of capital investment projects currently being prepared in the region. Most important is the programme of strategic road improvements extending into the 1980's and illustrated in Map 6.7. Among the major schemes planned are: the completion of the M11 south of Cambridge; northern and western bypasses for Cambridge; improvement of the A604 to the A1; the construction of a major link from the M1 to A1 in the west; the upgrading of the A45 from Cambridge eastwards to the Haven Ports; and a number of major bypasses. These include Newmarket, Bury St Edmunds and Ipswich the first two of which are already in progress or completed respectively. Progressive improvements to the A47, A17, and A11 will, with the other changes, strengthen the external links of the region, focusing the internal network on the Cambridge/Newmarket area. The present programme plans improvements first to the roads in the south and just outside the region, notably the A45 and M11. Not only are roads further to the north, such as the A47 and A11, being improved later, but the improvements are likely to be to somewhat lower standards. For instance the Swaffham bypass on the A47 is unlikely to be dualled for its whole length, despite the fact that the road carries heavy lorry traffic. It is also uncertain as to whether the A11 will be completely dualled. In the rail system, the external links are also likely to benefit, if proposals for electrification of the Cambridge/London and Ipswich/London lines are implemented. The Peterborough/Huntingdon/London service will benefit from the introduction of high-speed diesel trains in the late 1970's, but these are unlikely to be introduced on the Norwich-London line before the later 1980's. Again developments favour the south and west of the region, and to a lesser extent the main centres of East Anglia.

6.3.6. The possibility of improving the region's railway network and passenger services introduces an issue which could have a very important influence on where development occurs. The results of the context studies in chapter four, on the future of transport, showed the uncertainty that surrounds the question of personal mobility in the future. Increases in fuel costs, and safety regulations, are likely to make private transport much more expensive. The use of private cars could also be restricted on environmental grounds in a great many towns and cities. Reduced use of private cars would restrict the individual's choice of home and/or work place. Greater reliance on public transport would tend to limit new development to those settlements assured of reasonable services, as opposed to the more isolated parts of the region.

6.3.7 The growing interdependence of the region with Europe, the London metropolitan area, and the Midlands and North, is intensified by the development of the region's ports. East Anglian ports have trebled their share of the nation's trade from 2% in 1961 to 6% in 1971, and present forecasts see massive expansion. Total capacity in 1971 at the Haven Ports, King's Lynn, Great Yarmouth and Lowestoft, was some $10\frac{1}{2}$ million tons, and this is planned to rise to $25\frac{1}{2}$ million tons by 1980. This could represent more than 10% of the nation's trade. The types of facilities offered—for containerised, and roll-on/roll-off, traffic—the proximity to European Markets, a history of good labour relations, and efficient working methods, have given the various management boards the enthusiasm to undertake expansion. For instance the capacity of Felixstowe is planned to increase from around three million tons in 1971 to 10 million tons in 1980—and to 20 million tons by the mid 1990's. At Harwich a third quay providing handling capacity for 2 million tons a year is planned. Growth at the Haven Ports could generate further pressures in the Ipswich area, although a considerable amount of cargo shipped would travel to and from other regions, using the improved A45, and the railways. Current traffic loads suggest that there are potential problems associated with further port growth, particularly for the Norwich-Great Yarmouth road where few improvements are programmed.

6.3.8 Peterborough New Town will be the largest concentration of population in the region by 1990,

Map 6.7 Current Programme of Major Road Improvements

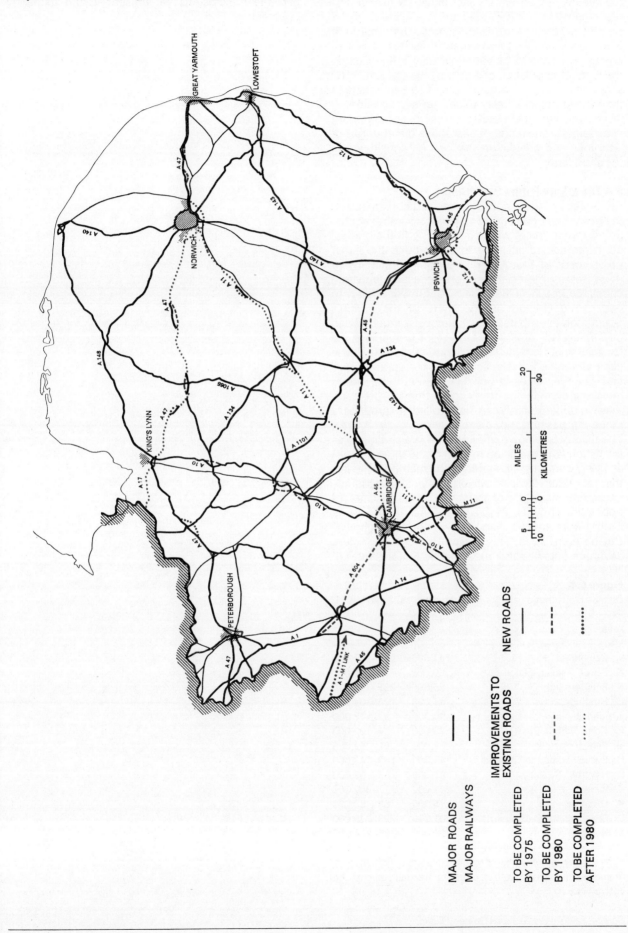

MAJOR ROADS
MAJOR RAILWAYS

IMPROVEMENTS TO
EXISTING ROADS

TO BE COMPLETED
BY 1975

TO BE COMPLETED
BY 1980

TO BE COMPLETED
AFTER 1980

NEW ROADS

with a sound base for further growth. This could lead to pressures for a diagonal route across the centre of the region, acting as an alternative to further improvements to the A45 after the completion of the present programme of road schemes. Peterborough New Town, and the town expansion schemes will, of course, continue to be very important influences on the rates of population and employment growth. The schemes are likely to attract a very high percentage of the mobile industry likely to set up in the region, at least until the mid 1980's. This is an important constraint on the range of alternative distributions of new jobs and population that can be considered in the short term.

6.4 The Likely Future Situation

6.4.1 Many of these opportunities and constraints on the growth of population and employment reflect the longstanding forces which are leading to the gradual concentration of activities in and around the larger urban areas of East Anglia. The general stability of these forces makes it possible to estimate within certain limits where the location of growth is likely to occur. The changes in the share of the region's population in each decade of the postwar period can be interpreted to provide a range of probable shifts for each area from the regional rate of growth. These can be modified to take account of the opportunities and constraints described above. With the future rates of growth for the region taken from chapter four, these modified shifts can be applied to produce a range of possible population levels in each area. The results are shown in Figure 6.4 which illustrates the estimated population in each of the thirteen areas at 1991. Careful examination of the method indicates that it is relatively insensitive to any single assumption. With this degree of assurance, the distribution of population shown in Figure 6.4 has been taken as the likely future situation, against which future choices can be considered. This means that any consistent deviation outside either the assumed regional rates of growth, or the area shifts from this mean, would require careful reconsideration both of the analysis and the conclusions we present in the following chapters.

Figure 6.4

Estimated distribution of population by areas 1971 and 1991

Area	1971	1991*
A. Cambridge	191,000	217–241,000
B. Fens (Wisbech-March-Ely)	80,000	72– 90,000
C. Peterborough	125,000	237–261,000
D. Huntingdon	91,000	138–164,000
E. Kings Lynn	90,000	97–117,000
F. North Norfolk Coast	95,000	84–102,000
G. Central Norfolk	62,000	61– 77,000
H. Bury St Edmunds-Thetford	141,000	189–213,000
I. Haverhill-Sudbury	65,000	88–108,000
J. Ipswich	242,000	277–307,000
K. Diss-Eye	75,000	68– 88,000
L. Great Yarmouth-Lowestoft	201,000	223–249,000
M. Norwich	223,000	256–284,000

*The ranges assume that present planned migration programmes are carried out, but no major new agreements are entered into.

Source: East Anglia Regional Strategy Team.

Chapter 7

Themes for Future Development

7.1 Introduction

7.1.1 The purpose of this chapter is to assess the possibilities of influencing the pattern of future population and employment within East Anglia. What choices are open, and what does each imply for the achievement of the objectives for the region? To answer these questions, within the background provided by chapter six, five ideal themes are considered for the location of new development. These themes are then compared for their likely performance against the objectives. This process of evaluation, much of which is necessarily in qualitative and imprecise terms, uses all the objectives described in chapter two. Rather more emphasis is placed, however, on those objectives concerned with benefits to people living in the region, and the way in which those benefits are distributed. The conclusions from this process provide the basis for the final chapter of this section. This sets out the principles and proposals which seem appropriate for the location of change within East Anglia.

7.2 The Development of Locational Themes

7.2.1 The major source of ideas for possible themes for the location of new development is the previous work on the future of the region referred to in Section A. Both the Economic Planning Council and the Consultative Committee have outlined a number of ideas to be taken forward. In summary form, these include:

(a) the possibility of increasing the growth and prosperity of the region as a whole by taking advantage of the potential of the four main centres, and of the other areas of the region that have recently demonstrated their ability to grow quickly;

(b) the need to consider the future of those areas which are relatively remote from the main centres, where the population has poorer job prospects, lower levels of services, and the market towns have an uncertain future;

(c) the possibility of concentrating growth into a number of selected centres to provide a wider range of services. This can be applied at various levels from the larger centres, to the small towns, and village development.

Two other possible themes are suggested by an examination of the objectives for the region. These are:

(d) the possibility of locating growth at centres which occupy particularly strong positions on the existing and projected transport network of the region. This could assist in spreading benefits to a wider area, in providing some support for public transport, and in ensuring increased priority for this network;

(e) the need to consider the conservation of natural and man-made assets in the region. This requires a careful balance of the economic pressures resulting from growth, between those conditions where conservation is impracticable and those where there is insufficient economic support for conservation.

7.2.2 These five possible themes for future development have to be represented in a more detailed form before the mixture of effects which they imply can be recognised. The actual circumstances within the region, together with the constraints and opportunities that exist for its future development, have to be taken into account. These factors were described in the previous chapter. It is also important to attempt where possible to measure the different effects of possible themes more precisely. This can be assisted by the way in which the themes are presented. This can create its own pitfalls, however, through the possibility that themes are represented in too much detail. The effects that are then measured may result from the nature of the representation, rather than from the underlying themes.

7.2.3 The most obvious aspect of the five themes that is capable of some form of measurement, is the future location of employment and population growth in different parts of the region in relation to the transport network. Employment opportunities are a major common element to a number of the objectives for the region: For this reason, a relatively simple method of estimating the effects of growth at different locations on employment opportunities was chosen. This method combines the access from place to place within the region provided by the major road network, with the employment provided at different locations, so as to provide a composite, and approximate, surface of the opportunities for employment across the region.

7.2.4 This method has the advantage of looking at the changes in employment opportunities open to the whole population, rather than simply to the additional population. It means, however, that the effects of changes may be submerged within the general pattern, and difficult to pinpoint. To overcome this, the formal representation of the five ideal themes has been couched in exaggerated terms. Firstly, the horizon is taken as 2001, rather than 1991, as this provides a much larger degree of change in re-

Map 7.1 Population Increase by Area, 1971–2001 (Control)

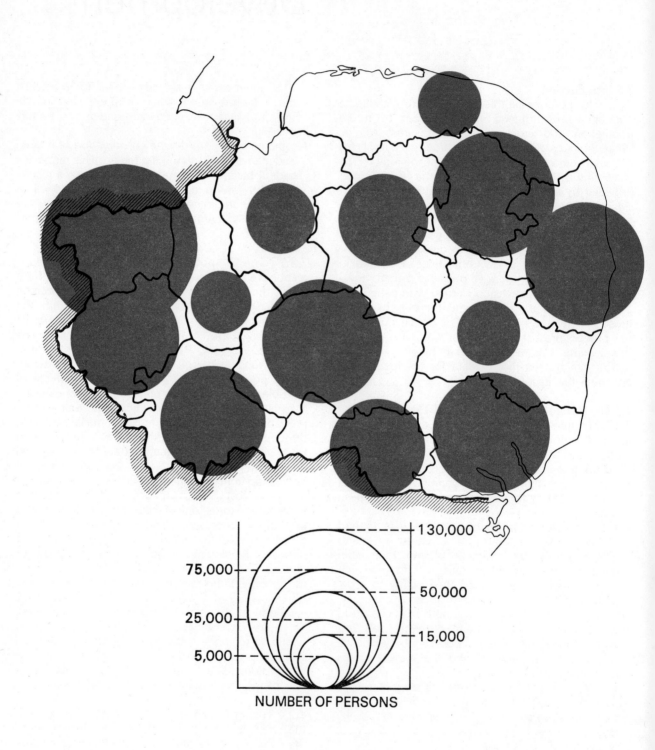

lation to those elements of population and employment that are expected to remain stable. Secondly, the changes occurring in different parts of the region have been taken outside the feasible limits set out in the previous chapter. A minimum or pessimistic estimate of the size of future population and employment was defined for each of the forty zones (described in Appendix A) into which East Anglia was subdivided by the amalgamation of local authority areas. It was then assumed that, for the purposes of this exercise only, the remaining population could be allocated between locations in the region. Finally, a sixth representation of the region in 2001 was formed, showing the 'most likely' pattern, on the basis of the continuation of present policies. This is shown on Map 7.1, generalised for thirteen areas, and provides a control theme for comparing the effects of the other themes. It must be emphasised, therefore, that much of the content of the remainder of this chapter is concerned with exaggerated and ideal patterns of development, as part of the process of understanding the different qualities of the themes that could apply to the future development of the region.

7.3 The Five Ideal Themes

7.3.1 In the following paragraphs, the themes are described in more detail and indicate the broad population and employment distribution, and any assumed modifications to the transport network required to support them. The major differences in population location from the control theme are shown on the accompanying Maps 7.2–7.6, and are summarised in Figure 7.1.

Figure 7.1

Proportions of regional population by area contained in locational themes

			Themes				
	1971	CONTROL	A	B	C	D	E
A. Cambridge	11·3	10·4	13·3	9·1	9·1	9·1	9·9
B. Fens	4·7	4·1	3·9	3·9	4·7	5·6	4·7
C. Peterborough	7·4	10·7	11·3	8·6	9·7	10·8	10·0
D. Huntingdon	5·4	6·4	7·1	5·2	5·2	5·3	6·0
E. King's Lynn	5·4	4·7	4·6	8·0	5·4	6·7	5·7
F. North Norfolk Coast	5·7	4·8	3·4	6·0	5·3	3·5	4·5
G. Central Norfolk	3·7	4·3	3·6	5·0	4·8	4·5	5·5
H. Bury St Edmunds-Thetford	8·4	9·0	8·4	11·0	8·3	8·5	9·5
I. Haverhill-Sudbury	3·9	4·7	4·6	4·1	4·1	4·2	4·3
J. Ipswich	14·4	12·9	13·9	11·7	11·7	13·7	12·5
K. Diss-Eye	4·5	3·9	3·6	5·3	4·8	4·4	4·6
L. Great Yarmouth-Lowestoft	11·9	11·5	9·7	11·6	12·4	11·9	10·7
M. Norwich	13·3	12·5	12·6	10·4	14·3	11·9	12·0

Source: East Anglia Regional Strategy Team

Theme diagrams start overleaf

Map 7.2 Theme A, 2001
(*Changing population distribution from control*)

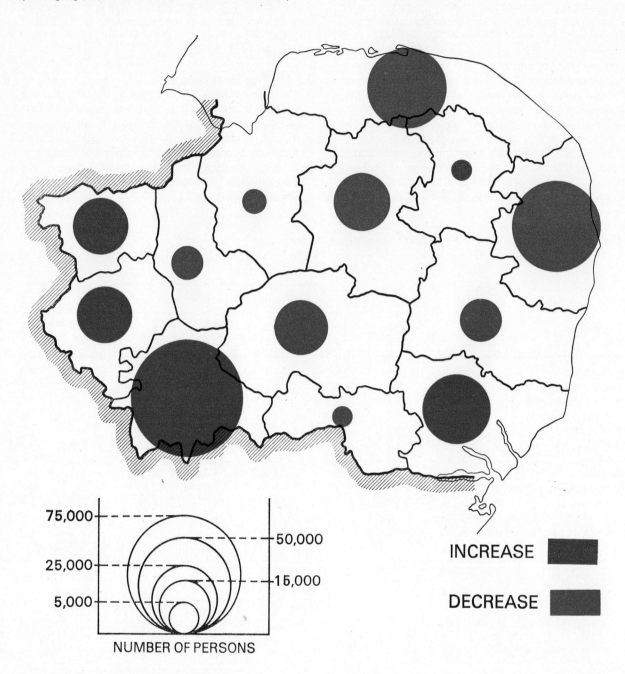

75,000
50,000
25,000
15,000
5,000

NUMBER OF PERSONS

INCREASE

DECREASE

7.3.2 Theme 'A': Maximum Growth

Development is suggested in areas with high potential for growth, in terms of past experience. Such areas would therefore exhibit one or more of the following characteristics:

(a) being within the influence of the London metropolitan area;

(b) benefiting from recent and planned route improvements, in particular from improvements on roads linking East Anglia with other regions;

(c) benefiting from the tendency for population and employment to concentrate in and around larger centres;

and

(d) having demonstrated an ability to generate growth in the recent past.

The south and west of the region are under the influence of all these growth pressures, with Cambridge, Peterborough and Ipswich the obvious candidates for large scale development. Other growth areas selected in this theme include secondary centres to these main towns—Huntingdon, Haverhill, and Bury St. Edmunds in particular. Growth on a somewhat smaller scale is proposed in Norwich, Great Yarmouth and Lowestoft, as their ability to absorb new development may be offset by their distance from London, and the fewer benefits accruing from route improvements. In all instances, concentration of employment is more marked than that of population; the spread of population growth around the centres widening the areas serviced by them.

Map 7.3 Theme B, 2001
(*Changing population distribution from control*)

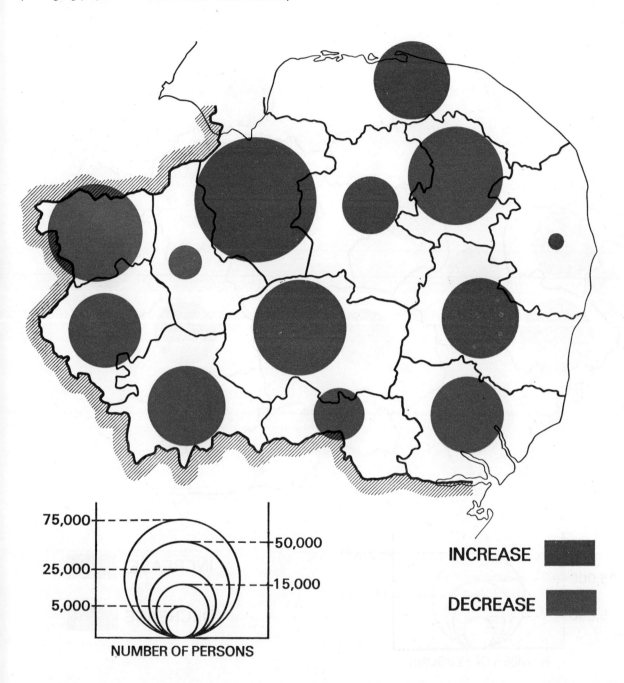

75,000
50,000
25,000
15,000
5,000

NUMBER OF PERSONS

INCREASE

DECREASE

7.3.3 Theme 'B': Selective Expansion

Development is suggested within a few selected centres serving the rural areas. Considerable parts of the region will continue to remain outside the direct influence of the growing centres, and will be unable to benefit from their facilities and services. If population and employment growth is steered towards the larger settlements that cater for these rural areas, the population within them could benefit from better services and employment opportunities. A substantial amount of growth is proposed at each of the selected 'growth points' of this theme. The scale implies major over-spill programmes, combined with policies restraining development in other settlements. The development of substantial service and employment bases in just a few centres is thought to have many longer-term benefits, producing more favourable conditions for self-sustained growth. However, the growth projected here involves the building up of five major centres at King's Lynn, Diss/Eye, Downham Market, Thetford, and Fakenham, and may well be beyond their physical capacities of development. Major growth is also proposed for the east coast areas, and in particular at Great Yarmouth and Lowestoft. Smaller growth areas selected are Bury St Edmunds and Mildenhall, both of which have had recent experience of fairly rapid growth, associated with existing schemes, and also service surrounding rural areas.

Map 7.4 Theme C, 2001
(*Changing population distribution from control*)

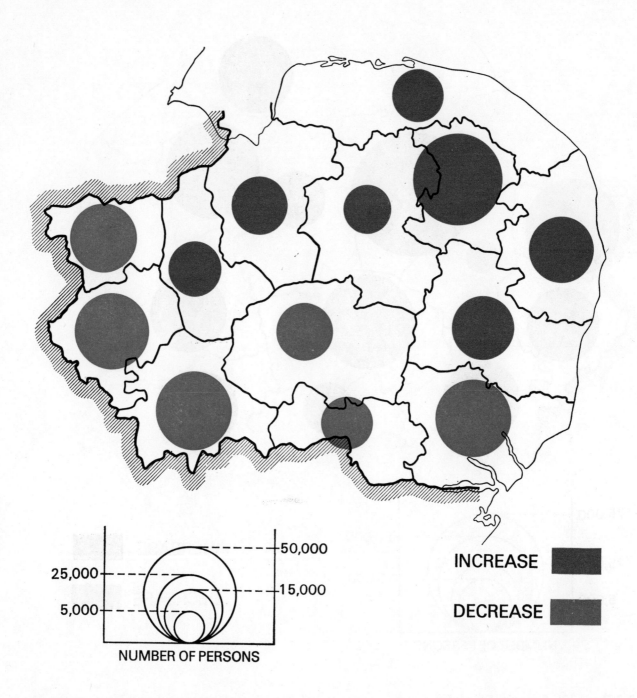

25,000 ----- 50,000

25,000 + --- ----- 15,000

5,000 + --- -----

NUMBER OF PERSONS

INCREASE

DECREASE

7.3.4 Theme 'C': Dispersed Growth

Development is again used to assist the rural areas. Particular emphasis is given to the north of the region, in the form of small scale development in many of the market towns. The amount of growth in population and employment that these towns can accommodate without difficulty is limited. Considerable expansion at Norwich is also proposed, as this could benefit the surrounding rural area of Norfolk. This may also strengthen the role of Norwich as a recognisable provincial centre within the region. Some growth at Peterborough, beyond the New Town target, could help strengthen the east/west A47 link, thereby making the north of the region more attractive to prospective employers. The theme proposes that about half of the population growth that might be influenced by location policies should be in the Norwich, Great Yarmouth and Peterborough areas, with employment more closely tied to their existing boundaries. Other development is distributed amongst twenty of the smaller towns in the north and centre of the region. Here population and employment growth are specifically linked, offering local job opportunities for those wishing to work, but lacking easy access to larger towns.

Map 7.5   Theme D, 2001
(*Changing population distribution from control*)

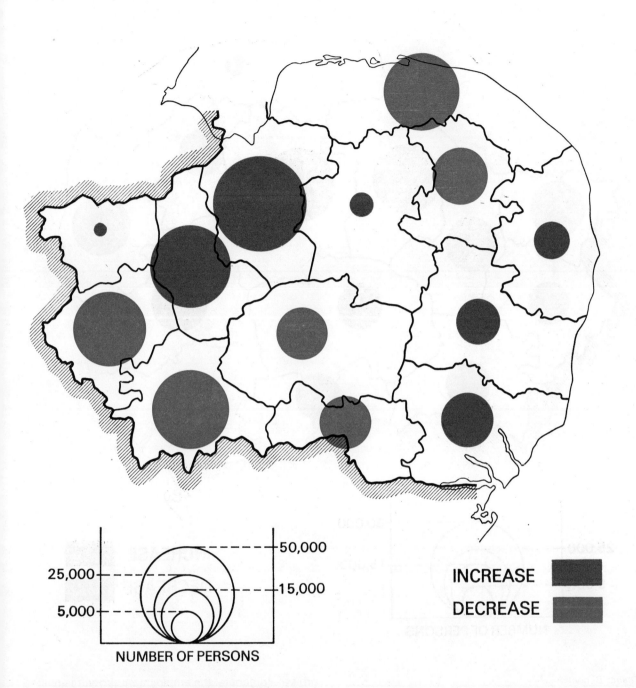

NUMBER OF PERSONS

50,000
25,000
15,000
5,000

INCREASE
DECREASE

7.3.5 Theme 'D': Strengthening of Transport Links

At present, major road improvements are being carried out, and are planned, in the south and west of the region. Such improvements encourage growth at the towns served by these roads, and planned railway investment could be a further stimulus to their growth. The cyclical process of population growth and further road improvements is self-sustaining. As a result the difference between the standards of roads in the south and west of the region, and the standards in the centre, north and east, is likely to widen. The encouragement of population and employment growth at centres with important road and/or rail connections, away from the south and west, may help to change the priorities in the improvement programmes as well as the standard of improvement currently planned. The routes selected for emphasis are:

(a) the A47 between Peterborough, Wisbech, Kings Lynn, Norwich and Great Yarmouth, to raise it to the standard of the improved A45 in the south;

(b) the A140, and also the rail link, between Norwich and Ipswich;

(c) the rail services between Peterborough, March, Ely and Thetford; between Ipswich and Lowestoft; between Kings Lynn and Cambridge;

(d) the A10 along the eastern edge of the Fens;

(e) the A143 between Great Yarmouth-Bungay-Diss.

The theme encourages growth at major route inter-

Theme 'D' continued overleaf

Map 7.6 Theme E, 2001
(*Changing population distribution from control*)

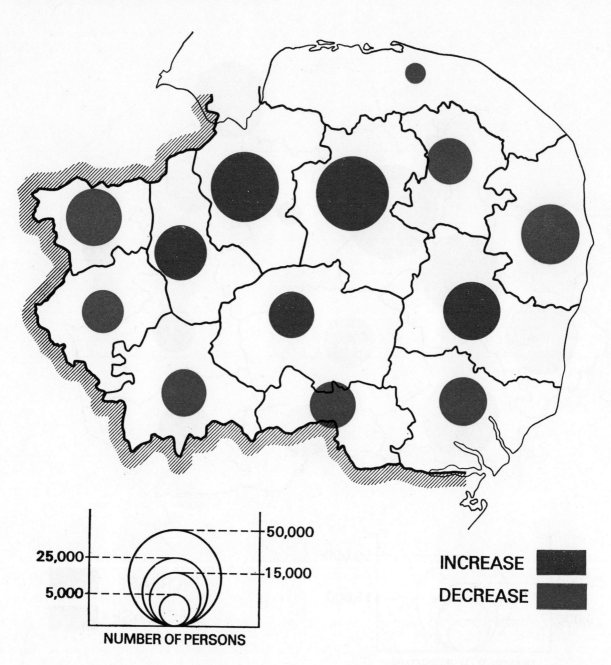

25,000

5,000

50,000

15,000

NUMBER OF PERSONS

INCREASE

DECREASE

Theme 'D' continued
sections in the centre, north, and north-east of the region, which will service local areas, and help to give an impetus to route improvement which in time may stimulate further growth. By concentrating employment growth at main centres, it may also encourage greater use of the public transport system between centres, and help to reduce the region's growing dependence on the private car. The centres selected for growth include Peterborough, Norwich, King's Lynn, Great Yarmouth, Lowestoft and Ipswich. Intermediate centres on connecting routes include Diss, Ely and Thetford; smaller towns which are accessible to the network, such as Fakenham, or on it, as are March, Downham Market, Swaffham, Wisbech and Bungay, are also selected for population

growth. In general the employment growth is related to the main and secondary centres, with population growth at smaller as well as at large settlements.

7.3.6 Theme 'E': Conservation of Environmental Assets
The primary concern of this theme is with locating future growth in those areas of the region where agricultural and environmental resources are least significant. Allied to this is the possibility of using growth to support conservation where local resources may be insufficient at present, and where recreational resources could support a larger population. In practice they take two forms. Firstly, there are three areas, in the form of north-south bands, where both agricultural and environmental assets are

Theme 'E' text continued above right

relatively insignificant. These lie either side of the Fens, and between Norwich and Ipswich. The second arises from the large number of small towns and villages in the region at a relatively low density. This suggests that in aggregate these settlements may have an unrealised potential to absorb further population, without making substantial inroads on agricultural land, and perhaps assisting local conservation policies. For this reason, the remaining growth is dispersed into towns and villages currently containing 500 or more people. In practice, therefore, the pattern taken by this theme is rather more dispersed than that represented by theme 'C'.

7.4 Evaluation of the Ideal Themes

7.4.1 These five themes are not intended to provide direct choices for the form of development of the whole region, as different themes will provide varying combinations of advantages for each part of the region. It is the purpose of this evaluation process to pick out from the themes that combination of features which seems most appropriate overall. To do this, all the objectives for the future of the region are considered, mainly in qualitative terms. In addition, the results obtained from the method of measuring employment opportunities, referred to earlier, are introduced as appropriate. Some further explanation of this method at this point is therefore necessary.

7.4.2. Basically, it seeks to provide a measure of the jobs available in different parts of the region. In very simple terms, the index calculated for a zone depends on two factors, (a) the total number of jobs available in particular areas, and (b) the 'costs' involved in travelling to jobs in different places. The index of 'job accessibility' for a zone will therefore increase if either new jobs are created within the 'commuting area', or if routes are improved, so that the 'commuting area' is widened to include jobs previously outside it. Nationally, motorway construction has possibly had the most far-reaching effects of this type in recent years. Over time, both these forces will have an impact on areas within East Anglia. The planned road improvements illustrated in Map 6.7 will combine with employment growth to alter the indices representing the 1971 situation. Each locational theme will provide measures of the index of employment opportunities for each of the forty zones for 2001.

7.4.3 The index of employment opportunities is closely linked to several other important factors in the future of the region. The most important of these are the opportunities to increase income, but it also has considerable relevance to the distribution of, say, shopping and health facilities. With careful interpretation, therefore, the general pattern it provides gives some indication of the distribution of opportunities in the region. At the same time, however, it cannot provide a measure of the absolute number or range of jobs available to an individual. For this reason, the results are expressed either in terms of the regional average or in differences from the control or 'most likely' theme. Similarly, it is unable to distinguish between differences in location within each zone, and does not include the rail network or the local road network, which could be significant in several parts of the region.

7.4.4 Each of the five major groups of objectives is considered in turn in the evaluation, drawing on the results from the index where appropriate. These objectives are concerned with (a) resources, (b) the relationship between the region and the national economy, (c) the distribution of improvements to the quality of life between different sectors of the population, (d) a similar concern with distribution, but between different parts of the region, and finally (e) the timing of these improvements.

7.5 Resource Objectives

7.5.1 The five resource objectives described in chapter two cover capital costs, running costs, labour resources, the rate at which land is developed, and the conservation of environmental resources. No single theme performs well in respect of all of these objectives. This is not surprising as a considerable degree of conflict is inherent in the objectives themselves. In general terms, the objectives of minimising the financial costs of new development are favoured by larger units, which are more likely in the urban areas. In contrast, the labour resources of the region are more likely to be under-used in the rural areas. The choice of location will be significant to the land and environmental objectives and whilst some dispersion will protect natural environmental resources man-made resources would benefit from an element of concentration.

7.5.2 In practice, both themes 'B' and 'D' perform reasonably well. Development is concentrated in a small number of centres, which should enable economies to be realised in both building and service provision. The rate at which land is developed can be restricted by building at a higher density. Employment growth is encouraged in areas now experiencing seasonal unemployment. On the other hand, these themes are not so successful as those of 'C' and 'E' in providing local employment for those unwilling or unable to commute. The other themes seem to perform less satisfactorily. Theme 'A' would appear to keep costs of development low, but excessive pressures around such a centre as Cambridge could bid up land prices and construction costs. The value of having an existing infrastructure of major roads and public utilities could be consequently reduced. The theme does little to improve the use of labour outside the growth areas, and creates intensive pressures on the environment in the south of the region. Theme 'E' performs excellently, as would be expected, for environmental resources but would incur high capital and maintenance costs. It provides for high activity rates, but not for a choice of jobs. To some extent theme 'C' shares the advantages and disadvantages of this theme ('E').

7.5.3 Several conclusions can be drawn to describe a pattern of location which would fulfil most of the resource objectives. The analysis suggests that population and employment growth should be promoted in a limited number of centres. This would enable economies of scale to be realised in both production processes and service provision. Environmental considerations imply that such growth should be encouraged in areas away from the south and west—areas of growth whatever policies are introduced. Labour resources can be used efficiently if a range of jobs can be provided. This also implies employment growth in an around a number of settlements which provide such job diversification, including some distant from the few main centres. If access to these growth centres can be improved through investment in both routes and transport, their labour pools can be extended. Growth encouraging route improvements, and providing some financial backing to a public transport system, is required.

7.6 The Region and the National Economy

7.6.1 The three objectives that fall within this group are concerned with the contribution that the region makes to the national economy, the support given to the region's economy, and shielding the region from the worst effects of fluctuations in the national economic situation. The priority given to the first objective is reduced by the principle, arising from Section B, that priority should be given to the location and composition of growth, rather than to its overall volume.

7.6.2 How well do the five themes perform? For the first objective, some indication is provided by the index of employment opportunities. The overall regional average of employment opportunities may be taken as representing the different capacities of the themes to vary the regional rate of growth. On this basis, in relation to the most likely situation, Theme 'A' performs best (+0·5%), with 'D' second (+0·3%), followed by 'E' (—0·4%), and 'B' and 'C' (—0·6%). This accords with expectations, except perhaps in the relative positions of 'B' and 'E', where the difference is very small. In contrast, Theme 'A' is unlikely to make a satisfactory contribution to the other two objectives because of the emphasis it places on developing links with the remainder of the country. Similarly, while 'C' and 'E' will not assist in building up these external links, the dispersal of growth they propose is unlikely to build up an economic base for self-sustained growth or of a nature likely to be sufficiently robust to resist disruption from external pressures. On this basis, the best performance seems likely for themes 'B' and 'D'. They offer the attraction of a considerable degree of concentration, encouraging the development of associated services, and a diversity of employment, affording some resilience against the decline of particular industries. The somewhat lower degree of concentration in theme 'D' is offset by its emphasis on the development of the route network, which will support an improved longterm potential in the regional economy.

7.6.3 The locational pattern achieving these national economy objectives would include concentration of population and employment, together with improvements to routes linking growth points with markets. The robustness of the regional economy can be built up if employment growth occurs in parts of the region serving local labour markets. Some diversification of employment is also implied. Growth in the north-east urban areas would encourage such local industries and services to develop.

7.7 The Quality of Life for different sectors of the Population

7.7.1 The distribution and quality of life objectives for the future of the region, as set out in chapter two, are very much interrelated. For the purposes of this evaluation therefore we have considered improvements to the quality of life in terms of the distribution between sectors of the population and between different parts of the region. Such improvements are related to income levels, the standards of public services, the goods and services offered by the private sector, and the mix and range of activities of the public and private sectors.

7.7.2 It is difficult to identify the effects of the five ideal themes on different sectors of the population. One way is to consider the extent to which particular sectors of the population are disproportionately represented in certain parts of the region. The rural areas contain a relatively large proportion of lower paid and unskilled workers. Themes 'C' and 'E' encourage a considerable amount of employment growth in these areas, directly helping to raise the proportion of people employed, and consequently household incomes. The effects of themes 'B' and 'D' are less direct, but could be more significant in the longer term. They offer in varying degrees the prospects of a better range of urban services, a wider range of jobs in the towns close to these areas, and improvements to the routes through them. On this basis, it is considered that 'B' and 'D' offer the best performance for this group of objectives.

7.8 The Quality of Life in different parts of the Region

7.8.1 The interpretation of this group of objectives has to recognise that the opportunities making up the quality of life are not equally distributed across the region. Similarly, the changes that will occur in the region irrespective of strategic policies will modify that pattern unequally. It is important, therefore, to attempt to establish both the existing distribution and the way in which it is likely to change before the effects of the five themes are considered. The index of employment opportunities, described earlier, has the advantage of providing a consistent method for each step, in the sense that it maintains a similar approach for all cases.

7.8.2 Using this index, the present distribution of employment opportunities is shown on Map 7.7, as deviations from the overall regional average. This indicates a pronounced peaking of opportunities around each urban area, and a general tendency for the level of opportunities to be higher towards the south and west of the region. The information shown on the map is summarised for thirteen areas of the region in the first column of Figure 7.2. On this basis, the five areas enjoying a level of opportunities above the regional average are around the four main centres and in the Huntingdon-St Neots area, which account for over half of the region's population. Equally striking are the two areas (the North Norfolk Coast, and the Diss-Eye area) below 80% of the regional average, and the two other areas (King's Lynn and Central Norfolk) below 90%.

7.8.3 The effect of the major programme of road investment in the region over the next decade has been considered separately from the question of population and employment growth. Increases in the costs of fuel could well outweigh the gains in access from

Figure 7.2
Expected changes in the relative index of employment opportunities by areas in East Anglia

Area	Present Situation (1971)	Effect of Future Road Programme		Control Theme, 2001	
		Relative Position	Percentage Increase over Present Situation	Relative Position	Percentage Increase over Present Situation
A. Cambridge	110·3	113·5	+2·9	108·3	—1·7
B. Fens	97·1	98·1	+1·0	97·3	+0·3
C. Peterborough	119·2	120·1	+0·8	130·4	+9·5
D. Huntingdon	104·1	107·8	+3·6	106·9	+2·6
E. King's Lynn	88·7	89·9	+1·4	88·7	0·0
F. North Norfolk Coast	71·6	71·0	—0·8	70·7	—1·3
G. Central Norfolk	87·6	88·3	+0·8	87·1	—0·5
H. Bury St Edmunds-Thetford	96·9	98·5	+1·7	99·9	+3·1
I. Haverhill-Sudbury	96·5	97·9	+1·5	96·3	—0·2
J. Ipswich	106·2	106·5	+0·2	101·3	—4·7
K. Diss-Eye	79·1	78·7	—0·5	78·0	—1·4
L. Great Yarmouth-Lowestoft	91·1	88·9	—2·4	85·9	—5·7
M. Norwich	111·2	106·1	—4·7	104·5	—6·1
Regional Average	100·0	100·0		100·0	

Source: East Anglia Regional Strategy Team

road improvement. For this reason, this programme is considered for its relative effects on different parts of the region only. This is shown in terms of the regional average on Map 7.8, and summarised again for the thirteen areas in Figure 7.2. This indicates that the majority of the region improves its relative position as a result of the road programme. The improvement is most marked in the south-west of the region, with the completion of the M11, and M1—A1 link, and along the route of the improved A45. Contrasted to this, however, is a substantial deterioration in the relative position of the Norwich and Great Yarmouth-Lowestoft areas. It may also be significant that the other two areas to show some relative deterioration are the North Norfolk Coast and the Diss-Eye areas which have the lowest index of opportunities at present.

7.8.4 The next step in evaluating this group of objectives is to consider the impact of the change produced by the most likely pattern of employment and population growth, represented by the control theme. The surface this produces in relation to the regional average is shown on Map 7.9, and is summarised in the last column of Figure 7.2. Since each new job created in the theme will be open to several people, we can explain the fact that the growth of employment opportunities is significantly faster than the actual growth of employment. This helps to place the results in the perspective that all areas should gain from growth in the future. The substantial increase in the relative level of employment opportunities in Peterborough, as a result of the completion of the New Town, is perhaps the most striking single feature of this control theme. Indeed, the only areas which show an improvement against the regional average are those adjacent to the New Town, or with a substantial planned migration programme. Taking the effect of this whole programme into account, the rural areas appear to maintain their position reasonably well, and the largest falls occur in and around the main urban areas including Great Yarmouth-Lowestoft. There is some possibility that the control theme understates the likely growth of these urban areas, compared with the forecasts adopted in chapter six, and that the method adopted to produce the index may not fully recognise the opportunities available to suburban areas surrounding the main centres. There is some basis, therefore, for considering that the actual position is likely to be relatively more evenly distributed than is shown by these results, with the important exception of the planned migration programme.

7.8.5 Even with these reservations, however, the control theme provides a consistent yardstick for examining the effects produced by the five ideal themes. These are shown on Maps 7.10 to 7.14, and summarised in Figure 7.3. The most striking feature of these results is the difference between theme 'A' and the other themes. Theme 'A' concentrates the improvements it produces largely to the south and west of the region, with little overlap with the remaining themes. The other four themes tend to produce improvements over much of the rest of the region, with 'B' and 'C' largely coincident in the areas influenced and tending further towards the north and east. Closer examination indicates that theme 'B' offers the best performance for five of the thirteen areas in Figure 7.3, including the four areas with the lowest index of opportunities at present. In contrast to this, the best performance of theme 'C' comes in the Norwich and Great Yarmouth-Lowestoft areas, whose relative position following the completion of the present road programme shows

Map 7.7 Access to Employment Opportunities, 1971
(*Deviation of Index from Regional Average*)

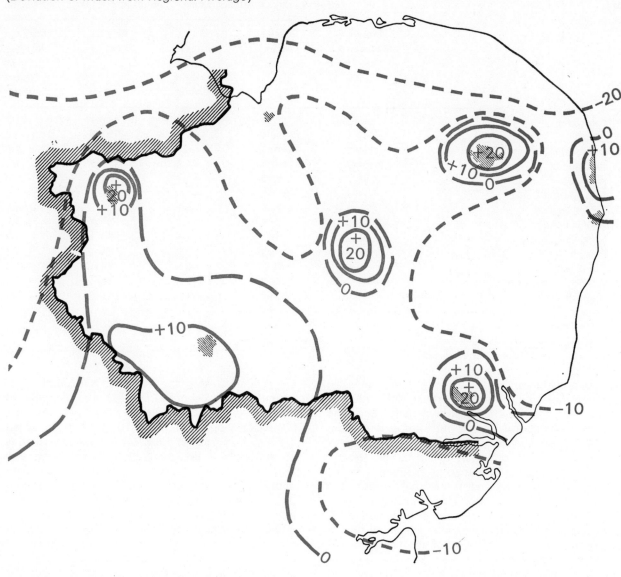

a substantial decline. The extent to which the different themes tend to reduce the overall disparities in opportunities can be assessed. To do this, the index for each area must be weighted by both the population change and the level of disparities that exist at present. The results are shown at the foot of Figure 7.3 and indicate that on this basis theme **'B'** performs considerably better in reducing the overall disparities in the index of opportunities across the region. Themes **'C'**, **'D'**, and **'E'** are closely grouped, with **'D'** being slightly poorer. Finally, it is clear that theme **'A'** does least well by a considerable margin in achieving this group of objectives.

7.8.6 From these results, using the index of employment opportunities, it seems clear that some degree of concentrated growth as represented by theme **'B'**, and around Norwich as in theme **'C'**, would be beneficial. The method used to produce the index, however, does not take account of some of the essential qualities of the other themes. This is particularly so for theme **'D'** which is based upon the encouragement of rail and bus public transport, and assistance in

gaining higher priority for improvements to the road network of the region. Consequently, the index is likely to understate the effects which it produces. Similarly, the more dispersed pattern of growth contained in theme **'E'** and in much of **'C'** has a considerable element of discretion in the location of growth in and around the small towns which cannot be represented by the index, and which would provide additional benefits. While the results appear to indicate a concentrated form of growth in the northern part of the region on a scale achievable only by a considerable planned migration programme, there are substantial reasons for adopting a less blunt approach. A combination of the elements of the four themes **'B'**, **'C'**, **'D'** and **'E'** would seem to be appropriate.

7.8.7 The inclusion in the assessment of factors not directly represented in the index of employment opportunities, tends to support this conclusion. A greater number and range of jobs in the northern part of the region would bring a wider choice of training opportunities, in both private and public schemes, to

Map 7.8 Effect of Current Road Investment Programme
(*Percentage change from the Relative Index in Map 7.7*)

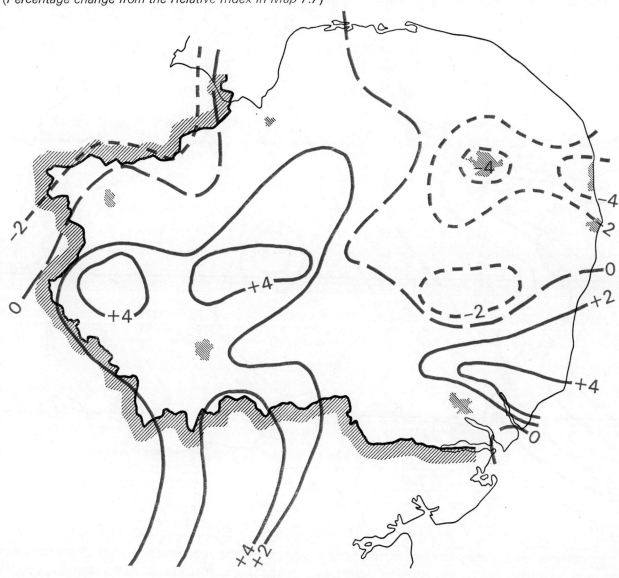

Figure 7.3
Notional change* in the relative index of employment opportunities produced by locational themes, 1971–2001

Area	Theme A	Theme B	Theme C	Theme D	Theme E
A. Cambridge	+2·2	—1·2	—1·6	—1·2	—0·1
B. Fens	—0·7	0·0	—0·2	+0·6	+0·9
C. Peterborough	—0·4	—0·8	—0·6	+0·3	+0·7
D. Huntingdon	+0·6	—1·7	—1·9	—1·2	—0·4
E. King's Lynn	—1·9	+5·5	+1·4	+4·8	+2·8
F. North Norfolk Coast	—3·5	+1·6	+1·0	—0·7	—0·1
G. Central Norfolk	—1·8	+2·5	+1·9	+0·5	+2·1
H. Bury St Edmunds-Thetford	—2·1	+10·1	+2·2	+3·6	—0·3
I. Haverhill-Sudbury	—0·5	—0·6	—1·0	—0·1	—0·3
J. Ipswich	—0·7	—0·6	—0·7	—0·6	—0·8
K. Diss-Eye	—2·9	+2·0	+1·1	+1·0	+0·4
L. Great Yarmouth-Lowestoft	—4·2	+0·7	+1·5	+0·2	—1·6
M. Norwich	—1·8	+0·3	+1·5	+1·3	+1·5
Weighted Results	1292	1507	1421	1404	1422

Source: East Anglia Regional Strategy Team

*Each result is given as the percentage change from the
control strategy given in Figure 7.2.

Map 7.9 Effect of the 2001 Control
(*Percentage change from the Relative Index in Map 7.7*)

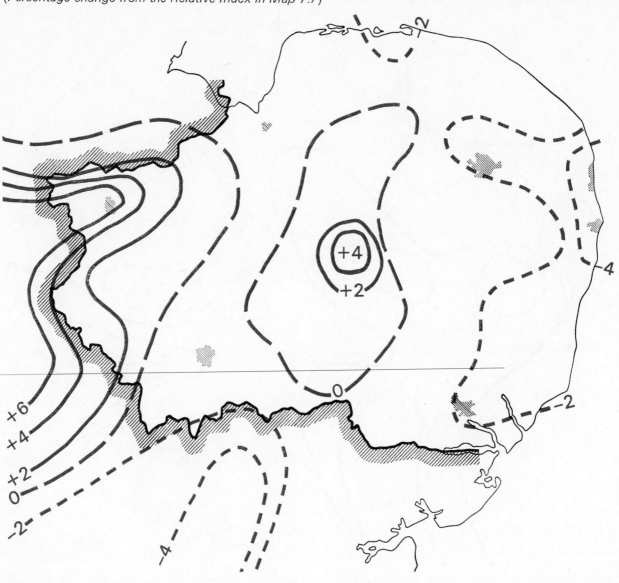

the local labour force. The increased competition for labour would tend to raise the overall level of wages in the area, including those in the traditional industries. At present, the rapid growth of population in the south and west of East Anglia is outpacing the rate at which social and recreational facilities can be provided. Some diversion of these pressures towards the north and centre of the region would bring advantages all round. It would help relieve the insistent demands in the south and west, allowing a more even pace of development. At the same time, it would encourage, in the north and centre, the development of those recreational resources that are now under-used, and provide a much-needed incentive to improve the general level of services there.

7.9 The Timing of Improvements to the Quality of Life

7.9.1 Two objectives concerned with the timing of growth were described in chapter two. One specified that improvements to the quality of life should be ensured in the future, and the second indicated that

short-term fluctuations in these improvements should be avoided if possible. How well are the five locational themes likely to perform in this respect? Perhaps the two themes likely to show the poorest performance are **'A'** and **'B'**. While theme **'A'** is likely to produce the fastest rate of growth for the region overall, it is most likely to create imbalance within the region, with serious pressure on services in the areas of rapid growth. Similarly, the achievement of theme **'B'** is dependent upon a programme of planned migration additional to that already in hand. As was demonstrated in chapter six, it is unlikely that this programme can be extended to any great degree until the next decade. It is, therefore, not only dependent upon factors external to the region for these decisions, but its major phase of development could coincide with the period of a substantial decrease in the supply of mobile employment associated with manufacturing industry, if the context study forecasts on the effects of automation are realised. Some queries on practicability also apply to themes **'C'** and **'E'**. In the case of **'C'** the scale of

Map 7.10 Effect of Theme A
(*Percentage change from the Relative Index for the 2001 Controls as shown in Map 7.9*)

expansion proposed in the Norwich area is likely to present problems even in the long-term. Similarly, a number of the areas suggested for substantial, if dispersed growth in theme **'E'** have a poor infrastructure. This reduces its practicability and places its realisation in the longer-term. In comparison, theme **'D'** presents fewer problems, except in the degree to which it requires some redirection of growth towards the north and east. It is, however, designed both to take advantage of the present transport network and to assist in the future development of that network. This suggests that it is likely to show the best performance against this group of objectives.

7.10 Conclusions

7.10.1 Three basic questions about the future location of development in East Anglia have structured the process of establishing and evaluating possible themes in this chapter. The first of these is the relative priority to be given to the faster growing areas, around the major centres and in the south and west of the region, as compared to the areas which are static or slow growing—in the rural areas, and to the north and east. The second question is the issue of whether future growth should be rather more concentrated or dispersed to achieve the greatest benefits. This involves both a choice of whether greater emphasis should be given to growth around major centres, secondary centres, the small market towns or the villages, and to the degree of selectiveness to be exercised at each of these levels. The third question, which overlaps the first two, is the nature of the future role of the planned migration programme in the location of future development in East Anglia.

7.10.2 The first question may be the simplest to answer. Theme **'A'** consciously favours additional development in the faster growing areas in the south-west of the region. The evaluation process suggests that this does not produce the extra benefits for the region as a whole which would compensate for the relative deterioration in the position of the remainder of the region, and there is no mechanism by which any such compensation could be carried out. It is

57

Map 7.11 Effect of Theme B
(*Percentage change from the Relative Index for the 2001 Controls as shown in Map 7.9*)

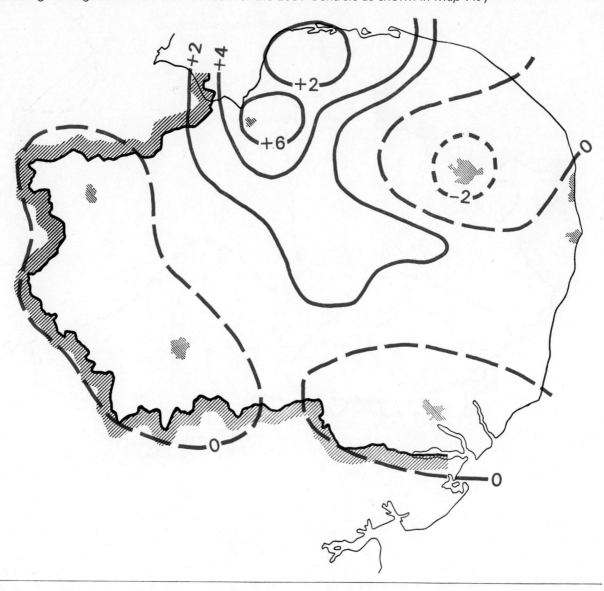

also evident that these areas also receive the greatest assistance from the road investment programme, strengthening their momentum for further growth. On this basis, it appears that strategic policies for the location of future development in the region should favour the encouragement of growth in the north and east of the region. This would also accord with the conclusions of the previous section, which indicated policies designed to influence the composition and location of growth, in contrast to achieving the maximum possible growth.

7.10.3 The prospects of the main urban areas are more varied. Peterborough is assured of an expanding future, while it seems inevitable that the pressures for growth in Cambridge will increase. The future of Ipswich is related to the growth of the Haven Ports, and to its strengthened connections with London. In the longer term, the future growth of the Norwich and Great Yarmouth-Lowestoft areas may be less certain than in the other centres. In principle, however, each of these main urban areas has demonstrated a capacity for sustained growth which is

expected to continue. It is perhaps more important, therefore, to consider the degree to which the continued growth of these centres will benefit the rural areas of the region. It has been recent experience that the area of dependence on these centres has been increasing with greater use and ownership of the private car. From the results of the context studies, and recent developments, it is no longer certain that the costs of motoring will enable this process to continue. Furthermore, it is a process which has progressively eroded the public transport system in these rural areas. It seems unlikely, therefore, that the whole of the rural areas of the region would be covered by the direct influence of the major centres, even if faster growth were promoted around them, and such an approach would carry the danger of a further decline in services. For these reasons, it is considered that future strategic policies for the growth of these main centres should be directed to complement the strengthening of the north and east of the region as proposed in the previous paragraph.

Map 7.12 Effect of Theme C
(*Percentage change from the Relative Index for the 2001 Controls as shown in Map 7.9*)

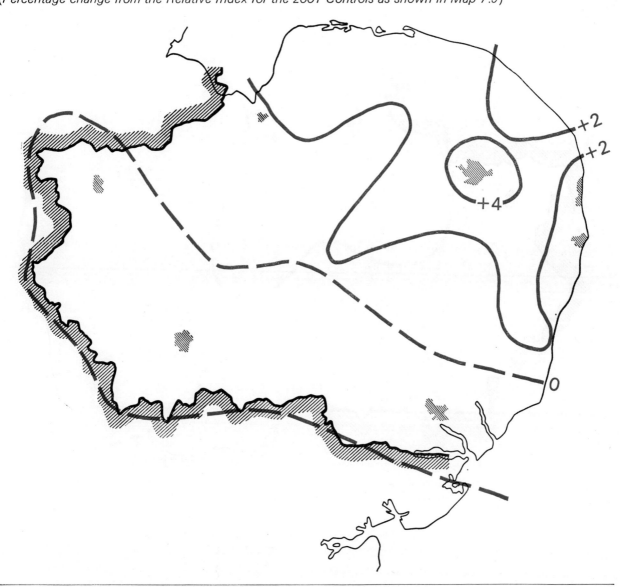

7.10.4 This conclusion provides a lead to the answer to the second question on the issue of concentrated or dispersed forms of development. In general, the evaluation process indicated that some concentration of development would be beneficial in providing a wider range of employment and service opportunities to many parts of the region. Perhaps the most successful theme on this basis was **'B'**, which placed stress on a considerable degree of concentrated development away from the main centres. This appears to indicate the encouragement of growth in a series of secondary centres at locations which are intermediate to the areas of influence of the main centres. The choice of these centres could adopt with advantage the basic principle of theme **'D'**, of locations at important intersections on the region's transport network.

7.10.5 It is much more difficult to be precise about the size of centre which would be suitable. Many of the small towns in the region are having difficulty in maintaining their present functions and do not possess the capacity for self-sustained growth. It is

evident, therefore, that in addition to location, size is an advantage, but local conditions are important, particularly the degree of enterprise present in both the private and public sectors. The scope for local initiative in these terms seems likely to increase under local government reorganisation. Perhaps the most robust approach is to consider the rate of development. An existing centre with a range of services is more likely to be capable of absorbing a certain volume of growth than is a much smaller town. On this basis, it is considered that a greater degree of concentration and selectiveness in the encouragement of growth is required, and that the rate of growth of any centre should be matched to its size and range of services, except in special circumstances.

7.10.6 This possibility of special circumstances brings in the third question on the future role of the planned migration programme. At present the main thrust of this programme is directed towards the south and west of the region, and is giving added impetus to the faster rates of growth experienced in these areas.

Map 7.13 Effect of Theme D
(*Percentage change from the Relative Index for the 2001 Controls as shown in Map 7.9*)

The conclusions reached above indicate that the possibility of redirecting this thrust towards areas further north and east should be considered where this is practicable in terms of the existing schemes. As a corollary to this, it is also evident that these planned migration schemes are a major instrument for priming growth in locations where this seems to be required. This could apply both to the build up in a concentrated form of the series of secondary centres suggested above, and to groups of small towns. On this basis, it is considered that the future of the planned migration programme should be positively designed to build up a strengthened framework of secondary towns, associated with improvements to the transport network.

Map 7.14   Effect of Theme E
(*Percentage change from the Relative Index for the 2001 Controls as shown in Map 7.9*)

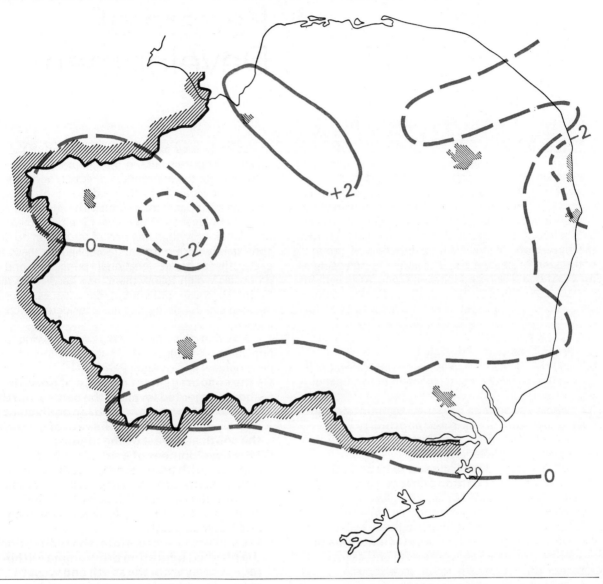

Chapter 8

The Future Pattern of Development

8.1 Introduction

8.1.1 This final chapter of Section C draws together the contents of the two previous chapters. It does so against the background of the principles for the region as a whole outlined in Section B. It begins by formalising the conclusions of the previous chapter as a set of broad locational principles, posed against the framework of the likely distribution of growth considered in chapter six. The regional perspective provided by these broad locational principles is then interpreted in the actual circumstances of the region. This gives rise to a set of more detailed proposals for consideration by central and local government.

8.2 Broad Locational Principles

8.2.1 Three of the principles with which Section B concluded are relevant to the content of this Section. These are:

B1 policies should be designed to maintain the diversity, and the sense of continuity with the past, that make East Anglia recognisably different;

B2 policies should be designed to be selective both in the composition and location of growth encouraged in East Anglia;

B5 policies should be designed to build up internal structures which are likely to be resilient to change, by a greater emphasis on securing longer-term potential and assets, rather than on realising the totality of short-term growth prospects.

The evaluation of the possible themes for the development of East Anglia has tended to reinforce these principles rather than indicate any substantial reasons for modifying them.

8.2.2 Future policies for the location of development within the region have also to be couched in terms of what is practically possible. In chapter six, the likely distribution of population within the region was forecasted, on the basis of a wide range of possible rates of growth for the region as a whole, and of similar ranges about the way this growth is expected to be distributed in the region. These ranges express the considerable uncertainty about both aspects of population growth, and no attempt has been made to force the results into precise targets. The opportunity has been taken rather to adopt the results as indicative of the discretion available to strategic policies at both the regional and local level to influence the distribution of population within the region. The broad locational principles which follow are set within this framework of discretion provided by the

forecasts. In their expression, and in that of the more detailed proposals later in the chapter, the intention is to indicate the appropriate direction and degree of movement away from the mid-point of the range towards its upper or lower limits. This also means that if, for any reason, the rates of employment and population growth in any part of the region do not lie consistently within the range implied by these forecasts, these broad locational principles and the proposals which follow them may need to be recast to match these different circumstances. Possible mechanisms for doing this are considered in chapter sixteen.

8.2.3 Within this framework, the following broad principles are suggested for the location of future development in East Anglia:

C1 the encouragement of a rate of growth above projected levels in the centre, north, and east of the region, with an equivalent exercise of restraint on the rate of growth in the south and west of the region;

C2 the development of a set of secondary centres, with associated growth in small towns, within those areas likely to remain outside the direct influence of the main centres of Cambridge, Ipswich, Norwich and Peterborough;

C3 as and when appropriate, the redirection of the planned migration programme within the region away from the south and west to support the development of secondary centres in the central, northern and eastern parts of the region;

C4 as and when appropriate, the gradual reorientation of the programme of road investment to support the improvement of major routes to the north and east, and across the centre of the region, and to provide a network of routes of good standard between the main and secondary centres;

C5 the encouragement of more concentrated forms of development to reduce the dependence of the region on the private car, to give more support to public transport, and to improve economies in the provision of a wider range of services to the rural areas;

C6 the selection of secondary centres and small towns for concentrated growth should be related to their locations at major intersections on the rail and road networks, the size and quality of the employment and

**services they offer at present, and their
ability, in social and environmental terms, to
absorb the required rate of development.**

8.2.4 Close scrutiny of these locational principles
will demonstrate that they are open to several inter-
pretations. Part of this ambiguity arises from the
need to maintain the discretion of those authorities
engaged in forward planning and making decisions
within the region. Some of it, however, is inherent in
any attempt to generalise. It is important that the
results of this examination of the future development
of the region should be stated as clearly as possible.
Without this, many of the decisions which will determine whether or not the principles stated here are
put into effect are more likely to be taken in the light
of national and local circumstances as they appear at
the time. The general framework used is again that of
the thirteen areas. The descriptions supporting the
proposals, together with Figure 8.1, are intended to
indicate the effects of the proposals in narrowing the
range of uncertainty over the future of each area.

8.3 The Proposals in Detail
8.3.1 The development of Peterborough New Town
will establish it as a major employment centre in the
north-east of the region. It also offers the prospect of
higher priority for route improvements across the
north and centre of the region, and with the Midlands
and the North. In the past, the commitment to growth
represented by the New Town has been justified
more in terms of the benefits it is expected to bring to
the relief of London's housing and congestion
problems rather than of the benefits it will bring to
the surrounding areas. As the momentum of growth
becomes more assured, it should be possible to relax
the present criterion of population growth within the
New Town area to take more account of the town's
function as a major sub-regional centre for a considerable area including the northern part of the Fens,
focused on Wisbech. Beyond the completion of the
New Town, provision will clearly have to be made for
the further growth resulting from the momentum
which has been established.
8.3.2 Both the Norwich and Great Yarmouth-
Lowestoft areas fall within the sectors of the region
where it is considered that the rate of growth could
usefully be stimulated. This may offset to some degree
the likely deterioration in the relative position of
both areas, resulting from the programme of future
road investment in and around the region. It could be
particularly important in the Norwich area, which
acts as a focus for the surrounding rural areas.
Norwich is also shielded by distance from the growing influence of the London metropolitan area on the
region, and its growth could also help maintain a
distinctive element of the region's identity. The
timing and rate of growth may present some
difficulties for the provision of services, and for the
environmental capacity of the town centre, under
pressure from the traffic and car parking that would
be associated with intensive employment growth.
Unrestrained growth of the commuting area towards
the north-east coast could also involve environmental conflicts. The location of further office and
industrial development outside the central area to the

west and south, in association with public transport
links to the centre of the region, would accord with
the regional perspective.
8.3.3 The Great Yarmouth-Lowestoft area includes a
major portion of the national holiday industry, and
also acts as a significant employment centre in other
terms. Its capacity to adapt to changing circumstances has been shown in the rate of growth maintained through a period when its communication
links have been reduced. Changes in fashion, and in
the economics of the holiday industry, may, however,
make the area vulnerable in the future. It is not clear
to what extent the involvement in North Sea oil and
gas exploration is a temporary phenomenon. Neither
is it certain that new activities will replace the old, in
as successful a way as has the food processing
industry in the recent past. This process of replacement may also be restricted by the shortage of
industrial land, and by a possible conflict with
environmental interests. These factors make the area
worth special study, particularly in respect of its
potentially unstable employment structure.
8.3.4 In those areas outside the direct influence of the
main centres of the region, the broad locational
principles indicate the development of a set of
secondary centres, intermediate in location to these
main centres. They would assist the provision of a
wider range of services and employment opportunities, encourage the improvement of a lattice of
connecting routes, and help support public transport
in these areas. The selection of secondary centres has
to be related to those existing centres that occupy
major intersections on the transport network, and
present a base which would allow a faster rate of
growth to be more easily absorbed. In these terms,
there is a shortage of candidates. In the north-south
belt in the centre of the region, the three candidates
that appear to meet these requirements are King's
Lynn, Thetford and Bury St Edmunds. These have the
added advantage of town expansion schemes
currently supporting faster growth. To the east, in
the area intermediate to Norwich and Ipswich, there
is no equivalent candidate, and the Diss/Eye area
appears to possess good rail and road access which
gives it preference, without the initial size and
employment base which would make it ideal.
8.3.5 King's Lynn occupies a strategic position on
east-west routes across the northern half of the
region, and is a terminal point of the rail and road
routes along the eastern edge of the Fens. It could
present some disadvantages as a secondary centre
both in the historic nature of its core, and in its
position to the west of the area that requires servicing.
For these reasons, it may be preferable to regard it as
the main focus of a growth zone orientated towards
the east and south, and including a number of smaller
market towns. This would be assisted by the road
system which converges in this general area for the
northern crossing of the Fens, and which fans out to
the east, creating a number of important intersections
at small towns.
8.3.6 Thetford is proving to be successful as a town
expansion scheme. It is on the A11 and on some
secondary rail and road routes. The neighbouring
Breckland partly restricts its function as a service
and employment centre for the rural areas, and further

growth could pose difficulties for the conservation of the area's ecology. Its encouragement as a secondary centre, however, could be beneficial in reducing the degree of dependence for employment on defence installations in the surrounding area, and could improve the case for a route across the centre of the region from the north-west to the south-east.

8.3.7 In its present role, Bury St Edmunds is perhaps closest to being a secondary centre, and its prospects for future vitality can only be improved by the development of the A45 as an important communications link. The loss of some local government functions could reduce its role as an employment and service centre, and it is, therefore, desirable that the momentum of the present town expansion scheme be maintained. It is not clear, however, whether any further stimulus will be required to maintain its status as a secondary centre.

8.3.8 The Diss/Eye area does not possess such a strong base for growth as the other candidates. It is, however, relatively central to an area where the general level of opportunities and services is comparatively low, and none of the other candidates in this area possesses such good rail and road connections. Growth would, nevertheless, pose some difficulties. Both towns have qualities requiring careful conservation, and growth on any scale would need co-ordination in planning and implementation between county and district authorities. In the perspective presented here, it appears to be the most suitable location in the region for any addition to the planned migration programme in the future. On this basis, it is suggested that a preparatory study to establish a secondary employment and service centre at Diss/Eye be undertaken. This would include consideration of a Town Development scheme, and be related to the structure plans prepared by the two counties.

8.3.9 The development of a set of secondary centres is unlikely to provide a complete answer to the future of the rural areas of the region. The 'Small Towns Study' demonstrated that the small market towns of the region could play a significant role in providing services and opportunities to the people who will continue to live in these areas. It is considered that the growth of a selected number of small towns should be encouraged in central and local government policies, and that the selection of candidates should be based on their location within the pattern of main and secondary centres suggested above, and on their position on the road and rail network. On this basis, the candidates which seem most suitable for careful consideration in the preparation of structure plans are Fakenham, Swaffham, Downham Market, Halesworth and March. In each case, a detailed examination of local circumstances is required, as with any other candidate identified by the local authorities.

8.3.10 The clearest example of a part of the region where policies of restraint are already in force is the Cambridge area. It is evident that the pressures on this area will increase substantially with improved road and rail links to London, and road links to the Midlands. From the regional perspective expressed in the broad locational principles, there is a strong presumption for the continuation of the present policies of restraint, with the expected growth channelled more towards the Fens and centre of the region. This would require, however, appropriate measures locally to counter the effects of restraint on the housing and employment structure of the area. The continuation of policies of village development, for example, would need to be matched by corresponding improvements to public transport into the city. There will also be difficulties in absorbing the growing pressures within the city itself. Both aspects have been the subject of a sub-regional study which looks towards the relaxation of present policies, and some encouragement of further growth, as a means of supporting measures to draw off these pressures. The acceptance of this approach appears to depend on the weight attached to the special character of Cambridge in relation to the wider regional perspective presented here, and to the practical difficulties of securing the total and consistent co-operation of all the interests involved in the future development of this area.

8.3.11 The presumption for some degree of restraint of growth in the Ipswich area is less marked. Its recent rate of growth has been affected by the uncertainty surrounding its possible designation as a New Town. Its future prospects seem more assured, with the expected growth of the Haven Ports, the developing role of Ipswich as an office centre, and increased commuting to London. The considerable environmental qualities of the coastal and inland areas indicate some degree of concentration of future growth around Ipswich itself, and the construction of the southern bypass should enable the implementation of conservation and traffic policies which will allow the city to absorb this growth. Outside the city, the directions in which growth could be beneficial in regional terms would be to the north and north-west, along the major road and rail routes towards Diss and Stowmarket.

8.3.12 Outside the main centres, the fastest rate of growth in the region has been experienced in the area centred on Huntingdon, St Neots and St Ives. This will be stimulated by the construction of the M1-A1 link, as well as by the existing town expansion schemes. In the medium term the continuation of this rapid rate of growth could lead to a loss of structure in the urban areas, problems of servicing, and the spread of a sense of uniformity, alleviated only by pockets of older development. This suggests that the town expansion schemes have served the purpose of stimulating growth, and that any further commitments are not required. There could be benefits, both locally and for the remainder of the region, in considering some curtailment of the present town development schemes if this is practicable. This would help to bring some restraint to the rate of growth and provide some possibility of bringing the development of secondary centres forward.

8.3.13 Further to the east, in the area of southern Suffolk, lie the town expansion schemes of Haverhill and Sudbury-Melford. This area is away from the main routes into and across the region, but unquestionably these schemes have assisted in bringing increased local prosperity. In the perspective presented here, the completion of these schemes would be reasonable, though any entry into further commitments would need to have strong justification in view of the requirements of the secondary centres.

8.3.14 Finally, it is necessary to consider the future of the coastal areas. Much of the North Norfolk coast, and the Suffolk coastal area, is extremely attractive and relatively unspoilt. These qualities help to compensate for the relatively low level of opportunities and services for people who live there. Further development would increase the pressures on these coasts, and there are no obvious reasons why there should be any major shifts in the present policies of restraint in these areas.

8.3.15 The broad locational principles also cover the question of priorities in the improvement of the strategic transport network of the region. As with the planned migration programme, the forward programme of transport investment extends over the next decade. At present, this programme places emphasis on the improvement of roads, rather than public transport, and within the road programme on links to the region, and across the south of the region. Some shift towards public transport seems likely, and there is also the prospect that some changes in priorities will occur towards the end of the programme. Some possibilities can be suggested. Firstly, there is a case for a higher priority in the longer term for routes in the north and east of the region, and for strengthening the internal network inside the region. This might be achieved through bypassing the more difficult bottlenecks in the attractive smaller towns and villages, and by the construction of short overtaking sections to break up traffic queues. Lastly, priority should be given to routes where there is no alternative rail route for freight or passengers. One example of this is the A47/A17, which provides an east-west route across the north of the region equivalent to that of the A45 to the south, and which would assist in supporting the growth of several centres located along it. In addition, a longer-term possibility is the improvement to a high standard of a diagonal route from the Ipswich area to the King's Lynn and Peterborough areas, across the centre of the region. This could remove some pressure from the Cambridge-Newmarket area, and strengthen the structure and prospects of the centre of the region.

8.3.16 Finally, as an illustration of the locational principles, it is possible to reinterpret the population forecasts for the different areas of the region made in chapter six. In Figure 8.1, these are presented to indicate the direction of the principles and proposals that have been described above, together with the degree to which these could reduce the range of uncertainty about the future population of each area. In each case, it has been assumed that the present planned migration programme will be completed. The application, however, of those proposals that could affect the scale and location of this programme would produce some increase in areas E, H, and K, and some reduction in area D. This would shift the range of population for each area, and that of the total population in the region as a whole, over and above that shown in Figure 8.1.

Figure 8.1

Effects of strategic proposals on population ranges, 1991
Population (in thousands)

Area	Without Proposals (as in Figure 6.6) (i)	With Proposals (ii)
A. Cambridge	217–241	217–233
B. Fens	72– 90	75– 87
C. Peterborough	237–261	241–257
D. Huntingdon	138–164	138–154
E. Kings Lynn	97–117	105–117
F. North Norfolk Coast	84–102	87– 99
G. Central Norfolk	61– 77	66– 76
H. Bury St Edmunds-Thetford	189–213	193–209
I. Haverhill-Sudbury	88–108	89–101
J. Ipswich	277–307	281–301
K. Diss-Eye	68– 88	75– 87
L. Great Yarmouth-Lowestoft	223–249	228–244
M. Norwich	256–284	266–284

Source: East Anglia Regional Strategy Team.

8.4 Conclusions

8.4.1 The detailed proposals are summarised below. Each will require careful consideration at local level, by central government, and by those agencies outside the region whose decisions could be affected by them:

(i) *the continuation of the present programme of development of Peterborough New Town, with more emphasis given to its function as a major employment and service centre for the surrounding area;*

(ii) *the encouragement of further growth in the area within the direct influence of Norwich, with emphasis on the location of future office and industrial development outside the central area towards the south and west;*

(iii) *a review in depth of the employment structure of the Great Yarmouth and Lowestoft areas, in relation to future prospects of the holiday industry and the environmental qualities of the surrounding areas;*

(iv) *to implement the development of a set of strengthened secondary employment and service centres—*

  (*a*) *the development of a growth zone in West Norfolk, extending existing town development agreements, focused on King's Lynn and including other areas to the south and east;*
  (*b*) *the further extension of the present town expansion scheme at Thetford;*
  (*c*) *the continuation of Bury St Edmunds' present function as a secondary centre;*
  (*d*) *the commissioning of a preparatory study to establish a secondary centre at Diss and Eye, including the possibility of a town expansion scheme,*

(v) *the selection of a number of small towns to act as growth points in association with the development of secondary centres;*

(vi) *in any further extension of the planned migration programme, priority should be given to:*

  (*a*) *Diss-Eye as a new location for town expansion;*
  (*b*) *King's Lynn and Thetford for extensions to existing schemes;*

(vii) *to assist in bringing forward the development of these secondary centres, a review of the future of the town expansion schemes in the south-west of the region, to include the following factors:*

  (*a*) *the peaking of future demands for services;*
  (*b*) *future employment needs of the second generation;*
  (*c*) *the impetus given by the schemes to migration above the levels set by the housing targets;*
  (*d*) *the possibility of increasing the contribution of the private sector;*
  (*e*) *the level of advanced public investment committed in these schemes;*

(viii) *the exercise of some restraint of growth in the Cambridge area consistent with maintaining the special character of the city centre;*

(ix) *the exercise of some restraint of growth in the Ipswich area, with development away from Ipswich itself encouraged to the north and north-west;*

(x) *the continuation of the general policy of restraint in the coastal areas, and in equivalent inland areas having environmentally sensitive qualities;*

(xi) *a shift in the priorities of the programme of transport investment towards:*

  (*a*) *public transport;*
  (*b*) *the development of routes in the north and east of the region;*
  (*c*) *improved connections between main and secondary centres;*
  (*d*) *road routes where no alternative rail service is practicable;*

(xii) *consideration should be given to the improvement of a strategic route connecting the Haven Ports with the King's Lynn-Peterborough areas.*

Section D

The Development of Services

The previous section examined how changes in the major elements of development, such as the distribution of population and employment, and the major transport network, could help achieve the regional objectives. In this section, we turn to the question of the contribution of public and private services to those objectives. Although it is difficult to anticipate all of the changes which could take place in these services, it seems likely that their effect could be at least as important in terms of achieving objectives, as changes in the pattern of development. The first of the chapters looks at the links provided by communications between people and the services they enjoy. It considers the future of public transport, and subsequently, the potential of both information services and telecommunications to overcome the difficulties which are experienced. In chapter ten, the provision of different services in the future is set against the background of circumstances likely to influence the pattern of social change within the region. This common background provides a basis for deriving a set of principles appropriate to the provision of all services, and from which proposals for individual services can be seen to originate. Proposals for the forward provision of health or educational facilities, for example, derive from the same perspective as do those for housing or public transport.

Chapter 9   Communications

9.1 Introduction

9.1.1 Previous sections of this report provide two principles which are of particular relevance for the development of services in East Anglia. The first of these is that policies should be designed to be adaptable and responsive to a wide variety of future circumstances, as it is impossible to predict in advance the precise nature of the changes likely to occur. The second principle is derived in the last section, indicating that policies should be designed to build up secondary centres and selected small towns. This is designed to extend the range of opportunities available in rural areas, improving access to services that are integrated in location, if not in actual operation.

9.1.2 At first sight, there would appear to be a conflict between these two broad principles. The concentration on secondary centres and selected small towns could imply the development of a rigid pattern of service provision at these places. Closer examination, however, indicates that this is an attempt to move away from the tendency to centralise on the main towns, with this subsidiary level allowing for more responsiveness in the provision of local services. Operating in this way, these towns will form part of the lattice within which service provision can be made. This can be illustrated by the whole field of communications, which helps to link people with the services they require. It does so by enabling people to travel to places where services are available, and services to be taken closer to where people live. In addition, other forms of communications offer the prospect of a speedier response, and could help to reduce some of the confusion that exists in people's minds about the content of different services.

9.1.3 In these terms, therefore, communications provide the essential framework within which other services are carried out. As a first step, the future of conventional public transport is examined. Secondly, we consider possible improvements to information services so as to produce direct contact between the public and services. This is followed by an exploration of the longer term possibilities in telecommunication developments. Broadly, this order of treatment reflects a timescale building up from present experience to the potential of systems whose capacity is not yet fully known.

9.2 Public Transport

9.2.1 In transport terms, East Anglia is very dependent upon the private car, both in the numbers of people who use it for essential purposes and in the way in which the form of new development assumes its continued use. Two-thirds of all households in the region have at least one car, with 12% having two or more, representing a higher level of car ownership than is found anywhere else in Britain. A high proportion of workers use the car for commuting to work in and around the main centres, and in the rural areas. The presence of an effective public transport system has not been an important factor in the selection of areas for development; in the post war period new housing development has been dispersed through many small villages. The dependency on the private car is increasing, and the social and economic life of large parts of the region is growing more vulnerable to any major change in the costs and availability of private transport. It also means increasing isolation and restriction of choice for those people unable or unwilling to drive, dependent upon public transport for access to the wide range of services normally located in urban areas. Many more will be dependent upon public transport for the informal visits that are taken for granted by those who use private cars, or who are working with others for most of the day.

9.2.2 This suggests that there will be a continued need for some form of public transport in the region as an alternative to the private car, to ensure that there is no further reduction in the level of opportunities open to people living in rural areas. At present, however, there seems little possibility of maintaining a self-financing, general purpose public transport system in the region, except in limited circumstances. The gradual reduction in the frequency and convenience of local services suggests a shrinking future for both rail and bus public transport.

9.2.3 The experience gained so far in the use of subsidies is not encouraging. The levels and frequency of service in any area are affected by the operational problems of vehicle and crew scheduling, and consequently the present pattern of subsidised services appears to have many arbitrary features. There are, however, no clear-cut criteria for deciding what constitutes a minimum or adequate level of service in any area. In addition, there is every indication that services will increase their losses over time, with the danger that local authorities could be drawn into a pattern of mounting subsidies without any clear rationale.

9.2.4 The net result has been a piecemeal system of support of public passenger transport in the region (Map 9.1). Almost all rail services are grant-aided by central government. This subsidy amounted to £2¼ million in 1972 and £3 million in 1973. The level of grant each year covers the long-run costs of

Map 9.1   Major Passenger Transport Routes receiving Subsidy, 1972

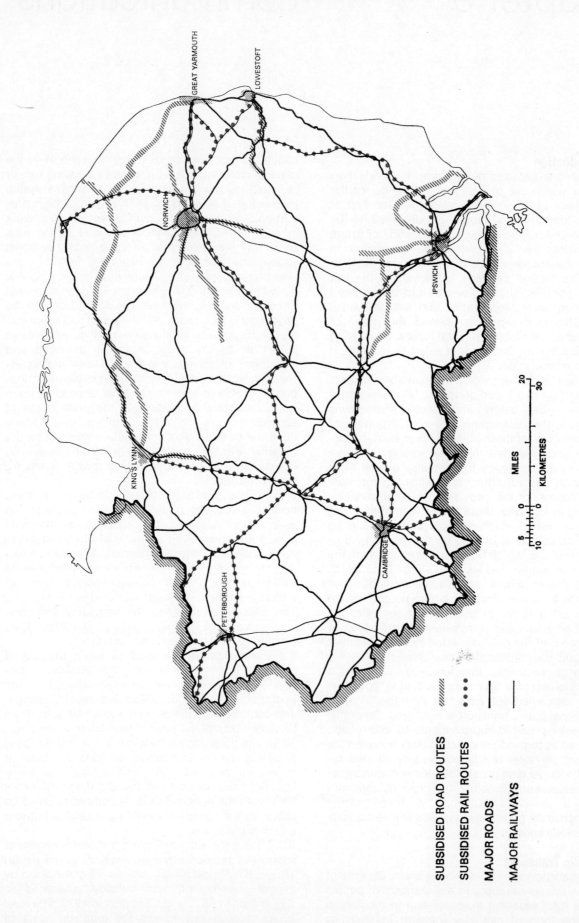

SUBSIDISED ROAD ROUTES

SUBSIDISED RAIL ROUTES

MAJOR ROADS

MAJOR RAILWAYS

maintaining the service at the existing standard, but gives no incentive either to withdraw a service, or to raise standards by further investment. The possibility of reducing operating costs by improving the condition of the track and signalling equipment is low because of heavy capital costs. The rail network is, therefore, likely to remain much as it is, but increasingly costly to maintain, unless there are major changes in national policy towards railway finance. In the longer term, the rural branch-line and local commuter services might be assisted by the development of more lightweight rolling stock. This would, however, require a shift in emphasis away from main-line technology in current research and development expenditure. In general, therefore, the rail system will continue to provide some useful links within the region, but it does not appear to be readily adaptable or capable of extension to meet the changing transport demands of the future.

9.2.5 The concern for mounting subsidies has limited local authority arrangements with the bus transport operators. In 1972 the main bus company received only £17,000 in operating subsidies, with less than half of this being a direct burden on local rates, although further grants were made by central government for the purchase of new buses. In cases where local authorities have not been prepared to meet the subsidy requested, services have usually been withdrawn. There have been no obvious benefits to the system as a whole from this piecemeal closure. The remaining network continues largely in the form inherited from the past. The method of subsidy tends to perpetuate this form, without encouraging experiments or innovation in services. Under present arrangements, therefore, there are limits to the extent to which the bus services can realise their potential for responding efficiently and sensitively to the circumstances of the region.

9.2.6 Local authorities have been more willing to develop their own special purpose transport services. The education and health services have both made extensive use of their own transport, paralleled in the private sector by the increasing numbers of firms providing transport for their workers. These services do not suffer the same financial limitations as do the general purpose road and rail services, because they are regarded as part of the main service for accounting purposes. They offer, in addition, a greater responsiveness to particular needs than does the existing general purpose system. These benefits, however, are not necessarily felt by the public at large, and there is some possibility of duplication.

9.2.7 The transfer of responsibilities for public transport to local authorities highlights many of these difficulties. Local authorities are now able to play a larger part than in the past in deciding the development of transport services and road investment in their areas. The transport plan and programme to be prepared by each authority will be implemented by them with the help of a transport block grant, allocated on certain agreed criteria by central government. Unfortunately, these criteria seem likely to favour the larger urban areas outside East Anglia. The scheme excludes the grant-aided rail system, although local authorities will still be able to help individual rail services. Even so, these proposals do provide an opportunity to develop a more co-ordinated public transport system, with greater scope for flexible arrangements between expenditure on roads and public transport.

9.2.8 Some service improvements will come through adjustments to the licencing system, and through modifications to postal and hospital/social car services, but overall these are unlikely to make more than marginal improvements to rural transport conditions. The adjustments made by the operators themselves to the pattern of bus services are likely to be far more significant. The main bus company aims to rethink this pattern on a hierarchical basis, separating inter-urban and rural services. The inter-urban services are planned to connect main and secondary centres in the region on a regular schedule, with rural services based on particular villages acting as feeders to this main network. Two important constraints on overall profitability, however, are likely to be continued traffic congestion in the main urban centres of the region, and the lack of guaranteed support to the rural link services.

9.2.9 In taking forward the pattern of public transport provision in the region there would appear to be three desirable aims: to provide an alternative to the private car; to provide an improved ability to adapt to local requirements; and to provide a consistent logic for the provision of financial support. It will not, however, be possible to achieve these aims unless several conditions are satisfied. The first of these is the recognition that a close association and understanding between local authorities and public transport operators will be necessary. The second condition is a readiness to consider a retrenchment from the present pattern of services, in order to widen the scope for any new approach. Thirdly, there is a need to recognise that the variety of local circumstances makes it impossible to draw up a standard of service which will fit the needs of all areas. And finally, it is necessary to allow for a fairly long period of operation before the effectiveness of a service can be assessed.

9.2.10 With these conditions, we can outline the nature of a public transport system designed to realise these aims. It would be based on a hierarchy of larger centres, secondary centres, and selected small towns. Connecting these towns would be services operating at fixed intervals or frequencies on a limited stop basis. Services could be by either rail or bus, with the choice between the two dependent upon the level of subsidy required, and upon the state of traffic conditions on the roads and in the towns. This would give a logic and structure to the provision of subsidies that does not exist at present, and would at the same time make clear the intention to maintain and build upon a particular framework of services.

9.2.11 On this basis, many small towns would become collecting points for the system. It is here that fixed schedules and frequency of service can give way to increased sensitivity in meeting local and individual needs. There may be some difficulties in responding to these needs. Local transport requirements will differ from one place to another, and each community will need to be involved in defining its service demands. To provide some upper limit and impose realism on this process, each community must have some responsibility for the finance and operation of the service at the local level. Parishes or groups of parishes, with their rating powers, may be the most suitable agencies to share in the cost of these locally identified services. They could be supported by a system of transport grants, designed to encourage a responsible, but imaginative, involvement. It is desirable for there to be as great a degree of variety as is dictated by local conditions, subject only to precautions against the actual misuse of grants.

9.2.12 It is clearly impossible to lay down a blueprint for such a system; there are bound to be several departures from the simplified version outlined above. It has advantages, however, in providing a logical and stable network of services in the region, and at the same time involves local people in a practical way in deciding and meeting their own needs. The possibility that an increasing proportion of public transport finance may come from local authority sources in the future could give added value to such involvement.

9.2.13 In developing the pattern of public transport priorities within the transport plans and programmes, there would appear to be considerable advantages in adding a regional dimension to the work of the local authorities. The joint use of staff, using the framework provided by the Consultative Committee, or any successor body, would assist in identifying transport priorities in conjunction with the major operators. The work might include not only the public transport links between main and secondary centres, but also the way in which these could be assisted by the pattern of development in the centres. In addition, experimental schemes for meeting the needs of local areas could be monitored, in order to help improve future systems both within and outside the region.

9.3 Information Services

9.3.1 Communications have so far been discussed in terms of getting people from one place to another. One aim of such movement is to put people in touch with a wide range of public and private services. Many people, however, are unaware of the services available to them, and are often deterred, by past experience, from attempting to discover what these could be. Many of these services have different administrative structures and boundaries for their local areas. This can mean that even the most determined person may be faced with visits to several different buildings in one or more centres. If the situation is a complex one, this may extend to a number of journeys over several days or weeks. For those who are old or immobile a large number of journeys can impose considerable costs and hardship. This suggests that we should aim to provide people with better access to a whole range of related services, preferably in reasonably close proximity to where they live. In addition, if people are to take a more constructive role in the development of local services they will need to be kept more fully informed than they are at present. There is increasing recognition of this fact amongst agencies and the public at large. The dissemination of information can also enable many public and voluntary workers to do their jobs with increasing sensitivity and effectiveness. Conditions in rural areas, where distances are greater, are however, likely to pose particular difficulties.

9.3.2 The provision of local information centres can be an effective response in these conditions. The sort of centres we have in mind would not provide a substitute for the regular contact possible between clients and staff, but would support such links by reducing the time taken up by routine enquiries. Over time these centres might provide a base for formal contacts, rather as the Post Office does at the present time. In many rural areas they could also provide a clearing-house for local transport needs, and perhaps a centre for voluntary workers. They would provide information about all the services operated by local government, and make particular days available when other statutory and voluntary agencies could be at hand. Both officials and elected representatives could use such centres for direct contact with local people. The small market towns could play a particularly significant role in this approach, in conjunction with their position as collecting points within the public transport system outlined above. They could well become centres for mobile facilities developed to take in surrounding areas, on the lines proposed for mobile consumer's advice centres. In the larger towns there is still likely to be a profusion of separate services, which may need to be brought much closer together in operations, if not premises.

9.4 Telecommunications

9.4.1 In the longer term, we can expect technological developments to produce more deep-seated changes in the ways people receive and pass on information. Telecommunication developments provide a new opportunity to overcome many of the difficulties we have identified. They can, for example, reduce some of the harsh disadvantages of physical remoteness, and help overcome social isolation. They offer, too, new opportunities for placing public and private services at the disposal of larger number of people. The simple public telephone system and the two-way radio have already widespread use in many fields of everyday life. More sophisticated developments are in use in business and commercial life, in East Anglia as well as nationally. Currently, research has been commissioned by the Department of Health and Social Security into the likely impact of health trends on telecommunications services during the remainder of this century. Equivalent studies are also under way in the fields of education and social services.

9.4.2 Some of the major technical limitations to improving the range and quality of information being transmitted are now being overcome. By the 1980's it will be possible to transmit immense amounts of information along a single channel, opening up the possibility of a telecommunications network, or grid, serving most parts of the region. Such a grid could be developed as a natural complement to the existing strategic road and rail network, on which it would depend for the distribution of goods. In this sense, a telecommunications network can be seen as part of the basic infrastructure for the region of the future. There are a number of benefits worth consideration by public bodies. In the first place it offers the chance to extend the range of opportunities open to people living in the main centres, to those living in much smaller settlements, irrespective of their age or income. Secondly, it extends to those now living in the main towns the opportunity to live away from a congested urban centre, without losing all 'urban' advantages. There is the obvious parallel with the effect of the private car in recent times. Thirdly it offers to everyone in the region some of the choices available in centres outside East Anglia itself. Particular public services benefiting from this would be education and training, health and social services, and the information services of government. In the private sector, employment, shopping, and entertainment would all stand to gain.

9.4.3 The evidence available to us indicates that a number of public services are already considering or going ahead with the installation of relatively low level facilities, sometimes connected to a central computing capacity. This has some parallels with the tendency of services to provide their own transport. In total, the amount of capital investment in equipment could be considerable, and there is a danger of some duplication of facilities. The opportunity could be taken in the public sector as a whole to encourage the development of a system common to all services. It could best be conceived as a hierarchy of networks, much as the road system is at present, where the capacity increases progressively with the size of centre linked. Thus the main, secondary, and selected smaller centres, will naturally play important roles. The basic unit will probably be the small town. Since there will remain many forms of contact between people outside the range of even the most sophisticated system, the need for bringing both services and people together in local centres will condition the network's development. It is at the level of the small town that access to information available further afield is assured. Similarly, where the service actually involves the physical movement of goods, then the small town can act as a collecting point. Below this level, contact with the local centre can be by either use of public or private transport, or by locally developed telecommunications systems, perhaps taking forward the possibilities of local broadcasting as an initial step. This common usage, and proximity to each other, could encourage closer integration of those services working in related fields. The opportunity to gain economies of scale in using a public system of this sort, might promote commercial usage in time, with mutual benefits.

9.4.4 We do not expect that such a system can be set up overnight. Even less do we suppose that it could go forward on the basis of the limited arguments presented here. It would require much co-operative effort on the part of public bodies in the region, and a willingness to invest in the future. It needs a careful programme of research and experimentation, possibly led by the Post Office, which would need to be balanced against other pressing needs. It does remain, nonetheless, a positive opportunity to bring benefits to all of the region's population, and a framework in which to take forward the planning of many individual services. It is clear that within parts of the EEC similar systems are being proposed, and developed, and may act as useful precedents.

9.5 Conclusions: The Setting for Service Provision

9.5.1 In this chapter we have looked at a number of ways in which communications can be developed to serve a region with an unevenly spread population. They can be adapted to conserve both manpower and capital resources, yet at the same time create conditions in which many people can fulfil their expectations of an improved standard of living. It implies that some form of concentration of population will continue to be necessary. It also implies that there will be little benefit in having a highly organised pattern of physical development if the services provided are administered in an inflexible way. The following principles reflect our view of how these elements can be reconciled in East Anglia:

D1 the public transport system in the region, particularly in the rural areas, should be rethought to provide an alternative to the private car, to match local requirements as closely as possible, and to provide a consistent basis for financial support.

D2 the flow of information between services and the public should be improved, to allow services to gain more understanding of the public's needs, and to improve the access of the public to available services;

D3 preparations for a telecommunications infrastructure should be put in hand, harnessing the opportunities presented by technological development to reduce the remoteness of rural areas.

Within these principles, the following proposals would seem most suitable:

(i) *financial support to public transport should be used to promote a comprehensive system of connecting services on a limited-stop basis, linking the major and secondary centres of the region with each other and with selected small towns, at regular and agreed intervals;*

(ii) *the choice of financial support between rail and bus services should be related to the amount of support required in either case, and to existing travel conditions;*

(iii) *the provision of public transport services focusing on the small towns should be defined on the basis of local needs, with communities, encouraged by an appropriate grant system, taking responsibility for the scope and continuity of the local services;*

(iv) *to support the preparation of transport plans, and the selection of transport priorities, local authorities should consider the joint use of staff on a regional basis, using the framework offered by the Consultative Committee, or any successor body.*

(v) *local information offices should be established to provide an improved point of contact between people and services;*

(vi) *these offices should be recognised in the area structure of services to increase informal contact between fieldworkers;*

(vii) *priority should be given to locating these offices in secondary centres and smaller towns, with mobile facilities developed for areas of scattered population.*

(viii) *in the longer term a telecommunications network should be set up, initially confined to the public services, but capable of extension to the private sector at a later date;*

(ix) *such a network should be capable of the rapid two-way transmission of complex information, in sound and picture, and linking all major, secondary, and smaller centres in the region;*

(x) *in the shorter term, experimental projects should be considered using the skills already available to the region through the local electronics industry, and through the GPO research headquarters at Ipswich.*

9.5.2 The proposals build upon the principles set out in Section C for the location of future development and those presented in 9.5.1. They indicate that it is possible to achieve both efficiency and sensitivity in the overall framework within which other services operate. The next chapter looks beyond communications to consider the other factors that must be accommodated in providing services. The contribution made by the public sector will be particularly important in this process of adapting and initiating developments to the benefit of East Anglia. That contribution is likely to be most effective if the future location of service facilities occurs within the setting which we suggest in this chapter and in Section C.

Chapter 10

The Provision of Services

10.1 Introduction

10.1.1 In this chapter, we move closer to those services which in different ways make up and support the fabric of people's daily lives. The context for doing so is provided by the strategic principles established earlier for the region as a whole, for the location of development, and for communications in the previous chapter. Within this context, two main influences will affect the forward planning of these services. The first of these is the changing views of the objectives of each service, and the practical means of achieving those objectives by the people directly concerned with them. Some reconsideration of the complementary roles of the public and private sectors may be associated with this. The second influence is the particular qualities of East Anglia. More general ideas on the provision of services may have to be considerably adapted if they are to fit regional circumstances effectively.

10.2 Strategic Principles for Service Provision

10.2.1 It is useful at this point to recapitulate on the strategic principles which are relevant in some form for service provision. From chapter five, these are:

B3 policies should be designed to be adaptable, with emphasis on small units of provision, in order to minimise the risk associated with a large degree of uncertainty;

B4 regional institutions should be developed, with appropriate powers and resources, to give a firmer basis for the forward planning of capital investment, and to shield the region from major disruptions from external sources;

B5 policies should be designed to build up internal structures in the region which are likely to be resilient to change, by a greater emphasis on securing longer term potential and assets, rather than on realising the totality of short-term growth prospects.

From chapter eight, two further strategic principles can be drawn:

C2 the development of a set of secondary centres, with associated growth in small towns, within those areas likely to remain outside the direct influence of the main centres;

C5 the encouragement of more concentrated forms of development to reduce the dependence of the region on the private car, to give more support to public transport, and to improve economies in the provision of a wider range of services to the rural areas.

10.2.2 These principles are couched in general terms, and have to be elaborated further to provide a set of principles which are of more direct relevance to service provision. To do so, we have to consider a number of points. The first of these is the relationship of the public and private sectors, both in the provision of services and in the planning of their future development. Secondly, the circumstances of East Anglia itself, both as at present, and in the way it is likely to change, will affect the general approach to providing services. It is only by interpreting these principles, to obtain firmer guidelines for services overall, that the particular question of the future direction of each service can be approached.

10.2.3 Each of the services considered in this chapter is directed towards a different need, and is organised to meet that need in its own distinctive way. This produces substantial variations in the respective roles played by the private and public sectors. In the period covered by this report, it cannot be assumed that these roles will remain fixed. Such an assumption appears reasonable for education, health and social services, where they will continue to be primarily the responsibility of the public sector. Similarly, shopping can be expected to remain the province of the private sector. It is less reasonable in those cases where both sectors are strongly represented, with evidence of an evolving relationship over time. In these instances, it is necessary to step back and consider what mix of private and public sector involvement is most appropriate to the circumstances of East Anglia.

10.2.4 This is made more complicated in that the major instrument for influencing the future development of any service is the activity of the public sector. Even where its role is a minor supporting one to the private sector, it remains as a major source of influence in a planning sense. As a result, it is tempting to assume that further extensions of the role of the public sector are required to bring about continued improvements in services. This would follow past trends in the growing importance of the public sector in most of the fields that affect people's lives. But the public sector has its own problems in acting as the initiator in these services. In its structure and accountability, it is more suited to carrying out routine tasks than to taking the lead in the face of an uncertain future. The process of acquiring additional responsibilities in a piecemeal fashion has also led to agencies, working in related fields, not fully recognising the need to develop their activities in sympathy one with another.

10.2.5 These difficulties have limited the ability of the public sector to respond to development and change in a positive manner. The recent round of reorganisations affecting many of the public services has illustrated some of the problems. Amongst these are the problems of securing an appropriate balance of local autonomy or discretion, of providing services efficiently to agreed national standards, of regulating the finance of public activities, and of coordinating the different services. Although some of these questions can only be resolved at the national level, a valuable contribution can be made at the regional level. Reorganisation also provides a major opportunity for concerted rethinking on service provision, perhaps on a more integrated basis. This is encouraged by circumstances in East Anglia, where a generally small and scattered population gives rise to conditions very different from the 'average' national picture.

10.2.6 Changes in the size and location of population growth within the region, for example, are an important determinant of where services must expand in the future. Estimates of population growth suggest that an additional 200–250,000 people will need to be catered for each decade to the end of the century. As the region continues to increase its share of the total population of the country, its allocation of resources for services will also increase. Figure 10.1 shows that the most likely pattern of population growth will increase the disparities between the three new counties, with the predominantly rural county of Norfolk falling relatively further behind. The diagram does conceal some important local variations, but strengthens the conclusions in chapter eight that the south and west of the region, and the main centres, will continue to claim by far the largest share of resources available for service provision.

10.2.7 This general pattern is reinforced by three factors which bear upon the nature of service provision. The first of these is the pressure at national level for the allocation of scarce resources to large population centres, where problems are readily visible and articulated. This suggests that national priorities are unlikely to coincide with those of East Anglia, over the period under consideration. The second factor is that the expressed demands for education, training, and social services, for example, are determined in part by people's expectations. As services are improved, and more people are made aware of them, the level of expectation increases, with the effect that demands do not taper off in response to such improved levels of service. Under these conditions, supply will continue to lag behind the apparent demand for services, emphasising the need to select priorities with care. The highest expectations for these services, moreover, are held by those who, by reason of education, social background, or experience, are most aware of them. The third factor is the preference of professional staff to work in areas which offer contact with people of similar background. In combination these social forces suggest that the main centres of the region, and those areas within easy reach of them, are likely to be assured of higher standards of services, in both public and private sectors. In contrast the remaining areas of the region may be at a considerable disadvantage. This situation will coincide with a general demand for services that are more responsive to individual needs, and organised in such a way that people can understand and make use of them without undue difficulty.

10.2.8 The shortage of resources in total will require the efficient location of capital projects, whether these are very large, as is a district hospital, or smaller, like a school or day centre. They are likely to be more effective if they are located to take account of the framework discussed in chapter eight. Their location will also be important as there will be a more general requirement for them to act as centres from which supporting services can be developed. They will need to take account of potential developments in other services, of which the telecommunications network of chapter nine is a good example. The first principle, therefore, aims to assure people living in all parts of the region of an effective presence of service facilities in the future, and, at the same time, of an efficient solution to the problem of resource shortages. In accordance with the general principles described earlier, the first principle for service provision is that:

D4 policies should be designed to strengthen the range of facilities available at secondary centres and selected small towns, so as to provide a structure resilient to short-term change, and a base on which to develop supporting activities.

10.2.9 The overall stability in the distribution of population suggests that there will be limited benefits from relying on this first principle to achieve an improved standard of service provision. The existing stock of public buildings likewise provides an important constraint in the short-term. Changes initiated within the different services are likely to bring their dependency on each other into sharper focus. The interrelationship of the demands for housing and social services, for example, is already established in the large cities, and may be equally applicable to more rural areas. In these conditions, it is necessary to consider a framework in which resources can be more easily transferred between services in accordance with their contribution to people's individual needs in a particular area. The piecemeal accumulation of powers to different agencies makes this transfer difficult. It will be eased in cases where agencies are brought together under umbrella organisations, as with the new health authorities. The limitations of the existing arrangements are, however, real, and will be difficult to overcome. At this stage it is important to establish the principle that the integration of services, and their substitution between each other, should be an objective of provision at different levels. While important strategic changes can be achieved at the regional level in allocating resources between services, for many purposes it will be important to develop this ability at a fairly local level, particularly in rural areas. The second principle is, therefore, that:

D5 policies should be designed to develop organisational structures at different levels,

Figure 10.1 Expected Population Growth of the Three East Anglia Counties, 1951–2001

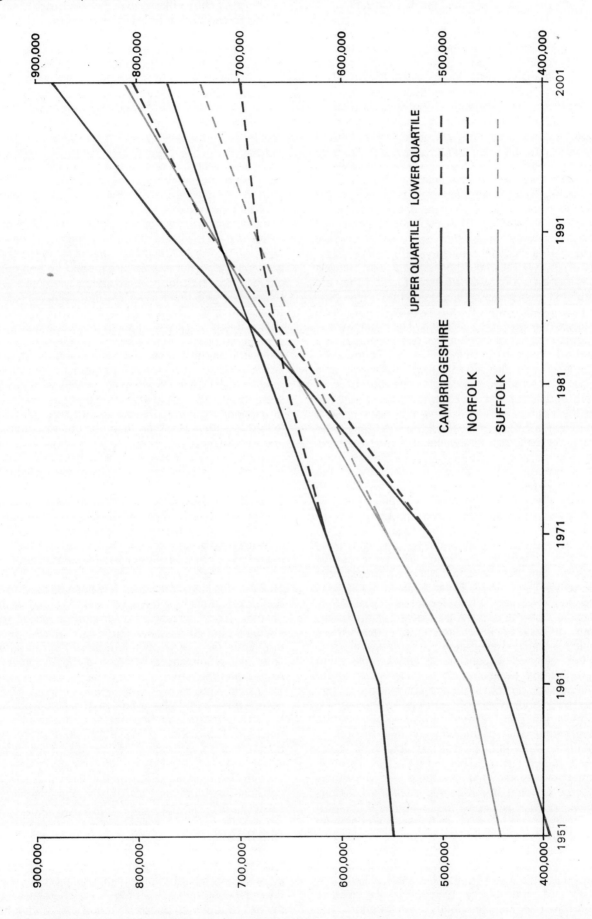

encouraging the integration of, and substitution between, services, so as to allow the most effective use of resources.

10.2.10 Progress towards this second principle is likely to be limited until there is a firmer base for forward planning. Improved methods of assessing the real effects of expenditure and policies will be required, as part of the process of improving the quality of services available to the region's population. The last few years have seen considerable progress along these lines, with the development of corporate planning techniques, and the ten-year planning exercises of social service departments, to be followed similarly by the area health authorities. We can expect such programmes to be introduced in other areas of service provision, and to be refined progressively. Exercises of this nature, however, will depend crucially upon the ability to recognise needs and anticipate problems before they arise. This ability will be more necessary if expectations prove to be as volatile as we expect, and if they are articulated more clearly and frequently. The proposals in chapter eight for a network of information centres is one way of realising this. The informational content of individual programmes will also need to be improved. Important changes in the population structure of particular areas in East Anglia will have to be monitored. For example, the numbers of elderly people will be swelled by retirement migration into the region. They will bring their own special requirements. In total they affect the size of the older population, which currently accounts for two-thirds of all expenditure on the health and social services. The proportion of the nation's elderly living in the region is expected to rise from 3·7% in 1971 to 4·5% by the end of the century, representing an additional 80–90,000 people over the age of 65. This increase will take place on an already 'top-heavy' base, in that the region currently contains many more people in the 65–75 and 75+ age groups than the national average. Many of these older people are likely to be living alone, on relatively fixed incomes, and often immobile, increasingly dependent on the good-will of others in the community. In areas of slowly growing population these problems will be exacerbated. In contrast, migrants to the planned expansion schemes will bring disproportionate demands for services catering for children, such as education and child welfare. They also require houses and jobs, not just for themselves, but for succeeding generations as well. These two broad elements of population are fairly simple to anticipate. More difficult, but probably more widespread, are problems associated with low incomes, both absolutely and relatively compared with others in the community. It will be important, for example, in East Anglia to anticipate the problems of the local person wishing to buy or rent a house, in competition with those from outside the region or working in high-wage areas. In these circumstances, it will be increasingly necessary for services to look closely, individually and together, into the needs of particular areas. This will require a much more positive involvement in the community than hitherto. The third principle, therefore, might be that:

D6 policies should be designed to give priority to recognising and anticipating the needs of those likely to require support, and to the diffusion of information.

10.2.11 Implicit in this third principle is the view that services will have to be more adaptable to social change. As the pace of social change increases, both expectations and problems are likely to differ from place to place, and over time. The uncertainty which is endemic in this situation requires flexibility of provision, and a willingness to consider a range of options at the local level. The emphasis given to service provision in one of the expanded towns or main centres is likely to be inappropriate to an older community on the coast. Similarly, elderly people in a developing market town are likely to need alternative solutions from those appropriate to older people in an isolated village. In such conditions, certain types of facility are unsuitable. Large establishments which demand heavy capital expenditure and commit resources for a long period ahead are more suited to areas where there is an assured demand over a long time span. There are few cases in East Anglia where this is so. It would seem more appropriate to give added priority to smaller and adaptable units of provision, coupled with advisory and mobile staffing arrangements. Experiments in methods of service provision, and perhaps the imaginative use of private sector resources, would also serve these general aims. In expenditure terms, the presumption would be in favour of current rather than capital expenditure, and would support block allocations of financial resources under most circumstances. The fourth principle for service provision, therefore, might be that:

D7 policies should be designed to be flexible in their use of adaptable units of provision, and in meeting variations in needs, so as to be more responsive to local circumstances, and to uncertainty over future demands.

10.2.12 This set of principles has been devised to be applicable to each of the services considered in this chapter. They represent an interpretation of the strategic principles for the region as a whole, set out in chapter five. Their common ground is the difference in circumstances between a region like East Anglia, and the national conditions in which policies for service provision are generally framed. As a group, these principles affirm that national policies have to undergo a degree of transformation before they are appropriate to East Anglia. Part of this transformation will require an increase in the extent of regional and local discretion in varying policies from the national norm. It is on this basis that we can consider the future direction of each of the individual services.

10.3 Housing
10.3.1 One commonly accepted measure of personal welfare is adequate housing, involving, wherever possible, a range of choice. A house is often one of the most important items a family may purchase, and the extent to which people's incomes are committed to spending on housing helps determine their

priorities in other fields, and the pattern of their needs. In a region where housing choice is affected both by rising expectations, and by the demands of a growing population, it is important that public policy anticipates some of the stresses that may occur. We can expect a more restricted choice of housing for some groups of the population unless the situation continually adapts to such changing conditions.

10.3.2 In recent years, expectations have moved clearly towards earlier and more widespread owner-occupation. They have been reinforced by the national structure of finance and taxation, with its general presumption towards owner-occupation as the main method of increasing housing choice. In this context, the public sector's housing programme has catered for those families unable to purchase their own home. In East Anglia, the movement towards owner-occupation has been strongly developed, and is likely to continue as the general level of economic activity rises in the region. The main centres, and the south and west of the region, will be most affected, although there are a number of exceptions to this general picture. There will be localised pressure for housing around the town expansion schemes, for example, as people seek to buy their own houses. More generally, there will be an intensification of the external pressures on the region's housing markets as greater economic and recreational contact is established with the South-East and with the Midlands. This will probably distort even further the structure of prices in the housing market that has persisted until very recently.

10.3.3 We can illustrate this distortion by the changing pattern of house prices over the last few years. In the last decade, from an average either at, or below, the national level, house prices in East Anglia are now only lower than those in the South East and South West regions. In 1971–72 prices for both new and existing dwellings increased more rapidly than in any other region, a situation which persisted during 1973 when the cost of newly-built houses rose on average over the previous year by almost twice the national percentage figure. The rapid rate of increase experienced over the last decade, moreover, has not been confined to a small number of favoured areas. The largest percentage increases appear to have been in those areas where prices were generally lowest at the beginning of the decade. Nor were they confined to any one type of property, as all groups experienced substantial increases. The reasons for this marked change in house price levels are complex. It is highly probable, however, that the impact of external demands has been of paramount importance. The difference between the price of a house in the South East, and its equivalent in East Anglia, seems to have widened in the decade, although some of the differences can be explained by general inflation. It appeared to produce a strong incentive on the part of certain groups of people to come and live in the region. The first source of pressure on house prices has been the growing number of commuters living in the south and west of the region and working in adjacent parts of the South East. The second source has been the retirement mover and second-home owner, attracted by cheaper prices and a pleasant environment. This group has produced a more widespread demand, searching for properties outside the main employment centres.

10.3.4 These external pressures have had a number of consequences. In areas where they have coincided with a strong demand from local employment centres (see Map 10.1), the growth of local commuting areas has been restricted. Elsewhere newcomers appear to have concentrated in particular areas, limiting the numbers of houses available to the local population. This concentration, when exercised, for example, by retirement migrants, can produce strains on certain local services, and make the community less equipped to care for itself. A more deep-seated result has been to introduce a growing disparity between the actual price of a home, and that which can be afforded by many local people. This situation can be evidenced for the region as a whole; in some areas there are more striking differences.

10.3.5 For most families the ability to purchase a house is closely related to the income they receive from employment. Income levels in East Anglia are well below the national average for most occupations. We can expect, therefore, that the regional population is at a disadvantage when competing with house purchasers from elsewhere. Figure 10.2 shows the extent of the difference between the income structure of mortgage borrowers and that of the regional population at large.

Figure 10.2

Comparison of incomes of house purchasers and regional population, 1971 and 1972

Income Range £'s	Percentage of full time employees[1]		Percentage of mortgage borrowers[2]	
	1971	1972	1971	1972
below 1400	49·3	35·7	24·3	10·6
1400–1600	16·0	15·8	16·4	14·3
1600–2000	19·4	25·6	23·0	20·6
above 2000	15·3	22·9	36·3	54·5

Sources:
(1) New Earnings Survey 1971–72.
(2) DOE 5% Mortgage Sample Survey 1971, 1972.

10.3.6 In these conditions it is the local first-time buyer who is most affected. There is some evidence that his position deteriorated between 1966 and 1971, a situation applicable to older as well as to new property (Figure 10.3). Regional comparisons on the same basis suggest that only in the South East and South West do first-time buyers experience greater problems. The East Anglian situation is similar in many ways to that of the South West, both regions drawing on the South East for recreational visitors and retirement migrants. This similarity lends support to the postulated influence of external factors upon the level of house prices in the region.

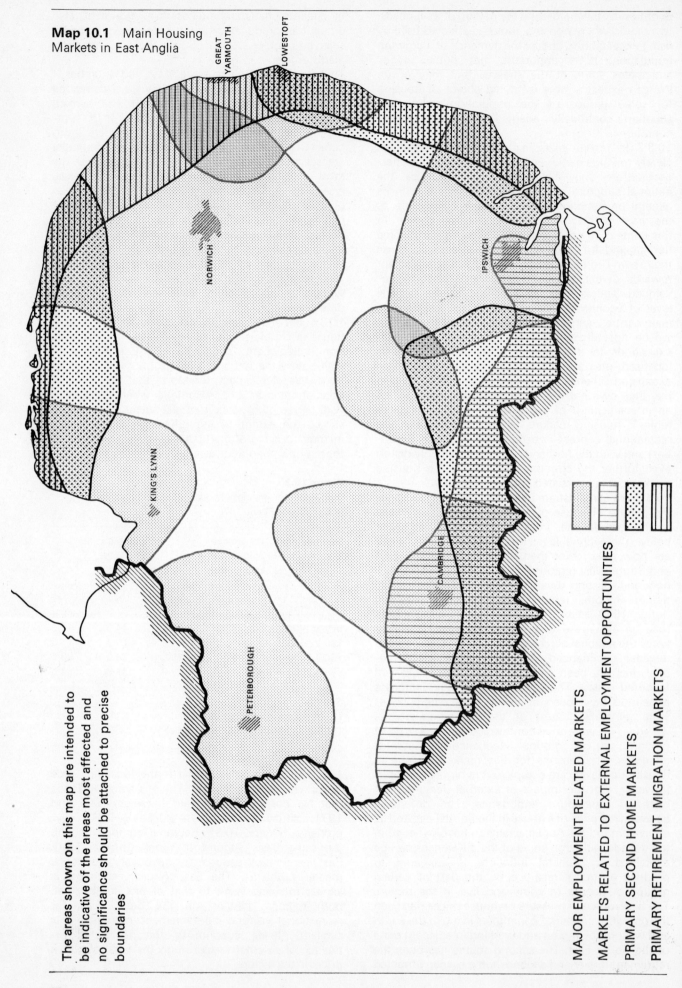

Map 10.1 Main Housing Markets in East Anglia

GREAT YARMOUTH

LOWESTOFT

NORWICH

IPSWICH

KING'S LYNN

CAMBRIDGE

PETERBOROUGH

The areas shown on this map are intended to be indicative of the areas most affected and no significance should be attached to precise boundaries

MAJOR EMPLOYMENT RELATED MARKETS

MARKETS RELATED TO EXTERNAL EMPLOYMENT OPPORTUNITIES

PRIMARY SECOND HOME MARKETS

PRIMARY RETIREMENT MIGRATION MARKETS

Figure 10.3

Excess of average price of three bedroom semi-detached houses sold, over maximum mortgage available to household with average annual earnings * by region 1966 and 1971

1966	Age of dwelling			
	Pre 1919 £	1919–44 £	1945–65 £	New £
North	407	467	817	734
Yorkshire and Humberside	221	81	341	267
North West	nil	258	568	260
East Midlands	nil	210	140	335
West Midlands	235	565	765	382
East Anglia	312	532	1,052	651
South East	1,213	1,943	1,573	1,344
South West	764	1,104	1,174	952
Wales	554	774	1,014	548

1971	Pre 1919 £	1919–44 £	1945–70 £	New £
North	795	585	885	383
Yorkshire and Humberside	18	nil	88	nil
North West	nil	227	387	nil
East Midlands	nil	nil	324	nil
West Midlands	nil	322	502	nil
East Anglia	584	794	1,324	1,021
South East	1,784	2,794	2,144	1,507
South West	1,146	1,496	1,416	887
Wales	283	833	833	138

*Defined as 2·6 times gross average earnings by region of men aged 18–64 in civil employment, for old property ; and 2·7 times gross average earnings, for new property. These multiples obtained from the average ratio of price to recorded income during the period 1966–71.

Source: Municipal Journal, Vol. 81, No. 28, 1973.

10.3.7 There are a number of ways in which this continuing deterioration in the prospects of local potential house buyers may be reversed. The most obvious one is to increase the total number of houses built in areas where the problems are most acute. The performance of the local construction industry in recent years, however, does not suggest that this will be possible without substantial changes. The number of private dwellings completed during each of the past five years has shown no marked increase. This reflects the fact that the demand for houses can fluctuate much more rapidly than the capacity of the construction industry, using tradition-al methods, to respond. This is partly a result of the structure of the industry in the region, where small, local firms make up almost 90% of the total. Such firms are most vulnerable to changes in the fortunes of the national economy, to material shortages, and to competition for skilled labour from larger firms and from other employment offering securer con-ditions. The smaller firms have been attracted to the more profitable sectors of the housing market,

represented by the new detached dwelling, and the older property ripe for improvement. The very large proportion of pre-1851 houses in the region, (15%), has ensured a ready supply for those wishing to move into the region and invest in local property.

10.3.8 The overall demand for housing that can be expected to arise from population change in the region, means that the annual rate of house building will need to be slightly faster than that experienced over the past five years. Such a rate should be within the overall capacity of the industry, on the basis of average annual completions, but will require a much steadier programme over a long period of time. The industry will need some support if this is to be achieved. The most appropriate form of support is open to question. It may need to include a regulating mechanism built into the capital structure of the industry, allowing it to ride the cycle of demands more easily. It will also need an assured supply of labour, materials, and serviced building land. Measures taken along these lines would help to achieve greater stability in the house building programme, and if they can be aligned with a clear forward planning procedure, then the private sector should be in a strong position to meet the demands made upon it.

10.3.9 A strengthened building programme in the private sector will not, by itself, relieve all the diffi-culties for the growing numbers of people requiring homes. Many will be dependent upon the rented sector, and particularly on the local authority. Recent experience suggests that there will need to be a substantial rethinking of current policies in the rented sector in the region as a whole. In the period 1966–72 there was a net increase of rented stock in the region of only 5,000 dwellings, compared with an increase of 72,000 in the owner occupied sector. The local authority programmes barely made up the loss experienced in the private rented sector of the market. Furthermore, without the town expansion schemes, there would have been a substantial decline in the total number of dwellings for rent. Since houses built in the planned schemes are, in the main, allocated to ex-London tenants, there has un-doubtedly been a real decline in rented houses available to the local population.

10.3.10 As the price of housing is likely to move further beyond the budget of many local people, an expanded programme of local authority building will be required. Such a programme could be aligned with the pattern of development set out in chapter eight, taking into account the planned migration proposals. Special emphasis would be required for new house-holds in rural areas, who are likely to be very seriously affected by rising house prices. Persistently low income levels, and a narrow range of job opportuni-ties for women, suggest that new local authority housing will be particularly required in both second-ary and smaller centres in rural areas. To help achieve this, whilst avoiding the heavy costs likely in a more dispersed pattern, we propose that a regional development fund should be considered in order to provide financial backing for approved schemes. Such a fund could be used to help defray some of the debt charges incurred by authorities providing a stock of housing in approved locations.

10.3.11 In addition to increasing the range of choice

in the rented sector, owner occupation will need to be supplemented in three important ways. Firstly, local authorities should play a more active role than they have done in the past, in enabling households to purchase their own homes. Secondly, joint schemes whereby private and public sectors agree to build houses and make these available to nominated households, such as existing local authority tenants, or those on waiting lists, are already possible, and have been initiated within the region. Finally, local authorities could also develop savings schemes, whereby tenants or potential tenants, might save towards the purchase of housing made available under the joint schemes envisaged.

10.3.12 One other aspect of housing choice remains outside the areas we have covered : that is a rented sector which does not depend upon employment or residential qualifications. There are obvious difficulties in relaxing such qualifications in the public sector. However, in some cases there may be special reasons why individual households do not wish to purchase their own home. They may be temporarily resident in an area, by reason of work or personal circumstance, or they may be new to the rented sector, as recent retirement migrants or previously tied-workers. They may also prefer to rent as of choice rather than buy. The numbers of such cases are likely to rise in the future, providing a market that could usefully be served by housing associations, as well as by a limited number of local authorities. Schemes could be supported by the National Housing Corporation, perhaps developed along regional lines, and with specific powers to initiate schemes in areas where this type of demand is likely to be high.

10.3.13 The ability of housing authorities to meet in these ways the variety of local housing needs will depend upon an informed reading of the local housing market, in relation to wider social and economic conditions. Their responsibility for meeting the housing needs of the elderly and homeless will lead in this direction, though it will be more difficult to anticipate the needs of transitory households. In all, such activity by housing authorities can only be part of the general movement to consider the interrelated nature of local services, and of a readiness to substitute one service for another where possible.

10 3 14 Within the principles set out in the previous part of this chapter, the more specific principle suggested to guide the development of housing policies is :

D8 policies should be designed, within the context of present national housing policies, to maintain the existing emphasis given to home ownership ; to encourage a specific rented sector not tied to residential or employment qualifications ; and to also direct public sector housing to the needs of those households excluded for various reasons from owner-occupation.

In the particular circumstances of East Anglia, we recommend that these principles could be met by the following proposals :

(xi) *the development of means of shielding the construction industry from short-term fluctuations in the demand for houses, both through improvements in the capital structure supporting the industry, and in ensuring a stable supply of materials and labour;*

(xii) *as an extension to (xi), local planning authorities should ensure an 8–10 years supply of serviced building land for housing, and carry out regular audits to this end, in conjunction with the building industry, in areas which form identifiable housing markets;*

(xiii) *the more widespread adoption by local authorities of means whereby newer households could be encouraged to obtain the benefits of owner-occupation, possibly by savings schemes, and joint schemes with private developers;*

(xiv) *the provision of a rented sector not tied to employment or residential qualifications, through either public or private enterprise, and possibly by the regionalisation of the National Housing Corporation, with appropriate powers and finance;*

(xv) *local authorities should attempt to identify and to meet the needs of those likely to be at some disadvantage in local housing markets, as a consequence of the marked concentration of groups of the population in certain areas, e.g. the elderly, retired migrants, young single workers, etc.*

(xvi) *an increased programme of local authority homes for rent, particularly in the rural areas, with emphasis given to secondary centres and selected small towns, located on public transport routes, and possibly given support through a regional development fund.*

10.4 Employment

10.4.1 Earlier chapters have emphasised the persistence of the overall distribution of employment opportunities across the region. This is evident, for example, in the pattern of opportunities for women to work, which helps to maintain lower average household incomes in rural areas. The lack of a ready supply of trained labour in many parts of the region hinders any marked change in this pattern. Furthermore, the ability of many people to take up those opportunities that do become available is impaired by their limited industrial experience. At the same time changes in the management and structure of firms have already led to a reduced direct involvement in local affairs, and local employment stability has become a less important factor influencing management decisions.

10.4.2 These developments have contributed towards a greater involvement by the public sector in the employment field. With the exception of the contribution of national distribution of industry policies to the planned migration programme, the main fields in which public bodies within the region are involved are those of industrial promotion, direct public service employment, and training. The extension of the public sector's activities into broader questions such as social accountability, ownership, and participation is unlikely to be a solely regional concern, and will hinge upon developments at the national level.

10.4.3 Local authorities are very much involved in promoting industrial activity, and in ensuring that local firms are supplied with a wide range of services. The experience of town expansion schemes shows the benefits that could be gained from a concerted effort amongst interested bodies in the region. Local government reorganisation offers an opportunity to reduce possible duplicated effort on the part of many authorities. With greater competition from new local authorities nationally, there is a strong case for establishing a clearer rationale in promotional activity. The first priority appears to be a more structured relationship between government departments, employers, trade unions, and local authorities, with the main objective being to advise authorities on the best means of mounting a co-ordinated promotional campaign within the region, based on the regular updating of local economic prospects. This would require some change in the activities of the Department of Industry in particular, and could be aided by closer formal working relationships established between the regional office, the county industrial promotion officers, and those of the district councils. Related to this, the second priority would be to recognise local variations in social and working conditions in any promotional activity. For instance, certain types of production processes may be less suited to rural conditions, where there is generally a resistance to highly automated production line work, and difficulty in implementing rigid work schedules.

10.4.4 Promotional activity should also be consistent with the pattern of development suggested in chapter eight. A system of incentives to encourage the decentralisation of small firms and functions from the main centres to small and secondary centres would bring benefits to both urban and rural areas. One possibility would be the selective use of funds specifically allocated for industrial promotion from each county's locally determined sector. This would help the framing of clearcut priorities, and ensure some continuity in promotional work. Local authorities themselves could play a more direct role in the process, by recognising the potential of their own role as employer. In many parts of the region, other public bodies are also significant employers. Over the period covered in this report, carefully considered shifts in public employment could have a useful effect on local job opportunities.

10.4.5 In the longer term, more fundamental changes in employment prospects could be brought about by training programmes designed to raise the general level of skills in the labour force. The relationship between the demand for training and the supply of places presents a number of difficulties for East Anglia. Some of these are familiar. The small scale nature of industry in the region means that one or two firms can dominate particular industries. As their future condition is much more uncertain than it is for an industry as a whole, it is consequently difficult to come to conclusions about the long term demand for training. This uncertainty is reinforced by the region's dependence upon external factors, both those related to the inflow of firms from the South East and elsewhere, and also those related to ownership and control. Two other features of the training situation are relevant. There is the general expectation of a need for greater adaptability at work, both within and between industries, and for continuous training for an increasing number of the work-force. Secondly, with a lower retirement age expected in the future, there are likely in this region to be a disproportionate number of older workers available for some sort of work. Both these features suggest that training programmes will need to be widened in their approach.

10.4.6 The emphasis of current training is strongly aligned to the demand arising within a well-defined occupational category in a particular industry. This is true of places offered on government courses, as well as in firms. The net result is to restrict the range of courses available and the number of places where courses can be taken. Government Training Centres will in time be established at Ipswich and Peterborough, to supplement that at Norwich, but are unlikely to directly benefit the central areas of the region where additional industrial expansion is expected. To some extent these limitations have been overcome by the development of the Training Opportunities Scheme (TOPS), which makes available courses at local education colleges and in firms at a number of the larger centres in the region. However, both schemes tend to operate strict entry criteria, specifying the timing and conditions of attendance. The TOPS, for example, requires that entrants must be prepared to terminate their employment before starting a course, and lays down a restriction on the duration of the course itself. The orientation of the training programme may thus be inappropriate both to the long term demand for adaptable rather than specific skills, and to the needs of a largely rural region with low levels of demand in any one industry or occupation, or in any one place.

10.4.7 For these reasons, a shift in emphasis towards developing programmes that give people a basic grounding, in a variety of technical and analytical skills, would be more appropriate in East Anglia. Such programmes would be orientated towards those functions that are increasingly common to a variety of occupations, leaving the sharpening of these skills to fit particular jobs as they arise, to training on the job, or to existing courses. In this way training opportunities could be extended to more people, and be better suited to a climate of uncertainty. The gradual build up of basic skills in the region's population could provide a more stable, yet adaptable, base for industrial expansion, and enable local workers to take fuller advantage of the employment opportunities subsequently made available.

10.4.8 Training programmes of this nature would have two main characteristics as operated in East Anglia. The first is that the content of the programmes should be structured to meet the problems of those unable to take long periods of time away from work or facing particular difficulties owing to age, financial commitments and social background. A prime objective would be to make available to these people the necessary adaptive skills in circumstances conducive to their continuing a normal family life. The second characteristic is that programmes would make full use of mobile units and local facilities, designed with regard to the needs of the rural parts of the region. In practice, there are a number of difficulties to overcome. In circumstances of full employment, and uncertainty as to future placements, the programmes themselves would need to be attractive, and flexible as to length and emphasis. Their content would depend upon a realistic assessment both of local employment conditions and of local aspirations.

10.4.9 The introduction of such training programmes would need to be preceded by experimental projects. Technically there appear to be no major obstacles. The concept of 'basic' skills is accepted, and these can be recognised. The content and emphasis of such a programme needs, however, to be worked up in the specific context of East Anglia. To this end, a joint experiment should be initiated, to be carried out in conjunction with local industrial and educational interests, and assessed on a long term basis. Its objectives would be twofold: firstly to define the basic skills appropriate to the region, and secondly the way these can be transmitted. The Training Services Agency, in their new role, could take a leading part in initiating and encouraging such an experimental programme.

10.4.10 The principle for employment policy in the region is framed within the general principles for service provision:

D9 policies should be designed to improve employment opportunities, particularly in those parts of the region outside the areas of dependence on the four main centres; and to improve the overall level of labour skills in the working population by appropriate training and educational programmes.

In particular we suggest that the following proposals are suitable to carry out that principle in practice:

(xvii) *the promotion of industrial development should be encouraged on a more concerted basis amongst local authorities, drawing on the experience of the town expansion programme;*

(xviii) *advice should be made available from national and regional bodies concerned with industrial and commercial development on a formal basis to local authorities, to enable them to assess their future potential;*

(xix) *local authorities and central government should have the joint responsibility for advising firms moving into the region, or from the larger centres, on local employment and social conditions;*

(xx) *part of the locally determined sector funds of local government could be specifically allocated for industrial promotion on the basis of priorities established at regional level and in structure plans;*

(xii) *local authorities should consider means of securing the movement of small firms, and of particular functions, to secondary centres and small towns from the major regional centres;*

(xxii) *training programmes in basic industrial and commercial skills should be developed, capable of refinement by existing training measures, and placing particular emphasis on mobile training methods, flexible in timing and content, and on co-operation with adult education projects;*

(xxiii) *an experimental project on these lines should be established within East Anglia, sponsored by the Training Services Agency in consultation with employers, unions, local education authorities, and local industrial promotion bodies.*

10.5 Education

10.5.1 Educational provision in the region is important on three counts. Firstly, it has a bearing upon the range of choice available to people in later years, both at home and at work. Secondly the provision of certain types of facility, such as nursery schools, can free more women to work if they wish and help raise household incomes. And lastly, it is itself a major category of public expenditure. Over the period considered in this report, there are certain to be considerable changes in educational thinking, and in the policies that are applied, many of which cannot be anticipated. We are, therefore, concerned with reviewing developments in education, both present and potential, as to how far they are suited to the particular conditions of East Anglia, as discussed earlier in the report.

10.5.2 Educational policy since the war has reflected a movement in favour of expanding educational choice for larger numbers of children. The recent expansion of the nursery school programme, and the raising of the school leaving age, illustrate one part of this process. Another is the concern for both the organisation of schools, and the size of school most appropriate to the educational horizons of children of different age groups. In the future, there is unlikely to be any retreat from this commitment to widen educational opportunities. In contrast the emphasis, and the means to do so, are much less certain, although more concern with the requirements of individual children is expected to lead to closer attention to the effect of family circumstances on education. Under these conditions, the ability of different parts of the region to adapt to changes in policies will be significant.

10.5.3 The opportunity to improve educational provision in East Anglia has been affected by the shortage of both financial and staff resources. Whilst new schools in themselves do not make for better education, they are much more likely to be designed to allow experimentation and readier adaptation to current thinking. As the bulk of capital expenditure in recent years has been on 'basic needs', that is on providing schools or classrooms simply to accommodate the growing school population, there have been only limited resources available for those areas experiencing slower growth or no growth at all. Figure 10.4 shows the general pattern over the last five years. The two authorities experiencing the most rapid population growth, Huntingdonshire and West Suffolk, were able to spend considerably larger sums over the five-year period than the slower growing authorities. Moreover, their expenditure per project tended to be higher, reflecting the scale of improvement or addition. In contrast, other authorities were both spending less each year, and also needing to spread their resources more piecemeal over a larger number of schemes.

10.5.4 It is unlikely that this broad pattern of differential expenditure will be reversed over the time period with which the strategy is concerned. The proposals in chapter eight would go some way to modify it, but will produce marginal change to a situation where suburban population growth, and planned migration, remain the main generators of school expenditure. In recognition of this sort of

Figure 10.4

Capital expenditure on major school projects
1969–70/1973–74 (£'000s)

Local Education Authorities	Total Expenditure over 5 years	Total No. of Projects	Average Annual Expenditure	Average Expenditure per Project
Norfolk	3619·7	48	723·9	75·4
Cambridgeshire	2598·3	31	519·7	83·8
Huntingdonshire	5159·2	44	1031·8	117·3
East Suffolk	3310·8	33	662·2	100·3
West Suffolk	6986·1	34	1397·2	205·5
Great Yarmouth	212·4	3	42·5	70·8
Ipswich	1029·9	7	206·0	147·1
Norwich	409·2	8	81·8	51·2
East Anglia	23325·6	208	4665·1	112·1

Source: DES 1973

problem for the more slowly growing areas, the improvement programme in recent years for primary schools has given some priority to replacing older buildings. In proportion to total expenditure, however, expenditure has been small, and opportunities for improvement greatest where the stock of old buildings coincided with population growth. For the region as a whole, it is estimated that some 30,000 children (20% of primary pupils) will remain by 1975 in primary schools built before 1903. In Norfolk, the proportion is likely to be considerably higher, corresponding to the large number of small, old schools throughout the rural areas. There are other implications of this situation, apart from constraining educational improvements. They include higher unit costs, largely in terms of staffing, and limitations on reorganisation proposals. Those authorities that have experienced population growth are, significantly, most advanced in putting reorganisation into effect.

10.5.5 To ease some of the difficulties in the region with limited resources, there are a number of complementary measures that could be taken. In the first place, the criteria for approving new expenditure should take into account the proposals for secondary and selected small towns in chapter eight. Apart from the benefits to accrue from the potential growth of such centres, secondary schools in particular should be able to take advantage of public transport and eventually of the proposed telecommunications network. For those areas benefiting from rapid population growth, much greater use might be made of adaptable and perhaps temporary units. This would recognise the uncertainty inherent in forecasts of the size of school population, especially in areas where the extent and composition of voluntary migration is a major and unpredictable factor. In part this may be a design problem, but flexible interpretation of the cost limits would help. To some extent such a measure could release financial resources for small projects in the slow growth areas. In this case there could usefully be consultation with other services operating in rural areas, so as to make joint usage an important objective. Despite these adjustments, there will

remain limited resources available to large parts of the region. There is a case for supplementing financial aid to these parts, but more importantly for freeing such aid to allow for local discretion. The difficulty of making rapid inroads into replacing old stock suggests that some priority should be given to strengthening support to teachers in many rural areas. This could take a number of forms. New ways of producing and distributing teaching material would be one possibility, perhaps extending some of the ideas from the Open University to schools, and making full use of local broadcasting possibilities. The use of teaching and technical support staff attached to a number of schools might be another.

10.5.6 In these circumstances, there may be advantages in relaxing the distinction between capital and revenue finance, replacing both by a system of block grants. The block grant could be closely aligned to expected population change, and based on a forward planning exercise approved by central government. This may produce benefits for those authorities finding it difficult to provide for a steady annual growth in school population, as with the new Cambridgeshire for example. A parallel system of supplementary grants could be available for use in slow growth or declining areas, where there could be substantial benefits from improvements to teaching support. Such a grant, for example, could be distributed to a small number of schools each year, rather than shared thinly amongst many.

10.5.7 An important and expanding area of educational provision is that of further education. National policy since the war has emphasised in turn the university and polytechnic branches of higher education, with consequently little development of the non-advanced further and adult education programme. There is some evidence to suggest that this trend is likely to be reversed over the period being considered, as opportunities are extended to those either leaving full-time education at an early stage, or returning for 'refresher' courses. At the same time there could be a move to coordinate all education for the 16–18 age groups, perhaps focusing on the local further education colleges.

10.5.8 The general emphasis of past policies has been of limited benefit to people in the region. University places, of course, are allocated nationally, and the absence of a polytechnic has hindered authorities in offering a range of advanced courses. To some extent, a change in policy towards extending such courses at further education colleges will benefit the region, extending the basis provided at Cambridge and Norwich. Any requirement, however, for students to live at home will cause difficulties in East Anglia unless there is greater expansion of non-university places locally. The four main centres of the region could each make claims for such expansion. They would need, however, the sort of resources available to polytechnics, and in total this is unlikely to be practicable. In these circumstances, a polytechnic based on a federal structure would be worth exploring. Some degree of specialisation could be possible, and the limited scale of expansion at each centre would help to maintain closer relationships between advanced and other forms of courses.

10.5.9 This development would have advantages in assisting further education colleges to play a more active role within the region. The needs of the older person, and those of the early school leaver, are likely to receive greater priority, as in national policies. Colleges can be expected to share the task of developing new courses and materials, and, at the same time, become more involved in local employment needs. Shortages of financial resources will make it difficult to provide the full range of facilities available to advanced course students. The choice may be between better buildings, and developments in taking courses to people in their homes or at work. There may be greater benefit from the latter approach, given the changes and circumstances anticipated in the region. More flexible ways of providing teaching material would need to be developed, using mobile classrooms, cassette television, course tutors, for example, as in current 'extension' courses. It follows that the building facilities available at the college base would need to include short stay accommodation. Elsewhere, a number of centres could be established, in conjunction with other welfare services, at the small towns, preferably giving priority to those on the proposed telecommunications network and accessible by public transport. The village colleges in Cambridgeshire provide a relevant example from the present.

10.5.10 There are a number of parallels between these developments and the training programme envisaged in 10.4. Both could usefully complement each other, sharing facilities, as on 'link' courses, and pursuing similar objectives. In order to bring into the same forum the various bodies concerned, a useful measure would be to use a restructured Regional Advisory Council for Further Education to initiate experimental projects, and to establish priorities within a framework of regional agencies as discussed in chapter fourteen.

10.5.11 On the basis, it is considered that the broad principle which is most appropriate to guiding the adaptation of educational policies to the particular circumstances of East Anglia should be as follows:

D10 policies should be designed to extend the ability of schools and colleges to respond to new developments in educational methods; to increase the range of opportunities to those unable to benefit fully from existing provision, particularly those living in rural areas, and those unaccustomed to learning by reason of age or background; to develop closer integration with other areas of service provision, especially training and leisure activities; to recognise the opportunities for educational provision in the proposed pattern of development.

It is proposed that within this context the following specific features be considered:

(xxiv) *upper and secondary schools should be developed in association with the proposed pattern of urban centres and communications;*
(xxv) *school building programmes should examine the use of small, adaptable, and temporary units, particularly in the field of nursery and primary education;*
(xxvi) *support for teachers in rural areas should be given special priority;*
(xxvii) *a system of block grants covering both capital and revenue financing should be introduced, along with a supplementary grant for use in areas experiencing slow population growth, as part of the development of an educational planning procedure;*
(xxviii) *more advanced courses should be made available, preferably within a federal polytechnic structure based on the main centres of the region;*
(xxix) *local further education colleges should jointly prepare a long-term programme to make course material readily available in the home and at work, perhaps on the lines pioneered by the Open University;*
(xxx) *the Regional Advisory Council for Further Education should assist in the promotion of education policies within the overall framework of development in East Anglia by their representation on regional bodies concerned with forward planning;*
(xxxi) *in providing educational facilities, in both school and further education sectors, the needs of other services such as training, social services, and public transport should be actively considered, possibly through the joint use of buildings and the development of common programmes.*

10.6 Health Services

10.6.1 The standard of health provision available to those living in the region plays an important part in determining their overall quality of life. The nature of the relationship between the supply of services and the effective demand for them ensures that there will continue to be a heavy pull upon available resources of finance and trained staff. Both these elements suggest that future priorities will have to be carefully considered in relation to the particular circumstances of East Anglia.

10.6.2 In recent years national policy for health care has given priority to the district general hospital. Capital programmes have been concentrated on establishing a network of sophisticated hospital facilities across the country, designed to serve populations of the order of 250,000. In attempting to provide a full range of diagnostic and treatment facilities, the basic size of the hospital unit has been enlarged considerably. This emphasis has been paralleled by a run-down in the small cottage hospital which previously made up a large part of total hospital accommodation. At the same time, health centres have been gradually developed so as to provide a firmer base for general practice. The reorganisation of the health service will serve to bring these different arms of policy closer together. The new planning procedures, for example, will ensure that most areas are working within the same national standards established by the Department of Health and Social Security.

10.6.3 In practice, the larger centres of East Anglia have benefited most from recent policies. The pattern of provision has, however, been modified as a result of the eccentric location of the four main centres. King's Lynn and Bury have had their own projects in recent years, and the particular conditions of the region have allowed lower bed-standards to be accepted. The limitations of previous provision meant that the region had few viable units on which to base such a programme. As a result, the majority of resources have been concentrated in the district hospital programme rather than on health centres and community provision. More recently, however, there has been a greater impetus in the direction of community support, the most noticeable features of which are the proposed community hospitals and the expansion of medical social workers. Progress in this direction over future years will nevertheless be constrained by a number of features in the region.

10.6.4 A community hospital programme would appear well-suited to East Anglia. It promises a pattern of provision adapted to a rural region with a dispersed population, and with a high proportion of elderly and immobile people. At the same time the present district hospital provision cannot be considered fully adequate. These competing claims indicate a need for a carefully worked out set of priorities. The district general hospital programme, as it stands, would commit considerable resources at a limited number of places over a long period. It is less flexible than some other items of health care, although nonetheless important in a comprehensive care system. The uncertainty that surrounds the future size of population at any one of the major centres suggests caution in planning large fixed facilities. The district hospital also requires extensive staffing, both technical and non-technical. There may be no difficulty in attracting specialist medical staff to the region, but the availability of general staff to carry out the routine tasks of any large establishment may be more limited. The suburban location of new sites will make access difficult for these staff, working as they do unusual hours and for relatively low pay. Thus, there may be a good case for reconsidering the district hospital programme, with a view to dispersing some functional units of the hospital around the main centres, consistent with maintaining viability. Four additional factors could affect this situation over the longer time period. In the first place, changes in medical practice may obviate some of the need for large and expensive facilities of limited general use. Secondly, the adaptation of telecommunications to medicine, particularly to diagnostic treatment, may make it less important to retain every function on one site. Thirdly, there may be greater possibilities for using common central services, such as kitchen and laundry facilities, where economies of scale could be maintained. And lastly, the expected spread of population away from the main centres may make it more difficult to provide a central location for any one unit. Each of these four factors lends some support to a review of the district hospital programme in the region.

10.6.5 A review of this nature could allow some release of resources for faster development of community medicine, including a community hospital and health centre programme. This would have the added advantage of providing an effective presence in areas away from the main centres. Such a presence could be used to develop support in the community and various forms of mobile provision. It would allow easier contact with other services, particularly the social services, and make joint usage of facilities a possibility. This more integrated pattern of provision would be most likely if development was aligned with that proposed in chapter eight, in secondary centres and selected small towns, so as to make most use of public transport, and the potential of any telecommunications network, linking these centres to the four main towns.

10.6.6 It is clear that the development of this approach would require considerable knowledge of local conditions, and of other services. The reorganised health service will be well-placed in this respect. The basic information on facilities, built up by the 'area profiles' for each of the new counties, will be supplemented by the work of the district health teams as they develop, and by advice from the community health councils. In order to make forward provision effective, however, there will be a greater need to draw on the information held by housing and social services agencies, and to discuss with them the priorities for a particular area. This might imply, for example, that one service would be best equipped to take the leading role in an area, with some saving of resources for other services. In circumstances of overall limitations on available resources, the remoter rural areas of the region would most benefit from such flexible local arrangements. Although the joint consultative committees at county level may have an effective role, there could also be benefits from closer participation at the regional level in resource allocation. In financial terms, the greater flexibility that could result from a freer transfer between capital and revenue funds would be more suited to a region like East Anglia.

10.6.7 In East Anglia, therefore, the strategic principle suggested for the forward provision of health services is:

D11 policies should be designed to encourage more flexible and smaller units of care, as part of a general move to integrate the working of health services with other welfare services.

In particular it is suggested that consideration should be given to the following proposals to put this principle into effect:

(xxxii) *a review of the district general hospital programme to include the possibility of using smaller functional units around the main centres, and of releasing resources to allow the more rapid development of community care;*

(xxxiii) *an increase in the priority given to the development of the community hospital and health centre programme in centres intermediate to the locations of the district hospitals;*

(xxxiv) *the location of fixed capital projects of health provision at the main and secondary centres, and at selected small towns lying on the proposed communications network, so as to gain the maximum benefits of an integrated pattern of development and transport for the region;*

(xxxv) *the establishment of mechanisms at regional and local levels for closer and more integrated working with other welfare services, and associated flexibility in the use of resources on a continuing basis.*

10.7 Social Services

10.7.1 The reorganisation of the social services that followed the 'Seebohm' report was the prelude to a period of considerable expansion. There are few indications that this trend will be reversed over the period with which the strategy is concerned. This means that, as in the health service, priorities will need to be carefully considered as demands on resources increase. Certainly, it is likely that the standard of the service will become a more important feature of people's expectations about the quality of life in the region.

10.7.2 Although services are provided under legislation, and priorities set at national level, local authorities have considerable discretion over individual elements in the services they provide. There has been, for example, only a small shift away from residential care in institutions towards rehabilitation within the community. This movement is likely to be strengthened, although it is uncertain whether the absolute demand for residential places will fall. It seems most likely that despite more effective support in the home and in the community, there will remain a demand for those services that can only be offered within some form of residential establishment.

10.7.3 The ten-year programmes recently completed by each local authority are a recognition of the need for forward planning. Very largely the primary concern is with the speed at which standards can be raised to the levels indicated nationally. This process will dominate the future programmes of local authorities, but there are a number of ways in which it could be carried out that would be more or less suited to East Anglian conditions. Existing differences in standards of provision between authorities reflect to a large extent historical circumstances. The presence of old residential establishments continue to place a considerable constraint on implementing current policies. It is, therefore, important in the context of uncertainty about both future population levels and future professional attitudes towards care, that present expenditure does not similarly close too many future options. Residential homes and other schemes built today may be ill-suited to the type of care thought appropriate in the future. Such schemes can impose considerable costs over a long time period, in both debt charges and everyday running costs. There will be some cases where large capital expenditure is inevitable. In others, there will be scope for using small and adaptable units of provision, some of which might be mobile. There is no reason why such units need to be less attractive or less functional. They would merely be a recognition of the small-scale and uncertain demands in a rural region, and appropriate, for example, to multiple use.

10.7.4 Consistent with this general approach could be the greater use of voluntary and community support. It is unlikely that the number of trained social workers will be adequate for the potential demands which could be met. In East Anglia these shortages are likely to be more acute in those parts of the region that can offer few alternative attractions to the professional worker. With a large and growing number of elderly people, and a dwindling base to many local communities, the dependence on voluntary support is greater than elsewhere. In these circumstances, greater use of voluntary support throughout the service may be necessary. Such support cannot be effective, however, without a minimum amount of training in local conditions. Professional social workers and local further education colleges could have a vital role, consistent with their own greater involvement in the community. There might be special training, for example, in working with migrant communities, as in the expanded towns, or with the elderly, as in 'retirement' villages.

10.7.5 The effective use of both buildings and staff will depend upon the recognition of local needs, and upon a feedback from the local community. A sensitive response to variations in local conditions is an important objective of this kind of service. This suggests that an important priority in the development of social services should be the establishment of methods of anticipating problems likely to arise, drawing on their contacts with local communities. The harnessing of this intelligence function would inevitably lead to a discussion of priorities to be achieved in other services as a means of avoiding potential problems. In the longer term, therefore, we expect to see a movement away from a concentration on problems, and on methods of ameliorating them, towards a more preventive approach. This would place much more emphasis on the effective management and allocation of resources at local levels, as part of a more integrated process of service provision. For example, in certain instances, this could mean that the needs of one group of the local population might best be met by either complementary action amongst different services, or by the expansion of one particular service at the expense of another.

10.7.6 The area structure of social services provides an existing basis upon which local conditions can be gauged. Area offices can also provide a point of contact for other services if sited appropriately, with access to housing, education, and health agencies, an important criterion. The pattern of development and communications proposed in chapters eight and nine would also ensure that client access is improved considerably. Beyond this broad framework, there must be dependence on the imaginative provision that can come only from extensive local knowledge and considerable discretion in detailed matters. Two developments which might be useful in encouraging these aims are, firstly, greater flexibility between capital and revenue funds, and secondly, more formal participation in resource allocation at the regional level. The first point could be met at present by the introduction of a block grant system to local authorities, based upon the prior approval of the ten-year planning document. This would ensure attention to national priorities, whilst at the same time encouraging a degree of local discretion. Special projects could remain outside such a system if necessary. The second point could be covered by the changes in agencies as discussed in chapter fourteen.

10.7.7 In the particular circumstances of East Anglia, it is suggested then that the future development of social services should be guided by the following principle:

D12 policies should be designed to encourage

more flexible forms of provision, based upon priorities agreed between related services, and having regard for the variety of local circumstances.

In particular, consideration should be given to the following proposals:

(xxxvi) *the greater use of small and flexible units of provision, in both residential and other forms of care, to allow scope for adaptation to changing ideas on methods of providing the service;*

(xxxvii) *the acceptance of greater use of voluntary effort in local communities and its encouragement by appropriate programmes of training;*

(xxxviii) *the location of capital projects at the main and secondary centres, and selected small towns, to gain the advantages of an integrated pattern of development and transport;*

(xxxix) *a greater emphasis on using intelligence gained about local conditions as a general source for deriving priorities and improving effectiveness in all welfare services;*

(xl) *the development of the area structure as the focus for a number of related services, in association with an enlarged degree of discretion and flexibility in the use of resources.*

10.8 Shopping

10.8.1 The range of shopping services available at centres within the region is an important index of personal choice. It also makes calls on public expenditure in the provision of infrastructure and other services, such as roads and social services respectively. The changes that are taking place in retailing and in the shopping habits of people have considerable implications, therefore, both for public and private sector resources, and for the range of opportunities available.

10.8.2 The present pattern of shopping provision in the region (see Map 10.2) has its roots largely in a system of marketing and retailing suited to a period when personal mobility was more limited. As the private car has extended mobility to a much larger section of the population, this pattern has evolved accordingly. The larger centres have consolidated their strong position in the hierarchy of centres, continuing to hold the advantage of a wider range of goods, and the possibility of lower prices stemming from a high turnover. An analysis of more recent change in the 1968–72 period suggests that even over such a short time-span these larger centres have been gaining at the expense of many smaller centres (see Map 10.3). Those that have suffered most tend to be in the remoter parts of the region, where the decline of the local population has accompanied the greater mobility available to those left behind, as documented in the 'Small Towns Study'. North Norfolk and Mid-Suffolk have been particularly affected in this way. In some cases, however, smaller towns have been able to benefit from their central position in areas of low population growth. The smaller towns along the A47, for example, have increased their importance in a local context.

10.8.3 Two factors have promised to modify the general process of concentration in shopping provision. The first is the commercial advantage to be gained from large self-service shopping units, demanding extensive space for display and car parking. The second is town-centre congestion, particularly on the main shopping days. Both these factors have served to reduce the advantages of a town centre site for many types of shop. The net effect has been to persuade retailing groups to look for out-of-town sites, often strategically situated near major road junctions. This search has not been confined to the major centres, as many of the smaller towns have experienced local traffic congestion and have a restricted number of central sites available.

10.8.4 The consequences of these changes could be twofold for East Anglia. In the first place, families in the rural areas, particularly those without their own personal transport, may not be assured of obtaining the benefits of a wide range of goods and lower prices. Secondly, the effectiveness of public investment in roads and other infrastructure may be reduced if either further development is encouraged, leading to local congestion, or if long-term viability is in doubt. Overall a balance has to be found between modern trends in retailing, and the desire to share the resulting benefits with a wider number of people, directly in shopping choice, and indirectly through the use of public funds.

10.8.5 The main centres are likely to continue in a dominant position as far as the range and variety of goods on offer is concerned. Changes in retail provision within their built-up area will require some adjustments to public transport and other service provision, and perhaps a reappraisal of urban road schemes. There should, nevertheless, be scope for alternatives to main centre shopping. In the perspective of this report, the most effective alternative would be the development of the secondary and smaller centres, as set out in chapter eight. Their potential includes acting as a focus for rural transport provision, as well as for a growing population. The close relationship between shopping provision and that of both welfare and other commercial activities suggests that the smaller centre can regain a stronger role. Such a role may be helped by turning the difficulties of congestion and parking in the larger centres to the advantage of such smaller centres.

10.8.6 For people with personal transport, weekend shopping is becoming more strongly associated with other activities, and they may choose not to make regular visits to any one shopping centre. The smaller centre that can offer easy access by car, an attractive shopping area, and possibly a major recreational feature, could succeed in developing a new role. More positive policies of purchase, access, and information, perhaps in association with the Regional Tourist Board, would help towns to develop their own individual character as well as their trade. In this context, the conservation of the historic centre would be an important objective of any commercial development, recognising that the small town's commercial viability may be closely dependent in the long term on its ability to remain attractive as a place to visit.

10.8.7 It would be consistent with this approach that large out-of-town developments would be encouraged only in special circumstances. In areas where there is rapid growth, existing centres may be unable to adjust and respond to change quickly enough, so

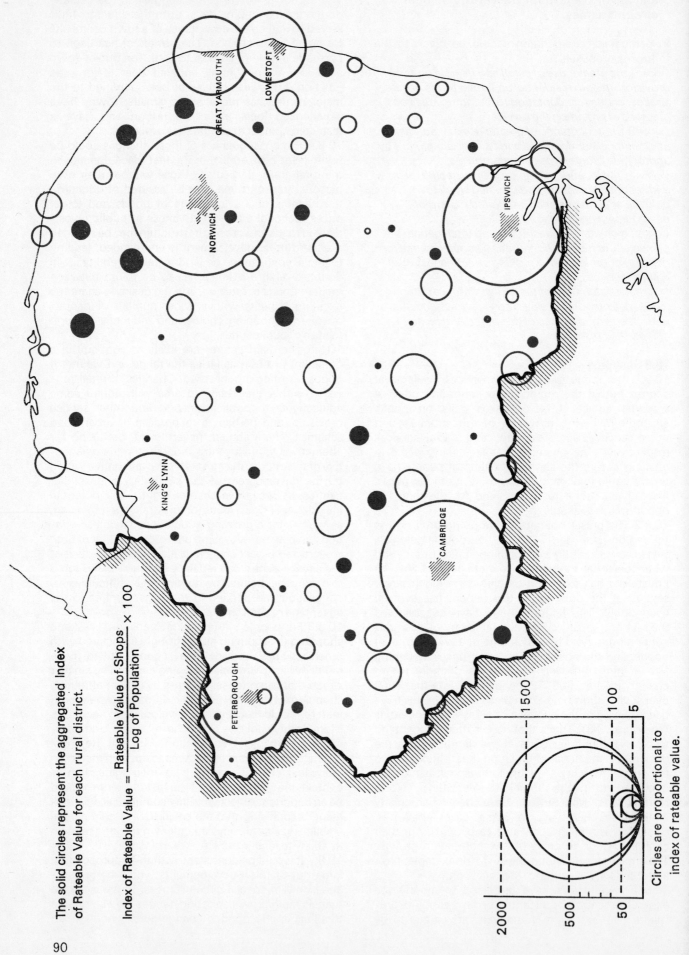

Map 10.2   Shopping Provision, 1972

The solid circles represent the aggregated Index of Rateable Value for each rural district.

Index of Rateable Value = $\dfrac{\text{Rateable Value of Shops}}{\text{Log of Population}} \times 100$

GREAT YARMOUTH

LOWESTOFT

NORWICH

IPSWICH

KING'S LYNN

CAMBRIDGE

PETERBOROUGH

2000

1500

500

100

50

5

Circles are proportional to index of rateable value.

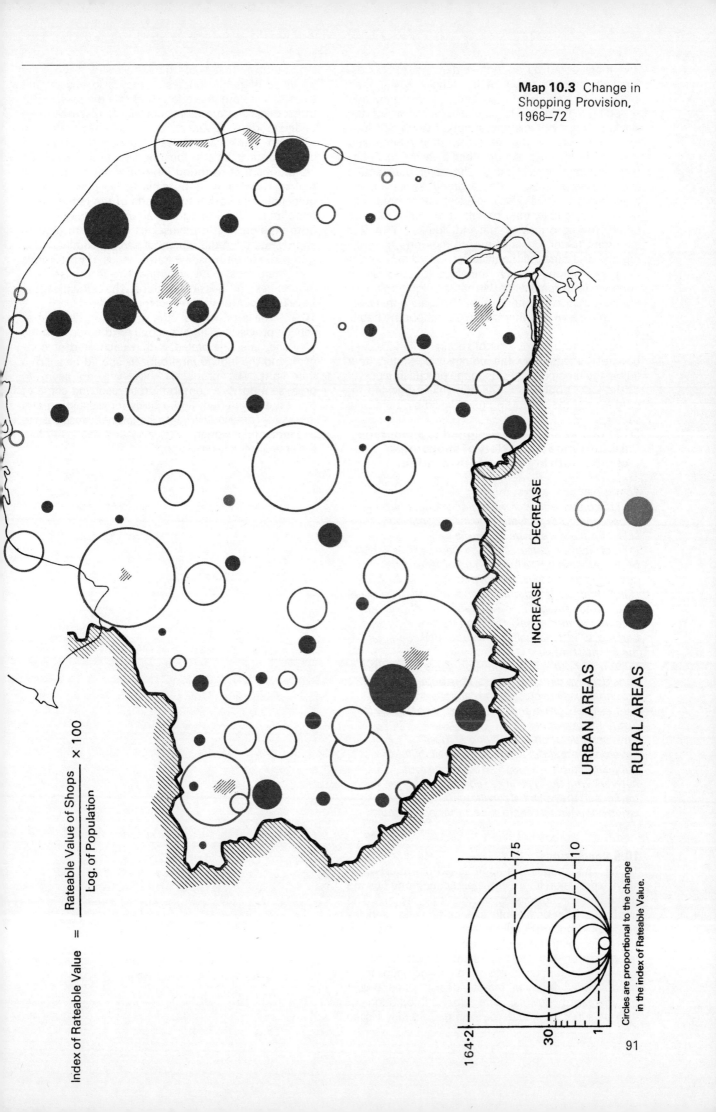

Map 10.3 Change in Shopping Provision, 1968–72

Index of Rateable Value $= \dfrac{\text{Rateable Value of Shops}}{\text{Log. of Population}} \times 100$

DECREASE

INCREASE

URBAN AREAS

RURAL AREAS

75

10

164·2

30

1

Circles are proportional to the change in the index of Rateable Value.

91

that there could be an unmet demand for goods. Similarly, there may be circumstances where road capacity is provided in advance of demand, and shopping developments can take up some of the slack. In these circumstances, out-of-town developments could be used to relieve existing centres and make more effective use of public investment. Technical and commercial changes, however, may require such developments to be regarded as essentially temporary in nature. The impact of telecommunications, for example, may be felt at an early stage in retail provision, making the individual visit a less important factor. Costs of private motoring may rise rapidly, and create difficulties for the weekly shopping expedition. It may, therefore, be unwise to approve developments of this nature, requiring heavy public investment, without some assurance that sites could have a valued alternative use if shopping habits change.

10.8.8 The future provision of shopping services will be most affected by the commercial factors that adjust the range of provision to the purchasing power of the local population. The principle suggested for guidance of the supporting role played by the public sector is :

D13 policies should be designed to encourage a wide range and variety of shopping choice, both in goods and in location.

To this end, we suggest that :
(xli) *the main centres of the region should continue to be regarded as providing the main opportunity to select from a wide range of goods;*
(xlii) *effective alternatives to the main centres should be encouraged by the building up of secondary centres and selected small towns;*
(xliii) *small centres should be encouraged to compete for trade advantages by developing non-shopping attractions, and by making adequate provision for car parking, whilst maintaining the essential character of their central areas;*
(xliv) *major out-of-town developments should be considered in circumstances where population growth is likely to outstrip the capacity of existing centres to absorb it, and for a period of time likely to justify the investment;*
(xlv) *consideration of the siting of these developments should include the availability of public transport, access to an adequate route network with the capacity to absorb additional traffic, and the potential for alternative use if and when commercial conditions and shopping habits change.*

10.9 Conclusions

10.9.1 This chapter has approached the question of service provision from a viewpoint conditioned by the particular circumstances facing the region. The implications for both public expenditure and agencies are spelled out more fully in section F, but it is clear that some of the proposals require a more positive interpretation of the role of the public sector. There is no reason to suppose that such a change needs to be accompanied by more remote decision taking and by increased powers. The closer integration of various services should, for example, actually lessen the confusion that exists in people's minds about the activities of public bodies. It may also ensure that decisions are put into effect, and that the reasons for those decisions are more thoroughly discussed and understood in advance. There is, nevertheless, a need to think more clearly about the level of discretion available to local bodies. In the uncertain conditions that surround long-term decisions in the region, it will not be possible to lay down precise guidelines applicable to all parts of the region or its population. The new agency arrangements operating in the region will in themselves not lead to general improvements in the quality of service administered. If they are to be sensitive to the needs of East Anglia then there must be a willingness to recognise local differences and possible options. The principles that have been put forward reflect this view.

10.9.2 These principles offer a common element to service provision. There is scope for difference in the way they are interpreted within each area of concern, and the individual proposals should be seen in that light. The proposals, however, do seem to promise a positive contribution to resolving some of the issues identified, and a basis for discussion and initiative. This would imply a sympathetic response to experiments designed to try new approaches within the area of service provision.

Section E

Environmental Resources and Recreation

The contents of this section parallel those of Section D in that they are both concerned with aspects of life in the region that are likely to be highly valued in the future. In this section, we turn to some of those qualities that make East Anglia recognisably different —qualities that are increasingly reflected in decisions about where people live and work. These qualities, mainly environmental in the broadest sense, have contributed in the past to the rapid growth of the region, and helped to make it an outlet for holidays and recreation. They also play a significant part in people's daily lives, not just in terms of where they live, but also in relation to their jobs, and later, during retirement. Most of these environmental qualities are under pressure from a scale and rate of change never before experienced in East Anglia. Some cannot be replaced once lost; others take a long time to renew themselves. If they are to be retained as a major asset for the future of the region, they will have to be consciously managed rather than left to chance.

In the first chapter of this section, we examine the nature of the demands on the environment. This is followed in chapter twelve by a brief survey of the changing condition of environmental resources, together with the pattern of recreational pressures within the region. The contents of these two chapters are drawn together in the final chapter as a statement of strategic principles for the management of the environment. For each of these principles, practical policy steps are considered, and these are summarised in the conclusions.

The content of these chapters is based on the work of a specially convened environmental working party. The interpretation made here may not coincide in detail with the views of individual members of the group, but would have had much less substance without their assistance.

Chapter 11

Demands on Environmental Resources

11.1 Introduction

11.1.1 From prehistoric times man has been extending his control over the environment. At different times the social and economic forces expressed through this control have combined to affect the environment in different ways. Many of the qualities we admire in East Anglia today are the product of the 18th and 19th centuries. In this period there was a strong movement to design landscape positively as part of the changes brought about by the enclosure movement in agriculture. The architecture of the towns and villages came under similar influences. Little of this heritage was disturbed by the industrial revolution and its aftermath, and it is only in the present day that the pace of change is posing serious questions.

11.1.2 The fixed element in the environment of East Anglia is the landform which is, for the most part, no more than undulating. This throws into greater prominence the coastline and those elements which clothe the land surface. Many of these elements are man-made, with little of the natural vegetation remaining. Even so, the region possesses a wide variety of habitats which support an extensive plant and animal life. Together these are qualities helping to make East Anglia recognisably different, and an attractive area in which to live and work. But the environment is more than this. In all its aspects, it is a resource which is available for a large number of uses both now and in the future. The quality of this resource, and the way in which it is affected by the pressures upon it, are the subject of this and the next chapter.

11.2 The Demands made on the Environment

11.2.1 Since the war, increased mechanisation of farming and the extension of the area of arable farmland and urban development have had dramatic effects on the countryside. In the towns, relatively standardised forms of building, and changes in transport, have often served to alter their character. These influences are mainly functional, and, unlike earlier periods, when human development was not so rapid or pervasive, can result in the widespread destruction of many of those qualities which are essential to attractive and healthy environments. These functional uses must form the structural elements of the countryside and urban areas, but their scale and speed of change means that they have to be counterbalanced by a much more conscious process of management which recognises the other major demands on the environment.

11.2.2 The first of the demands which has to be recognised in the management of environment is **scientific and educational.** At one level, this is concerned with those features of the environment which support life; for example, the need to maintain clean air and water. In addition, man has been and will continue to be dependent upon a variety of other species for use and study. The environments of the region are part of the potential stock of knowledge. Where they have been explored in detail, they have a continuing educational function. Where they are still largely unknown, they offer an outlet for human curiosity into the past and into natural surroundings. There is much that is not known about the history of the occupation of the region, the evidence for which lies beneath both the towns and the countryside.

11.2.3 Many of these environmental resources are irreplaceable. Some can only be renewed over a very long period and it would seem to be incumbent on the present generation to leave for its successors at least an equal amount and variety of environmental resources as it inherited. The environment can also be a valuable safeguard for the future. There may well be circumstances where man may unwittingly go beyond conditions which are either essential or extremely important to life, as he explores new and complex methods of controlling and using his environment. The maintenance of plant and animal species, and examples of earlier technologies, could prove to be sound insurance.

11.2.4 There is a further **ethical** reason why species and their habitats should be protected. This is the question of the extent to which there should be a right of survival for species, where their interests conflict with human activities. Species cannot exist divorced from others, and to maintain this ecological balance, there must be an inter-relationship of habitats. It is not certain at the regional scale exactly what this inter-relationship is, but a minimum of continuity between habitats seems to be required to enable the necessary movement of wildlife. This could be achieved by a natural lattice of habitats across the region, avoiding extensive areas sterilised by agricultural or urban uses.

11.2.5 A further category of demands is the pleasure derived from environment in the various activities that people perform. This includes the environments within which they live, work or travel, for recreation or holidays. This **aesthetic function** that the environment performs is one of its most important. At the same time it is the most difficult to define adequately. For most people such pleasure derives from environmental elements inherited from the past. But changes are taking place, especially in agriculture which in many respects functions as any other commercial operation. This suggests that it is important to create environments that meet the practical requirements of these activities, but at the same time will be as high in quality as the legacy inherited from the past. 11.2.6 Demands on environment as a **background to day-to-day activities** and recreation will clearly be related to the distribution of population in the region. The growth of the region's population to the end of the century seems likely to increase the stock of buildings by at least a third. The quality achieved in this development will therefore have a considerable effect both on the visual appearance of East Anglia, and on the domestic and working environments of its people. More formal provision of facilities such as swimming baths, sports halls and entertainment centres is closely tied to the distribution of population, and tends to be concentrated in the larger towns. The low density of population in the region means that there are problems of access from the rural areas, and that the overall level of provision is likely to be lower than in other regions where population is more concentrated.

11.2.7 The recreational demands of the population living in the region are, however, only part of the total demand on the environmental resources of East Anglia. This ranges from the foreign visitor, who tends to concentrate on Cambridge and Norwich, and the British holidaymaker, to the more informal requirements of people from neighbouring regions who take short breaks in East Anglia. In looking at both the present and future form of these demands from **recreation and tourism,** a convenient distinction can be drawn between the tourist and holidaymaker whose visits tend to be planned in advance, and the more informal and diverse requirements of the tripper both from within and outside the region.

11.2.8 In 1968, the British Tourist Authority estimated that about 1,650,000 holidays were taken in East Anglia. The number seems to be increasing by about 30,000 a year. Nationally, the proportion of the population taking holidays remained static in the sixties, and the growth occurred in second holidays which nearly doubled. In both cases, East Anglia's share was just under 10%. The results of the context studies were optimistic in that there could be a slightly faster rate of growth of the numbers of holidays taken in the region. With a range of assumptions, the possible growth in holidays is shown in Figure 11.1.

Figure 11.1

Notional future levels of holidays taken in East Anglia 1968–2001 (in thousands)

	Expected Increase	Number of Holidays
1968		1,650
1968–81	385–440	
1981		2,035–2,090
1981–91	350–400	
1991		2,385–2,490
1991–2001	350–500	
2001		2,735–2,990

Source: East Anglia Regional Strategy Team.

11.3 The Value of Environment

11.3.1 A major problem in assessing these demands is the extent to which they are measurable. Some demands, for example, agriculture, urban development, and roads can be valued. Others covering the need for wild life, and the needs of future generations, are much more difficult to translate into specific monetary terms. A similar problem applies to aesthetic pleasure. It is not possible to compare beauty and usefulness. One is valued for its own sake, the other for its results. The concept of an environment valued for its own sake is important. It requires environment to be kept and enhanced as a basic framework in the region within which other uses must fit. It then becomes available for the various demands upon it, while avoiding the problem of placing values on qualities which are often intangible.

11.4 Landscape for East Anglia

11.4.1 It remains, before concluding this chapter, to try to define the type of landscape principles that might in general terms be developed. Landscape appreciation is largely an aesthetic experience which is subjective and personal and will vary with individuals and over time. Does this mean, as is often popularly stated, that an aesthetic experience, from for example, a painting, a piece of architecture, or a landscape, is no more than a matter of opinion? Whilst many attempts have been made to find an answer to this question, it has been held recently that the aesthetic quality of an object lies in its capacity for producing aesthetic experience. This capacity lies in the object and not the observer, and it has been suggested that this capacity lies in qualities that the object may have with regard to unity, vividness (or imageability) and variety.

11.4.2 **Unity** is the extent to which a landscape represents a cohesive state. Usually there is some expression of dominance in that some elements are more important than others. The landscape will appear whole so long as subordinate parts do not represent chaotic competition, repeating each other to the point of monotony. **Vividness** lies in the strength of the single composition and is the total impression that is built up. Some landscapes give an impression that is unique. In East Anglia, the Broads, the Fens, the North Norfolk Coast, and Dedham Vale are all examples of landscapes which identify themselves in this way. **Variety** is the number of different objects and relationships that are found in landscape. In this sense it falls within a definite pattern and is important for the qualities of unity and vividness mentioned above. It should also be noted that extreme variety (with no vividness or unity) becomes monotonous, as does a lack of variety.

11.4.3 In addition to these qualities, it is important to make a distinction between the foreground, middleground and background of a scene. In the foreground, the details of the scene are displayed; these have the greatest impact on sight, smell and hearing. This is where variety in both vegetation and wildlife is most significant. The middleground is where parts of the landscape which give it vividness are most important. It is also where man-made features can be most easily incorporated. In the background the main elements of landform and blocks of vegetation provide the unity of the landscape. The sequence and speed with which the landscape is observed will affect the emphasis given to these different elements. A person on foot will concentrate on the variety in the foreground, preferring occasional glimpses of the middleground and background to the monotony of the wide panoramic scene. An observer in a car may be much more frustrated by being enclosed in this way.

11.4.4 The relative flatness of East Anglia means that tree cover will provide the main source of visual unity and image. The nature of modern agriculture suggests that over parts of the region the main landscape features may be copses or blocks of woodlands which are more compatible with it than the traditional hedgerows. The increasing dominance of buildings in the countryside suggests that large scale planting is required to blend them into the landscape. Sensitive management of roadside verges, waterways and footpaths is needed to give variety to scenes. To afford movement for wildlife, inter-field hedgerows linking main woodlands will be necessary, while stocks of land which can develop naturally through their stages of succession would give a variety of wildlife habitats.

11.5 Conclusions: The Management of Environmental Resources

11.5.1 The wide spectrum of demands on environmental resources results in a large number of interests and agencies being involved in their management. This fragmentation makes it difficult to gain a comprehensive view of the condition of these resources, and the ways in which they are changing. It also increases the difficulties of securing any overall approach to their management, and may also be reflected in the low level of direct expenditure on the environment. For all these reasons there appears to be a need for a focus for the management of the region's environmental resources at the regional level, which would bring together all the public and voluntary bodies involved in shaping their future.

11.5.2 The further difficulty of placing a value on these resources means that they have to be treated as public goods, with responsibility for them assured by the public sector in the form of direct expenditure, together with systems of grants and regulatory controls over activities in the private sector. One of the clearest examples of this is the statutory provision for historic buildings and conservation areas. The principles adopted in this legislation have not been applied in equivalent form to the countryside and landscape qualities. The activities of the public sector would need to extend beyond conservation in the countryside to no less than the positive design of landscape, and the conscious management of all forms of environmental resources.

11.5.3 The content of this chapter can then be summed up as a list of requirements which seem essential to the management of environmental resources. These are:

(a) to safeguard a high quality and variety of environments for present and succeeding generations;

(b) to safeguard a wide variety of habitats for plant and animal life;

(c) to secure the positive design of landscapes: in parallel with, and enhancing the visual quality of, modern agriculture practice and urban development; and in a way which allows for their slow rate of maturation;

(d) to satisfy the requirements of the population of the region for: high quality in their everyday environments; variety in their informal recreation; a range of formal activities for more active participation;

(e) to recognise and make provision for the likely growth in holidays and tourism in the region;

(f) to identify and make more accessible those qualities of visual interest, and historic quality which are attractive to formal recreation and tourism;

(g) to provide for the exploration and retention of the more significant sites of archaeological, historic and architectural interest;

(h) to provide a joint focus for bodies involved in shaping the future of the environment;

(i) to secure an appropriate system of expenditure, grants and controls for the management of the environment.

11.5.4 These outline requirements have to be translated into practical form. In the next chapter this process is begun by looking at the condition of environmental resources in East Anglia, and the way it is changing in response to the pressures upon it.

Chapter 12

The Condition and Use of Environmental Resources

12.1 Introduction

12.1.1 The requirements that must underlie the management of the environment have to be considered against actual circumstances in East Anglia. The first step is to establish the condition of the stock of environmental resources of the region, and the way in which that stock has been responding to the pressures upon it. Following this, the patterns of tourist and recreational activity within the region are analysed in turn. From these sources it is possible to reach firm conclusions on the possibility of reconciling demands in the future. This provides the basis on which strategic policies for the management of environmental resources can be considered in chapter thirteen.

12.2 The Stock of Environmental Resources

12.2.1 East Anglia possesses a considerable variety of environments. This is reflected in Map 12.1 which divides the region into fourteen distinctive sub-regions, each with its own set of environmental characteristics. These combine the nature of the physical landform, the use of the land, and such surface features as vegetation and urban areas. Perhaps the best-known of these sub-regions are the Broadland, with its recreational waterways, the flat, rich farming lands of the Fens, and the heaths and forests of the Breckland. Of no less importance are the sands and saltmarsh of the North Norfolk Coast, the sandlings, shingle and estuaries of the Suffolk Coast, the historic villages of the Stour Valley, and the coastal resorts around Great Yarmouth and Lowestoft, and in West Norfolk. Much of the remainder of the region forms the belt of intensive cereal farming, which runs in a horseshoe shape from Mid-Norfolk southwards to the Ipswich area, westwards to Cambridge, and then northwards through West Huntingdon to Peterborough. Within this belt, a number of separate sub-regions can be identified such as the Ouse Valley in West Hunts, and the chalk uplands of South Cambridgeshire.

12.2.2 The fertility of East Anglian soils, together with the climate, ensure that agriculture has continued to be the dominant user of the land surface. As shown in Figure 12.1, it accounts for 84%, with arable farming occupying 69%. The areas of land of highest agricultural quality are shown on Map 12.2. Of the remaining 16% of the land surface, woodland and built-up areas occupy 6% each, leaving a further 4% covered by inland water, verges, nature reserves, etc. The coastline is an important element in its own right, with about a quarter of its length built up.

Figure 12,1

Land uses in East Anglia, 1972

	Percentage
Arable Land	69
Grassland/Heathland	15
Woodland	6
Built up areas	6
Inland water, nature reserves, road verges, etc.	4

Source: East Anglia Regional Strategy Team.

12.2.3 Over the past twenty years the built-up areas have been expanding at the expense of other uses, and arable farmland has been gaining over other non-urban uses. The degree of expansion of the built-up areas has been offset by the return of military holdings to agriculture, so that the net loss of agricultural land has been kept to 0·4%, but the growth of the developed areas has been at least treble this. More significant has been the change in agriculture itself, where the expansion of the arable area of the region has led to a reduction in the grass and heathlands by a third. The greatest reduction has been in West Hunts, South Cambridgeshire, the Stour Valley and High Suffolk, and the remaining grass and heathlands tend to be concentrated in river valleys and around settlements. In the same period the total area of woodland has declined by a quarter, and the increase in the coniferous plantations of the Forestry Commission only serves to emphasise the more rapid decrease in the deciduous woodlands under private ownership.

12.2.4 The scale of the population growth expected in East Anglia to the end of the century means that the built-up area will continue to grow, covering perhaps 8 to 9% of the region's surface. Further returns to agricultural use from military purposes are likely to be small, so that the area in agricultural use will decrease correspondingly. The prosperity of arable farming is expected to continue, so that grass, heath and woodland may come under increased pressures for conversion to arable use. Much of the grass and heathland is found close to urban areas, and is therefore particularly vulnerable. A significant proportion may be taken for development. Similarly, such cover may occupy areas in river valleys where future sand and gravel extraction will occur. Broadly, therefore, the areas occupied by buildings and arable farming are expected to increase, with equivalent reductions in the area of grass, heath and woodland.

Map 12.1
Environment and Recreation
Sub-Regions

Sub-regions are amalgamations of complete zones

SUB-REGIONAL BOUNDARY

ZONAL BOUNDARY

13 GREAT YARMOUTH AND LOWESTOFT

12 BROADLAND

11 NORTH COAST

10 MID NORFOLK

9 WAVENEY VALLEY

14 EAST COAST

8 HIGH SUFFOLK

7 STOUR VALLEY

6 BRECKLAND

5 WEST COAST

4 FENLAND

3 CAMBRIDGE

2 WEST HUNTS

1 SOKE OF PETERBOROUGH

Map 12.2 Agricultural Land Quality

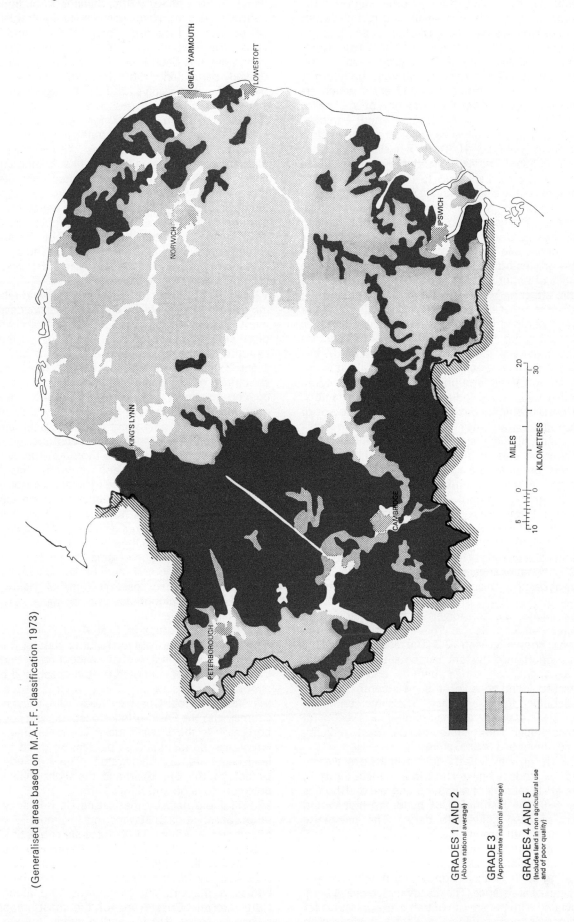

(Generalised areas based on M.A.F.F. classification 1973)

GREAT YARMOUTH

LOWESTOFT

NORWICH

IPSWICH

KING'S LYNN

CAMBRIDGE

PETERBOROUGH

MILES

KILOMETRES

20
30

0
0

5
10

GRADES 1 AND 2
(Above national average)

GRADE 3
(Approximate national average)

GRADES 4 AND 5
(Includes land in non agricultural use
and of poor quality)

12.2.5 The circumstances of East Anglia indicate that problems from the pollution of the environment should be less severe than in other regions. The amount of derelict land is small, and mainly results from rail closures and the extraction of sand, gravel and brickclays in the valleys of the Ouse, Nene, Gipping and Wensum. A high proportion of this justifies restoration in conjunction with the return to other uses of the additional 4,000 acres which are likely to be required for the extraction of river valley minerals by the end of the century. About a third of the rivers in the region were considered to be below first class quality in 1970, with just over a tenth grossly polluted. The worst standards were associated with the larger urban areas to the south and west, with some of the slower moving rivers also experiencing some pollution from the leaching of agricultural chemicals. The use of pesticides in the arable farming areas has produced a number of side-effects, the most noticeable of which is the effect of chlorohydrocarbons on bird life. In the coastal waters the sources of pollution are untreated sewage and trade waste, affecting mainly the larger estuaries and the north-east coast of Norfolk. Over two-thirds of the sewage pumped into the sea around East Anglia is untreated, compared to well under half nationally.

12.2.6 In general, the level of air pollution is low because of the extensive rural areas. It is highest in the area around Peterborough where brick production, together with heavy industry, are the main factors. The levels of sulphur dioxide in the air of the towns of East Anglia is four times higher than in the surrounding countryside, and significantly is also higher than in the urban areas of the South-East, where stricter controls on domestic smoke emission have been enforced. A seasonal problem also occurs with the annual burning of stubble in the arable farming areas. In general the levels of noise again reflect the character of East Anglia. Both military and civil aircraft movements, however, contribute to intensive noise levels covering at least a third of the region.

12.2.7 In national terms, the buildings and urban areas of East Anglia are a considerable environmental resource. Two-thirds of its towns, and at least half of its villages are considered to be of historic and architectural importance. Their distribution in the region is shown on Map 12.3. The retention of such a high proportion of historic settlements reflects both the prosperity of earlier periods and the more depressed conditions of the nineteenth century, which helped to preserve them. The same conditions have also assisted in maintaining a wealth of archaeological sites, although the vast majority remain unmapped or unexplored.

12.2.8 The growth of East Anglia over the past twenty years has produced mixed blessings in these terms. In some areas retirement migration and second homes have seen the restoration of buildings that would otherwise have fallen into decay. The prosperity associated with growth has provided an economic use for buildings of character. Nationally, legislation provided for historic buildings and conservation areas, including some financial support for private owners, has been of assistance. The disadvantages have been associated with the growth of traffic, the pressures for development and rebuilding, and the loss of function of some types of building. The effects of the growth in road transport take many forms, ranging from vibration from heavy traffic, damage to buildings in narrow streets from large vehicles, to the problems of car parking and the realignment of roads and junctions. The adaptation of historic centres to these conditions has been both slow and costly, and has proved particularly difficult in Cambridge. Even more difficult to resolve has been the question of the smaller towns and villages, away from those major routes with high priority for improvement, but subject to a steady growth of traffic and an increasing proportion of heavy vehicles. Many otherwise pleasant streets in small towns like Fakenham and Halesworth have been badly affected compared to those in a town such as Diss, where geographical circumstance has isolated it from the worst effects of through traffic. The extent of the problem is made clear by the fact that less than half of the historic settlements have plans for by-passes, and many of these are not yet included in forward investment programmes for the next decade.

12.2.9 The pressures for redevelopment and rebuilding can often be met by careful and sensitive development control, which can maintain the visual character of an area. More serious may be the loss of internal structures or the remains buried below the buildings. Many buildings of visual quality often conceal structures of an earlier date, with brick facades coating medieval construction. Similarly, modern methods of building have foundations which effectively destroy very important archaeological remains below them. The planning of Peterborough New Town was accompanied by a thorough survey of its archaeological potential, and provision has been made for excavation and the incorporation of many sites into the recreational facilities being developed. There are other centres, however, such as Bury St Edmunds and King's Lynn, which are of much greater significance and where the next decade could see the considerable destruction of remains. Similarly, in rural areas, the extension of agricultural activity on to marginal lands may destroy remains below the ground. Deep ploughing, for example, can be particularly destructive.

12.2.10 Several areas in East Anglia are officially designated as Areas of Outstanding Natural Beauty. Map 12.4 shows that, with the exception of Dedham Vale, they are concentrated on the coast, and cover almost half of its length. The two largest areas are the North Norfolk Coast between King's Lynn and Cromer, and the East Suffolk Coast, running south of Lowestoft to the Stour Estuary. The remaining areas which can be identified as possessing good quality landscape are also illustrated. They include the Broadland, the Breckland and the slight chalk scarp between Royston and King's Lynn.

12.2.11 Land held by the Nature Conservancy and other conservation trusts amounts to almost 3% of the region and a further 68,000 acres are subject to 'Site of Special Scientific Interest' (SSSI) protection under the 1949 National Parks and Access to the Countryside Act. By far the largest area owned by these bodies is the virtually continuous strip along the North Norfolk Coast (one of the most important coasts in Great Britain, and possibly Europe, for

Map 12.3 Historic Towns and Villages

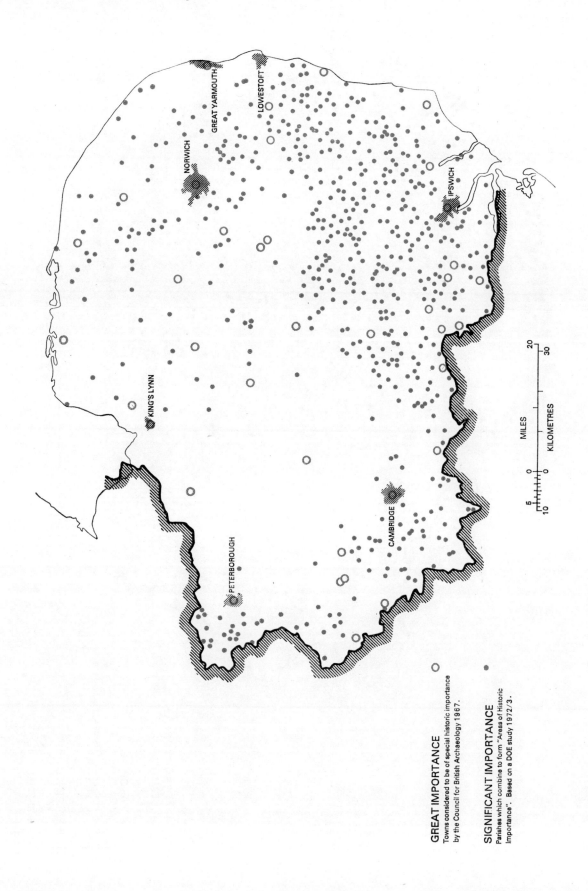

GREAT YARMOUTH

LOWESTOFT

NORWICH

IPSWICH

KING'S LYNN

CAMBRIDGE

PETERBOROUGH

MILES

KILOMETRES

GREAT IMPORTANCE
Towns considered to be of special historic importance
by the Council for British Archaeology 1967.

SIGNIFICANT IMPORTANCE
Parishes which combine to form "Areas of Historic
Importance". Based on a DOE study 1972/3.

Map 12.4   Landscape Areas and Sites of Ecological Importance

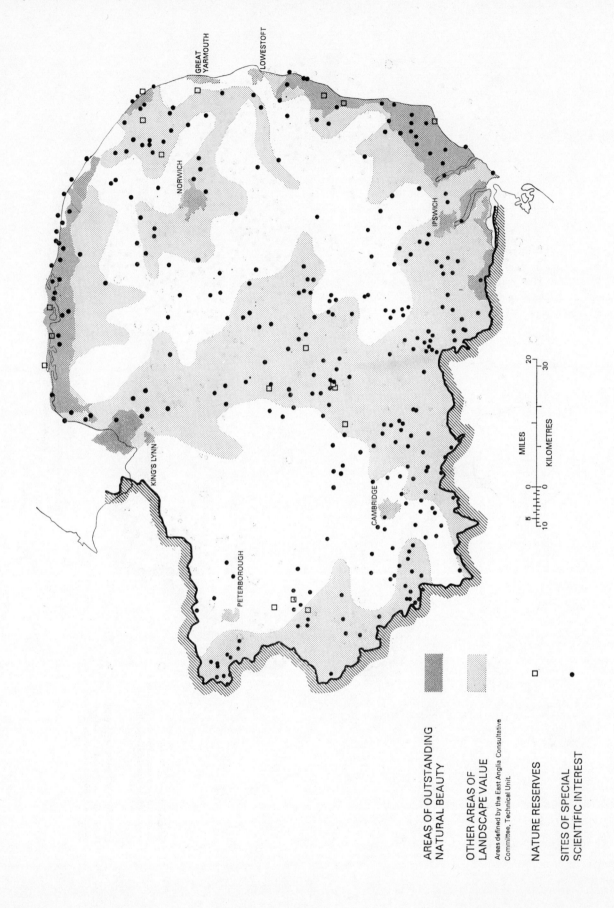

AREAS OF OUTSTANDING
NATURAL BEAUTY

OTHER AREAS OF
LANDSCAPE VALUE
Areas defined by the East Anglia Consultative
Committee, Technical Unit.

NATURE RESERVES

SITES OF SPECIAL
SCIENTIFIC INTEREST

GREAT
YARMOUTH

LOWESTOFT

NORWICH

IPSWICH

KING'S LYNN

CAMBRIDGE

PETERBOROUGH

MILES

KILOMETRES

ecological and physiographical study), with the remainder being situated in Broadland, Breckland, the East Coast, west of Peterborough, and in mid Hunts. The SSSI's, totalling 283 sites, are generally distributed according to the pattern of the Nature Reserves described above, although their greater concentration in the sub-regions to the south reflects the importance attached to the ancient woodland that they protect. This forms the climax of vegetation in this part of East Anglia.

12.2.12 The habitats provided by the region for plant and animal life are of considerable importance. The region is both a destination and staging post for migratory birds, and three-quarters of British breeding birds reside there at some time, including the Avocet and Bittern. Similar proportions of British animal life and plant types are present, including a third of the rare wildflower species. Many plant and animal species require special habitats, associated either with the coasts or the marginal grass, heath and woodlands which are under pressure for conversion. Deciduous woodlands alone, for example, contain four-fifths of the region's woodland bird species.

12.2.13 The vegetation cover of East Anglia is, therefore, very significant for the habitats it provides and for the variety it contributes to a relatively flat countryside. The hedgerows are of importance on both counts—they support a greater variety of plant species than do woodlands, and are an important element in the landscape. Many of the hedgerows in the region result from the enclosure movement, but many others are much older, originating as boundaries to estates and direct enclosures from the woodland, and therefore have a considerable historic importance of their own. Changing methods of arable farming have increased the rate of hedgerow loss in recent years. Figure 12.2 shows that half of the hedges in the region have disappeared since the war, and while the rate has slowed recently, a further half of those remaining could go by the end of the century. The rate of removal has been greatest in the

west of the region, but may be more severe in ecological terms in the south-east where the hedge-rows are generally older and richer in species.

12.2.14 Of the common hedgerow trees in the region, oak and elm are the dominant types, with ash only half as frequent. Many of the oaks in particular are relics of the early nineteenth century, planted to meet the demand for shipbuilding. Many of these single trees are old and the number of saplings, at 8% of the total, is far below replacement rate. In Norfolk 68% of the oaks, 38% of the elms and 27% of the ash are dead or dying, while a third and a quarter of the oak trees in Huntingdonshire/Cambridgeshire and Suffolk respectively appear to be in a similar condition. This process may have been speeded up by changes in agricultural practice, especially those of improved drainage with subsequent lowering of the water table, the use of fertilisers, and the use of deep ploughing around the roots of trees. This suggests that the next two decades will see a gradual but dramatic reduction of the single hedgerow trees, particularly the oak, as an element in the landscape of East Anglia.

12.2.15 About 80,000 acres of woodland are in private ownership and do not receive commercial timber grants. These include the most important broadleaf woodlands, containing the greatest variety of habitats and species. The woodlands in private ownership tend to be mainly located in the intensive cereal farming areas, whilst those of the Forestry Commission are concentrated in the Breckland and on the East Coast. Thus the areas of woodland which are particularly significant as habitats and landscape features are also those subject to pressure for conversion to arable use.

12.3 Holidays and Tourism

12.3.1 Environmental policies for the region must take into account the effects of holiday and tourist activity, as well as the changing stock of natural resources. Different types of holiday, for example, produce varying effects on the environment and must be managed appropriately. Chapter eleven showed that in total the number of holidays likely to be taken in the region would increase substantially. Furthermore, this growth would be in the form of second holidays, and this feature has a number of implications for the type of accommodation required and for the expenditure levels of holidaymakers in the region. Figure 12.3 shows that East Anglia differs considerably in the accommodation it provides at present, especially in the hotel and caravan sectors. The tendency in second holidays is to choose self-catering accommodation in caravans, chalets and second homes. This seems likely to reinforce rather than provide balance to the existing structure of holiday accommodation in the region.

12.3.2 The growing proportion of self-catering accommodation has been reflected in a relative decline of the older, more traditional, holiday resorts, and a considerable growth in areas adjacent to these centres. In Felixstowe for example, the number of hotels and boarding houses was reduced by 56% between 1953 and 1966, while in Norfolk the number of static caravans has risen by 34% between 1961 and 1971. Furthermore, the region has 5% of

Figure 12.2

Hedgerow removal in East Anglia, 1945–70

County	1946 Miles of hedge	1966	1970 Miles of hedge	% Decrease 1946–70
Norfolk	17,612	n/a	9,139	—48
Suffolk	16,798	n/a	12,669	—25
Huntingdonshire	5,624	1,348	586*	—90
Cambridgeshire, Soke of Peterborough, and Isle of Ely	14,642	n/a	4,278	—71
Total for East Anglia	*54,676*	*n/a*	*26,672*	*—51*

*Estimated.

Sources:

E. Teather 1970.

W. Baird and J. Tarrant 1973.

Nature Conservancy 1967 and 1968.

Figure 12.3
Proportion of nights spent on holiday by type of accommodation, 1971

Accommodation (Adults only)	East Anglia & Essex %	England %
Serviced		
Hotel amd guest houses	12	23
Some holiday camps, paying guests in private houses	6	6
Self service		
Self service holiday camps, rented accommodation, tents, caravans, cottages, etc.	33	20
With friends or relatives	41	46
Other		
Boats and miscellaneous accommodation	8	5
Total	**100**	**100**

Source: British Home Tourism Survey, 1971

the national total of touring caravans of which the overall numbers are expected to grow rapidly. Second homes in the region are also expected to grow quickly. At present the majority are found close to the coasts and on the southern edge of the region, (Map 10.1).

12.3.3 Almost 80% of holidays taken in the region are spent by the sea, and the coastal areas, together with the Broadland, contain almost 90% of all accommodation. While the coast is the main attraction, the distribution of accommodation is not evenly spread. Norfolk is the main holiday area with roughly 80% of the total. Within Norfolk, this accommodation is concentrated in three main areas. The largest is on the east coast around Great Yarmouth, stretching north to Hemsby, and including the Broadland to the west, where there is accommodation for almost 100,000 people. On the coast in the Hunstanton area there is accommodation for 23,000, with a further 42,000 people provided for between Cromer and Wells. In Suffolk, with only about a quarter of the holidaymakers of Norfolk, the major concentration lies south of Yarmouth including Lowestoft and Kessingland, whilst elsewhere Southwold, Aldeburgh, and Felixstowe provide smaller amounts of accommodation. Norwich and Cambridge can together take 3,000 overnight visitors at any one time.

12.3.4 It is not possible to estimate the amount of employment provided directly by the holiday industry. It is known to create problems of seasonal unemployment, which can become acute in larger centres such as Great Yarmouth. It does, however, provide opportunities for female employment, particularly for those not seeking a permanent job. In addition to this, the benefits the region receives from the expenditure of holidaymakers are not clear. East Anglian holidays are cheaper on average

than those elsewhere, as Figure 12.4 shows. Further reductions in hotel accommodation, and the growth of self-catering, are likely to increase this difference and may reduce the flow of income to the traditional holiday centres, whilst placing more strain on the environment and road system of the surrounding areas. The urban centres attracting tourists seem much more likely to benefit from holiday income.

Figure 12.4
Items included in the cost of holiday accommodation, 1971

	East Anglia and Essex	England
Bed and Breakfast	3%	8%
Bed and Breakfast and 1 meal	6%	11%
Full Board	12%	17%

Source: National Travel Survey 1971

12.4 The Pattern of Recreational Demands

12.4.1 The pattern of recreational demands upon the environment appears to be influenced by two major factors. The first is that the supply of recreational attractions will affect the extent to which latent demand becomes effective. The second is that since recreation is more informal than either holidays or tourism, it is less likely to be undertaken at great distances from home. These factors suggested that the accessibility model, as described in chapter seven, could be used to explore the relationship between the distribution of population and recreational attractions. The major difficulty in so doing has been the construction of a composite index of recreational attractions for the forty zones. Those included range from the coast-line, areas of outstanding natural beauty, historic towns, houses, and gardens open to the public, to inland waters, rivers, zoos and wildlife parks, nature reserves, woodlands and heaths.

12.4.2 Doubt must surround any system of relative weights attached to individual features to produce a composite index. It is therefore a very approximate measure, and cannot be adopted for detailed purposes. With these reservations, however, the distribution that results for East Anglia (Map 12.5) shows a reasonably clear pattern. The eastern and northern parts of the region are clearly the most attractive areas, with the coastal areas being most significant. By comparison, the western half of the region, together with much of the centre, has fewer attractions. The two areas which emerge with the lowest index are the flat and relatively featureless Fens and the area between Norwich, Thetford and Ipswich. These two areas, together with the area of more intermediate quality to the south are part of the zone of intensive arable farming where the marginal lands are under most pressure for conversion.

12.4.3 The surface shown in Map 12.6 shows the 'population potential' of the region at 1971. This shows the relative levels of access between people across the region and is taken as broadly representative of the pressure of latent demand for recreation. Clearly, the main weight of this demand is to the south and west of the region and outside the

Map 12.5 Distribution of Recreational Attractions, 1972

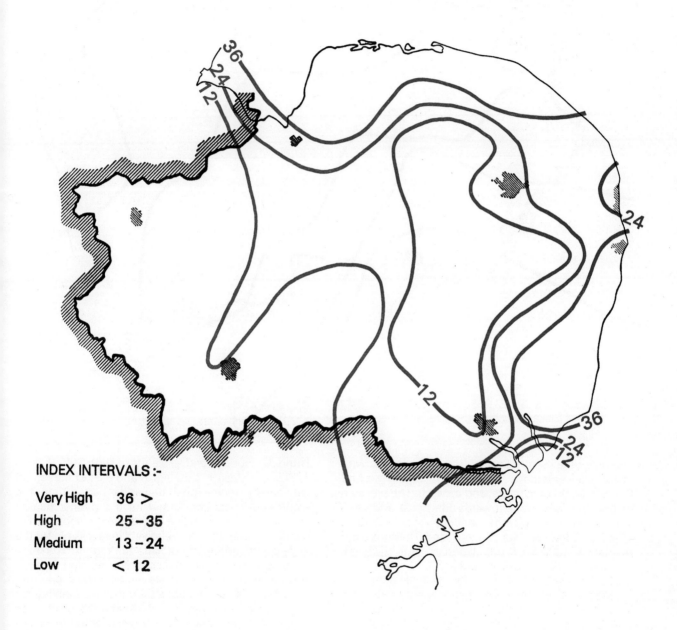

INDEX INTERVALS :-

Very High	36 >
High	25 – 35
Medium	13 – 24
Low	< 12

region in the South East and the Midlands, with major concentrations within the region around Peterborough, Cambridge, and Ipswich. The pressure of demand falls away towards the north and east, interrupted only by the medium sized centres, (Bury St Edmunds, King's Lynn, and Thetford) and the concentration of population in the Norwich, Great Yarmouth, Lowestoft area.

12.4.4 Combining the composite index of recreational attractions with the costs of movement produces a surface of accessibility to recreation, which is illustrated in Map 12.7. This shows that in relation to the regional average the highest levels of opportunity are on the north and east coasts, especially close to King's Lynn and the East Suffolk coast just north of Ipswich. Relatively high areas of opportunity extend from these areas to include parts of Mid Norfolk and the Breckland. Areas of medium opportunities include Broadland, Mid Norfolk, the Stour and Waveney Valleys, whilst the areas of lowest opportunities lie on the western fringes of the region—including the Soke of Peterborough, much of the Fens, West

Hunts, Cambridge and also parts of High Suffolk.

12.4.5 It is clear that the north and east of the region can satisfy recreational demands better than the south and west. The former have a greater quality and quantity of attractive recreational resources. On the other hand, they are relatively inaccessible for the large population living outside the region. The main attractions are the coastlines of Norfolk and Suffolk, and the southern havens are already under pressure from demands for sailing, although the suitability for on-water activity varies considerably from place to place. Another area where intense pressure is felt is the Broadland. The final major environmental resource, lying this time more to the centre of the region, is the Breckland. Recreation here is based on forest and heath, and is informal in that there is little to be exploited commercially. There is some evidence that the picnic sites in the area are used by holidaymakers en route to the coast. In the south and west of the region the situation is in many ways the reverse of that found to the north and east. Better communications, higher population and a relative

Map 12.7 Access to Recreational Opportunities, 1971
(*Deviation of Index from Regional Average*)

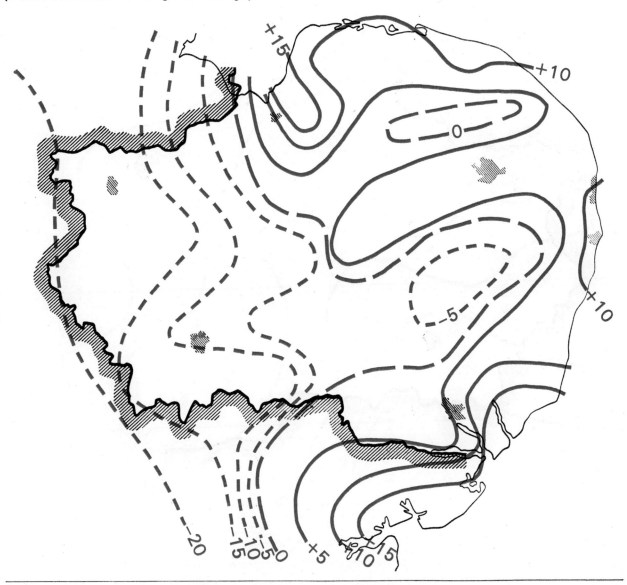

paucity of recreational facilities leads to pressure on existing facilities and a need for new recreational provision.

12.4.6 The main recreational area in this western half of the region is the Ouse and associated Fenland waterways. These are only intensively used in the southern areas around St Neots and St Ives. Less intensive use in the north of the river system arises from a smaller population and from the less attractive form of the river itself. The use of the river banks for picnics or other forms of informal recreation is growing, and some conflicts are arising from multiple use of the system. Elsewhere in the Fens, because of the high quality and value of land, there is a general shortage of recreational facilities. Along the southern edge of the region, a considerable source of recreational attraction lies in the historic villages of High Suffolk and the Stour Valley. This area, along with North Essex, is likely to come under most severe pressure from the South East as routes are improved.

12.4.7 This analysis of the present-day situation has

been taken forward towards the end of the century to assess the implications of changes both in the scale and distribution of population and in the transport networks of the region. The impact of these changes upon the 'population potential' is illustrated in Map 12.8, using the most likely population at 1991. Compared with Map 12.6, it demonstrates a fairly marked increase in population potential across the region, although the slope from the south-west towards the north-east remains a dominant characteristic. While road improvements within the region, particularly those concerning the A11, A45, and A47, are of significance in improving access, links to other regions will be more dramatic in their effect of increasing the volume of demand. The only modification that might be made to the pattern comes from the suggested principles and proposals for the location of growth in chapter eight. In general terms, these policies would restrain population growth rates in the south and west of the region and encourage those in the centre, north and east of the region, producing a marginal shift in demand towards the

Map 12.8 Population Potential, 1991
The contour intervals are indicative of the relative differences in the accessibility of people to people

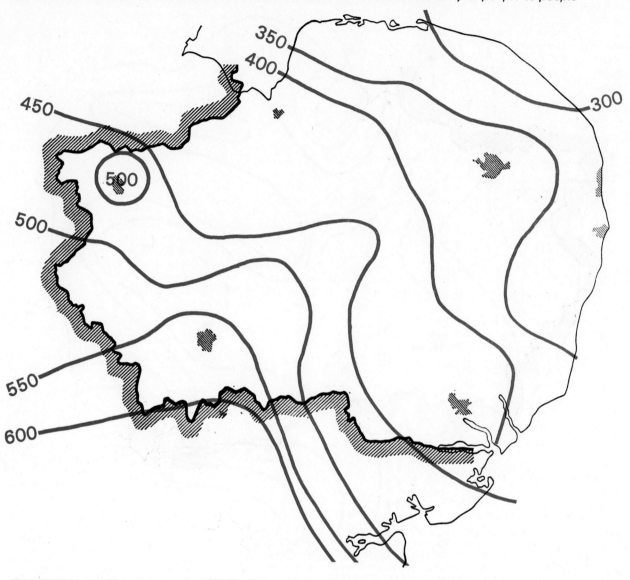

most attractive areas.

12.4.8 The marked variation in the distribution of recreational attractions across the region gives some indication of the quality of local environment enjoyed by people living and working in those areas. The composite index of recreational attractions, however, includes a number of features that are especially developed for active recreational use. These are less significant as a backcloth against which people conduct their lives. An index of environmental quality which includes landscape, historic features, tree cover, and water, amongst others, has therefore been created, and is shown in Map 12.9. In the areas where the landscape is generally flat and featureless, the rate of removal of woodland and hedgerow is most rapid. These areas also tend to experience rapid population growth, which suggests that policies of landscape reconstruction are required for local environment around urban settlements. Elsewhere in the region, particularly on the east coast where there is an attractive, but sensitive, environment, policies should be directed towards maintaining the stock of resources. Overall this suggests that there is some parallel between the need for improving local environmental quality and that for increasing the range of recreational attractions.

Map 12.9 Distribution of Environmental Qualities, 1972

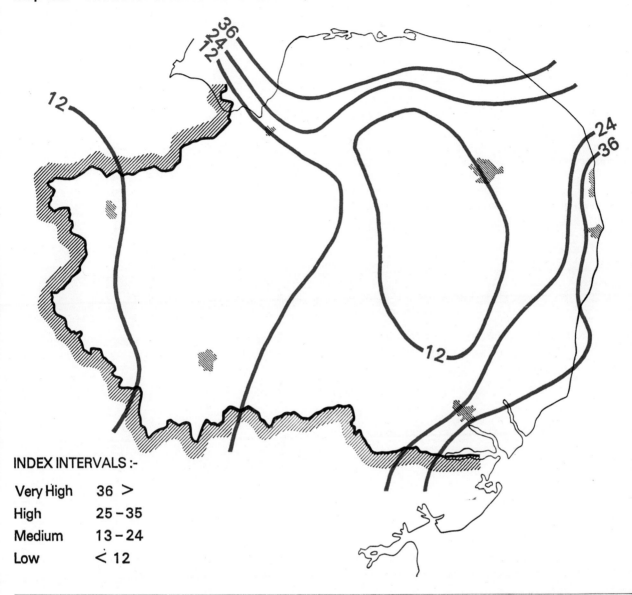

INDEX INTERVALS :-

Very High	36 >
High	25 – 35
Medium	13 – 24
Low	< 12

12.5 Conclusions

12.5.1 What overall conclusions can be drawn from this analysis for the future management of environmental resources in East Anglia? The first and most important conclusion is that the environments of the region have to be treated as a basic resource, and recognised as such, in much more deliberate policies of management. This requires a number of approaches. Firstly, policies designed to safeguard a minimum standard of resource across the whole region are necessary, with special reference to those features which are irreplaceable. Secondly, those elements which are significant in national and local terms require to be identified and conserved. Thirdly, priority may need to be given to existing resources which may be under pressure from other intensive demands. Finally, in areas where this competition has been and will continue to be severe, positive policies for reconstructing the environment and the landscape are called for.

12.5.2 The sheer intensity and pace of change in some uses of the environment create difficulties. No single demand requires all the properties of the environment for its own fulfilment. The remaining qualities are irrelevant to that specific demand—at best to be tolerated, and at worst to be removed when they are inconvenient. The most intensive demands are also likely to be the most intolerant towards other qualities. In these terms, it is possible to recognise different classes of conflict between demands.

12.5.3 The first of these conflicts is the intensive demand which, by its nature, threatens to destroy those qualities which it requires itself. In East Anglia, the clearest example of this is intensive recreation on the coasts, the Broads and the Breckland. This type of situation appears to require policies designed to modify the demand, and to increase the capacity of this type of area to accept it. The second class of conflict is where two intensive demands are in direct competition. It is evident in this chapter that the areas of intensive arable farming and the areas of intensive recreation do not coincide in East Anglia. There is, however, considerable conflict between the arable areas and local population pressures. The conflict is

111

unlikely to be resolved to any significant degree by policies designed to divert either or both of these pressures. In these areas of conflict, it will be necessary to find approaches which satisfy the essential requirements of both demands.

12.5.4 Two other possible areas of policy may be worthy of consideration. The first is concerned with those areas where different demands appear to be able to co-exist and where there is greater potential for improving the stock of resources as an end in itself. These areas may also be capable of absorbing some of the pressures diverted from more intensively used areas. The second takes another form. The overall perception of the environment of East Anglia is strongly influenced by the way in which people move through it by a combination of routes and stopping places. There would appear to be considerable scope for policies designed to use this complex pattern of movement in the priorities given to different types of resources at different locations.

Chapter 13

The Management of Environmental Resources

13.1 Introduction

13.1.1 The previous two chapters provide the basis for considering policies for the future of the environmental resources of East Anglia. As a first step, the conclusions of the previous chapter are restated as a set of broad strategic principles, followed by consideration of the practical proposals which seem most suited to putting those principles into operation.

13.2 Broad Strategic Principles

13.2.1 The scale and rapidity of change in some of the major uses of the region's environments means that it is no longer possible to assume that they will continue to possess high quality and variety. These attributes can only be ensured by much more deliberate and conscious policies which seek to manage the condition of the environment positively and effectively. The following set of strategic principles can be identified to help achieve this overall aim:

E1 policies should be designed to enable the progressive strengthening and remodelling of the environment and landscape of the region in relation to changes in land management;

E2 policies should be based on a general commitment to the conservation of all indigenous species of animal and plant life, together with habitats for migratory species;

E3 policies should be designed to identify and retain sites and buildings of archaeological, historic and architectural interest or significance;

E4 policies in areas subject to intensive recreation should be designed to keep such pressures within the environmental capacities of these areas;

E5 policies in areas subject to competing demands from intensive arable farming and local population pressures should be designed to reconcile the conflicts that occur;

E6 policies in areas not subject to intensive demands should be designed to improve the stock of resources and to allow the diversion of recreational demands from other areas;

E7 policies for the development of recreational uses in the future should be associated with the pattern of movement of holidaymakers and recreational traffic across the region;

E8 policies should be designed to secure effective co-operation between responsible agencies, in association with programmes of education and research, and the achievement of appropriate levels of funding.

The remainder of this chapter considers the policies and proposals which appear to flow from these principles.

13.3 The Strengthening of Environmental Resources

13.3.1 Policies to ensure a healthy stock of environmental resources fall into two categories. In those parts of the region where extensive removal of environmental resources has resulted from intensive arable farming, policies for environmental reconstruction are necessary, in order to design positive landscape forms which are compatible with modern farming. An outline of the form these might take was given in chapter eleven. In the remainder of the region rather more emphasis could be placed on the conservation of existing resources. In some cases this might go beyond the more extensive use of specific controls, such as tree preservation orders, towards the designation of 'rural' conservation areas, which would be similar in principle to those at present restricted to urban areas.

13.3.2 It is also important that a diversity of habitats for wildlife should be maintained across the region. This can be partly achieved within the framework suggested above. There would appear, however, to be some benefit from the linking of habitats by linear features. In this respect, tree belts, hedgerows and road verges will be most significant. The retention of significant tree belts, particularly of deciduous trees, and of major hedgerows would seem to be desirable. This process could be assisted in the arable areas by identifying the older hedgerows. These are important as pre-enclosure boundary features of manors and estates, possibly from Saxon times, and also contain the widest range of species. The most important contribution to habitats resulting from modern construction is the road verge, which with proper attention and management can become a very important habitat for plant species. But there is also a need to conserve a number of specific habitats including scrub, meadow, heath, marl pits, gravel workings, ponds and fen. This coverage may need to be more widespread than under the present 'Sites of Special Scientific Interest' system.

13.3.3 Policies for the management of the landscape also require sensitive design and siting of buildings in the countryside. Much of this can be achieved through development control, with the exception that exempts non-residential agricultural buildings of less than 5,000 square feet from requiring planning permission. The successful integration of buildings into the landscape could be helped if all agricultural buildings were subject to planning control. A system of voluntary agreements which would achieve the same aim would be preferable. Two such approaches might be adopted. Firstly, freedom from planning permission on agricultural buildings could be subject to challenge by the local planning authority. Under this system a farmer would notify the local planning authority of his intention to develop, and permission would be assumed unless the authority challenged the development within a given time. Secondly, development in accordance with land management schemes described later, covering all aspects of the future development of farm holdings, could be deemed to have planning permission.

13.3.4 The brief survey of pollution questions in chapter twelve suggests some field in which policies could be developed. The proportion of derelict land justifying treatment, and the likely use of river valleys for sand and gravel extraction, suggest that more priority could be given to restoration, particularly for forms of recreation using inland water. Secondly, there are grounds for the firm application of the clean air legislation in use in urban areas. Allied to this, although the seasonal problem of straw burning may only be resolved by the development of economic uses for this raw material, some relief in the short-term could be secured by incorporating the N.F.U. code of practice, or its equivalent, into bye-laws. Finally, continued vigilance is required to ensure that the use of new types of chemical fertiliser or pesticide does not damage wildlife and plantlife habitats.

13.3.5 The conservation of historic and architecturally significant buildings, and archaeological remains in urban areas, poses a series of related issues. Considerable protection to buildings has been achieved through the listing of buildings of importance, though there must be concern about the rate of disappearance even of buildings on the list. Such concern is augmented by the absence of information about the structures of buildings. Some re-appraisal of listed buildings has taken place in West Suffolk, a practice that could be usefully extended to other parts of the region. It would also be an advantage if powers were available to ensure inspection and recording of structures above a specified age prior to demolition.

13.3.6 In the more general field of conservation areas, it is not clear whether further powers are required. More significant at this level may be the attempt to ensure that these areas are kept in economic use while avoiding pressures for redevelopment or basic alterations to structure. This approach formed part of the evaluation process for the location of population and employment growth outlined in chapter seven. It is evident, however, that some of the towns and areas selected for growth are also very significant for both conservation and archaeological reasons. In these towns, the pressures that result will require corresponding emphasis on appropriate conservation measures in advance of growth. The techniques of

modern construction are such that while the external facades of buildings can be retained, the gutting of interiors and deep foundations can destroy very important sources of information about urban history. In some towns, the next decade could eliminate much of this material. To overcome the immediate problem, it is considered that the built-up area in each town at the end of the 18th century should be defined as an 'area of historic significance'. In these areas, additional powers would be necessary for prior notification and approval of the demolition of buildings. In addition, the possibility of significant archaeological remains should constitute a reason for refusing planning permission for buildings with deep foundations, unless an adequate period for the exploration of the site is made available. In the same areas, there could also be a presumption against major re-development. Ensuring that new construction is restricted to the frontage and height of existing sites and buildings could produce this effect.

13.3.7 The protection of archaeological sites outside the urban areas presents another set of difficulties. For the earlier prehistoric periods, few traces of human occupation are known, and most discoveries are made fortuitously through excavations and quarrying for roadworks, redevelopment, and sand and gravel working. The scale of these operations in East Anglia will increase over the next few years, and more systematic observation of these operations would be an advantage. The assurance of this, if the trained staff is available, could be increased if the right of access for observation was made a requirement in contracts given by public bodies, and included as a condition on planning permission for private development.

13.3.8 For more recent periods, the problems range from identifying significant sites to ensuring that excavation occurs if they are threatened by development. The immediate need is for much more systematic recording of known sites, together with the identification of other areas which are likely to be significant. Allied to this much more positive steps may be required to open up archaeological sites as features for recreational areas. At present, knowledge of East Anglia's prehistory and historic situation is limited to a small number of experts. A programme of excavation and recording, allied to recreation, could give more impetus to public awareness, and to the possibility of increased funds. The initiative in Peterborough New Town could provide a prototype for urban areas, and the same principle could be extended to rural areas in conjunction with the route network proposed above.

13.3.9 The proposals above can only be realised with appropriate funding, staffing and organisation. At present, the numbers of full-time trained archaeologists are very small, and they are scattered through a number of bodies. There are current proposals for archaeological units, possibly at regional level, to be backed by central and local government funds. If these are realised, the situation will improve, though support from the public sector must compete with other social priorities. It may be of considerable importance, therefore, to ensure close linkages with educational and recreational interests to gain wider public interest in sites and their meaning.

13.3.10 The management of the environment in these terms will not be achieved without the active co-operation of all the interests involved. For East Anglia, the appearance and resources of its countryside will continue to be a primary factor, and the farmer is the person responsible for day-to-day decisions. It is essential, therefore, that he should be aware of and accept the kinds of policies suggested above, and as a first step it is suggested that they should be included in programmes of agricultural education. Coupled with this, we consider that land management schemes for farms should be encouraged. These would cover the future development of the farm, including buildings, tree groups and hedgerows. They would also include questions of changes to rights of way and footpaths which interfere with arable cropping. With an outline scheme, agreed by the Ministry of Agriculture, Fisheries and Food, and the local authorities, the details would go ahead subject only to notification to both bodies, with a presumption of the appropriate grants from the Ministry and planning permission, etc., from the local authorities. In this way, the provisions of the Countryside Act, 1968, could be put into practice more effectively than at present through closer co-ordination between agricultural and environmental interests.

13.4 Areas of Intensive Recreation

13.4.1 The only places in East Anglia expressly designed for intensive recreation are the holiday resorts; the others are all subject to potential conflicts. This is particularly so in the non-urban areas, where the attractions lie in a sensitive mix of vegetation and animal life. This ecological balance can be disturbed by the volume of use by visitors and the economic pressures which they bring. The coasts of Norfolk and Suffolk, the Broadland and the Breckland are under increasing pressure, which could exceed each area's capacity, spoiling the very characteristics which make them attractive. There is no easy and complete solution to this problem. In each case the need is for an agency to take continuing responsibility for the management function of keeping demand within capacity.

13.4.2 In each of these areas, therefore, it is considered that joint management committees, with appropriate powers and finance, should be established. They could be linked together for better effect at the regional level to form a body concerned with overall environmental management. The nucleus of these committees, with the possible exception of the Broadland, could be formed by the county and district authorities, subject to the proviso that all other major interests should be actively represented. The first steps towards this have been taken in some areas in the form of joint advisory committees, and here the requirement is for a strengthening of these bodies to allow them to exercise a more positive role. In the Broadland, the recreational demands for use of the waterways suggests that the Regional Water Authority may be the most appropriate body to exercise the necessary management. This approach would require some form of consultative committee to include all the major interests, and the additional possibility of designation as a national park should be kept under review.

13.4.3 Two distinct strands of policy are necessary for such management. Within the areas themselves, the first priority is to obtain practical estimates of their capacity to absorb visitors. This should be accompanied by policies designed to 'harden' some parts to increase their capacities. As a corollary to this, other areas should be developed to divert some of the pressures. The development of the Southern Broads would be an example of this. Elsewhere, this approach would need to realise the potential of other parts of the region for more intensive use. The clearest example of this is the Great Ouse river system, though some of the inland areas of high landscape quality could also offer some relief.

13.4.4 On this basis, it is considered that a joint management committee for the promotion of the recreational use of the Great Ouse river system should be established. As this recreational use would centre on the use of water, the Regional Water Authority appears once again to be the most appropriate body to take a leading role in the formation of this committee. It should consider:

(a) improvements to navigation, including the link between the Ouse and the Nene, and some reinstatement of parts of the system which are no longer navigable;

(b) the assessment of the potential capacity of the river system for different types of recreational use, and the need for additional moorings;

(c) the encouragement of off-water facilities, including picnic areas, and commercial facilities at appropriate locations;

(d) a programme of planting to soften and improve the appearance of those areas which are visually dull or monotonous.

13.5 Areas of Competing Demands

13.5.1 The areas of intensive arable farming have seen the most radical transformation of the landscape by the removal of trees and hedgerows. They have also seen a large-scale reduction in grass and heathland by conversion to arable use. Particularly in the south-west of the region, where village development policies have been pursued, the areas in intensive arable use coincide with local population pressures for extensions to the built-up area and for recreation. As a result, the two types of demand have been brought into confrontation by the progressive elimination of the intervening transitional areas. For agriculture this can mean serious problems of trespass. For the local population, it can mean restrictions on their ability to walk away from roads on grassland and in woods. It has also meant that habitats for animal and plant life in the grassland areas have been reduced.

13.5.2 There is again no easy and simple solution to this form of competition. Neither the demands of arable farming nor the local population can be transferred elsewhere on a scale which would ameliorate the situation. The continuation of pressures for population growth could lead to further housing developments separated from bare stretches of arable land only by apparently forbidding, but easily penetrated, post and wire fences. Two approaches could assist in reducing this conflict.

Firstly, these areas are in most urgent need of landscape reconstruction, as discussed above. This could be combined with measures to integrate settlements into the countryside through tree planting, both in the short-term and as part of longer-term landscaping policies. Secondly, where possible, this planting should be linked with access to sites for local recreation purposes.

13.6 Areas of Potential

13.6.1 In the remaining areas of the region, the intensity of particular demands is lower, and the level of conflict between competing demands reduced as a result. Population pressures, for example, are lower, and recreation consists of drives through pleasant countryside with short stops in towns and villages of interest. The appearance of the landscape and habitats has been changed to a lesser degree by the removal of hedgerows and trees. Particularly to the north and east, low levels of employment opportunities suggest that some encouragement of greater recreational use would be beneficial to the areas themselves, and would assist in diverting pressures from areas of more intensive demand. It could also bring an improved level of economic support to the conservation of the towns and villages.

13.6.2 There may be considerable changes in these areas in the future. The marginal grass, heath and woodlands are likely to be under pressure for conversion to arable farming. The vegetation cover of these areas has a large number of old and dying single trees, which are not being replaced as they disappear. These changes suggest that a considerable remodelling of the landscape is occurring. Such areas offer, therefore, a considerable potential for applying appropriate landscape policies, working in parallel with the changes that will take place.

13.7 Movement Through the Environment

13.7.1 The majority of people see the environment as they move through it. This is true both of day-to-day life as well as of conscious recreation. The visual impression of East Anglia gained through journeys along its major road and rail routes can be a decisive factor in the minds of those considering setting up new firms or seeking employment in the region. The proposal that recreational pressures should be spread more evenly across and around the region can therefore be defined. The major road and rail routes, together with a recreational route network, would provide a basis for the development of formal recreation sites in the region.

13.7.2 For recreational policies, the route system could be associated with a programme of grants and incentives, possibly agreed on a joint basis by the local authorities and the Regional Tourist Board, for a variety of types of provision. This would include country parks, overnight accommodation for touring caravans, picnic areas, toilets, overtaking stretches of dual carriageways, the development of motels and eating facilities, and the development of historic sites and buildings for visiting. Greater use of both public and commercial facilities could be supported by a series of information pamphlets, which could set out not only these facilities but also specialised subjects

such as historic churches, Roman East Anglia, and the architectural qualities of particular towns and villages. In this way, both visitors and people living in East Anglia could gain a heightened appreciation of their environment. Within the areas visible from these routes and major bypasses, consideration could be given to landscape policies which serve to enclose the middleground.

13.7.3 Within this route network, some provision would have to be made for recreation on foot. The clearest example of this is the development of long distance footpaths. The development of a coastal footpath should continue, and the extension of present paths along the Devil's Dyke and Peddars Way could be considered. If present restrictions could be lifted, the river banks also offer a considerable potential, enhanced as they are by the habitats for animal and plant life in the adjoining grasslands. More locally, around formal recreation sites and villages, recreation on foot will require landscape policies which retain much more interest and variety in the foreground. This places more emphasis on hedgerows, trees, heath and grassland. The retention of commonlands, and the use of preservation orders, together with planting schemes, would have priority in these locations. In some of the formal recreation sites the theme could be the maintenance of small areas of traditional landscapes. In this way, some of the traditional country skills might be retained, e.g. the layering of hedges by hand.

13.8 Research and Implementation

13.8.1 The policies suggested above rest on a framework of information which is inadequate for the purpose. In attempting to relate ecology and recreation, it is quickly apparent that knowledge of the capacity of environments to absorb recreational use is limited. Similarly, the vegetation cover of the region, which is important both for the landscape and habitats, is undergoing considerable change. Information on its age and condition, and the rate at which it is either being replaced or not replaced, is sparse. The destruction of archaeological sites in urban and rural areas is a problem, but there is inadequate knowledge of the sites that exist and the rate of destruction. Recreational patterns are changing, but these changes are only partially understood. In each of these cases, there are urgent needs for basic research which can only serve to enlighten those responsible for making decisions.

13.8.2 Allied to such research is the need for more widespread education and a greater understanding of all these aspects of the environment. Much of the information which is available is in the hands of experts in each field and it is difficult for the layman to gain access to it in terms which are comprehensible to him. While the time of experts is clearly precious, it has also to be recognised that the public support and funding required to maintain such resources in the face of intensive and immediate demands will only come if a greater degree of understanding is achieved. This may require the active support of local newspapers and radio stations, development of adult education sessions, and the inclusion of environmental studies in primary and secondary school syllabuses.

13.8.3 Many of the policies discussed above for the treatment of landscape, the environment and recreational pressures, imply a regional approach. The joint management committees for the areas under most intensive recreational pressures would not, in isolation, produce effective measures to divert pressures to other parts of the region. This indicates the need for an overseeing agency at the regional level which is able to produce effective forward plans and reconcile the conflicting interests involved with the environment. The nucleus of this body would be formed by representatives of the three County Councils, the Ministry of Agriculture, Fisheries and Food, the Countryside Commission, the Nature Conservancy, the Forestry Commission, the Regional Water Authority, the Regional Sports Council and the Regional Tourist Board, but should also extend to cover private interests. It could well be associated formally with the type of overall regional agency discussed in the next chapter. Its main functions would be to ensure that both the activities and forward planning of its constituent members reflected agreed priorities for the management of both environmental resources and recreation pressures, and that adequate funding was made available for this purpose.

13.8.4. The implementation of the proposals would clearly fall to local authorities or other public agencies, such as those described above. This would, however, require the involvement and co-operation of private individuals and organisations. To do this, a system of grants and incentives would be required in addition to the direct expenditure by the public sector. In this perspective it is useful to look at current levels of expenditure on the environment in East Anglia. At present, it appears that the local authorities spend about £6,000–£10,000 annually on tree planting. Since the war there has been an estimated net loss of over thirteen million trees. Planting schemes to replace this loss, and allowing for some trees failing to survive, could cost between £150,000 to £300,000 annually, without compensation for the land and agricultural production lost. This may be compared with the level of farm improvement grants paid over the past five years. These have risen from over £2,000,000 in 1968 to £6,750,000 in 1972, reflecting the increased prosperity and confidence in agriculture and arable farming in that period. This suggests that planting costs for replacement of trees in the region could be as little as 5% of farm improvement grants.

13.8.5 This particular example suggests that the costs of managing the region's environmental resources would not be out of scale with other systems of grants and incentives by the public sector. The problem at present is that the environment is not represented in current priorities in public expenditure, and this will be difficult to rectify when such expenditure is growing at a slow rate, or in the absence of bodies which can make effective use of funds. If possible, and at the appropriate time, it is considered that higher priority for these resources might be achieved by the provision of specific grants for a temporary period of ten years, thereby allowing desirable patterns of expenditure to be established. With this momentum, the specific grants could then be included within the general block grant.

13.8.6 One special problem remains in East Anglia. The appearance of the region depends upon the prosperity of agriculture. Recently, however, values of farming land have increased to an extent which do not reflect an adequate return from agricultural production alone. This may create pressures on agriculture to show improved returns in the short-term, perhaps to the detriment of the landscape and standards of good husbandry. Should this prove to be the case, there may well be grounds for considering policies to restore the relationship of the basic value of land with its long-term potential for agricultural production. The measures to do this could provide a source of funds for environmental management.

13.9 Conclusions

13.9.1 In this chapter a large number of proposals covering a wide range of subjects have been put forward. It is convenient therefore to provide a summary of these proposals at this point so that they can be given careful consideration.

13.9.2 Policies to strengthen and conserve Environmental Resources

Within the strategic principles for the strengthening of the environment and landscape, the conservation of animal and plant life, and the conservation of features of archaeological, historic and architectural significance, the following proposals are suggested for further consideration:

(i) *the emphasis in future landscape policies should be on blocks of woodlands, copses, and hedgerows separating large fields;*

(ii) *the more widespread use of tree preservation orders, extended to cover hedgerows;*

(iii) *the designation of rural conservation areas on similar principles to those applied to built up areas;*

(iv) *the retention of a lattice of linear habitats, including belts of deciduous trees and older hedgerows, with a variety of species of historic significance;*

(v) *the development of road verges as habitats for plant life;*

(vi) *the sensitive control of the siting, form, materials and screening of agricultural buildings by appropriate modifications to present planning procedures;*

(vii) *the restoration of derelict land, and future sand and gravel working sites in river valleys, for recreational purposes;*

(viii) *the more active application of clean air legislation in urban areas, and the inclusion in local authority by-laws of current codes of practice for stubble burning;*

(ix) *the reappraisal of current lists of buildings of architectural and historic merit, together with powers to inspect and record structures above a specified age prior to any proposed demolition;*

(x) *the designation of 'areas of historic significance' within towns recognised to be of historic importance, and within these areas:*

    (a) *powers to allow the prior notification and approval of the demolition of buildings;*

    (b) *proposals for deep foundations to constitute reasons for the refusal of planning permission, without corresponding provision for exploring*

the possibility of significant archaeological material;
(c) a general presumption against major redevelopment extending beyond the frontages and heights of existing sites and buildings;
(xi) *provision for access for systematic observation of major construction projects for archaeological purposes to be included in contracts by public bodies and as a condition on planning permission;*
(xii) *a programme of identification and recording of significant archaeological sites, with consideration given to designation as Historic Monuments;*
(xiii) *an increase in the numbers of full-time archaeological staff;*
(xiv) *land management schemes covering the future development of farm holdings should be encouraged on a tripartite basis between farmers, the Ministry of Agriculture, Fisheries and Food, and local authorities.*

13.9.3 Policies for Areas of Intensive Recreation
Within areas subject to pressure from intensive recreation, the following proposals appear appropriate :
(xv) *the establishment of joint management committees for the North Norfolk and East Suffolk coasts, the Broadland, the Breckland and the Great Ouse river system;*
(xvi) *the leading role in the formation and activities of these committees should be taken by the appropriate county and district authorities, except in the Broads and the Great Ouse river system, where the Regional Water Authority would be most appropriate;*
(xvii) *in each case, the committee should include all major public and private interests in each area;*
(xviii) *active steps should be taken by the committee to estimate the environmental capacity of the area to absorb visitors and, where necessary, divert visitors elsewhere and harden the environments to accept increased use;*
(xix) *consideration should be given to the development of the Southern Broads for recreational use;*
(xx) *in the Great Ouse river system policies should be designed to promote recreation, through additional moorings, off-water facilities and planting schemes.*

13.9.4 Policies for Areas of Competing Demands
For the reconciliation of conflicts between competing demands the following policies seem desirable :
(xii) *a long term programme should be developed to reshape the environment and landscape;*
(xxii) *the closer integration of settlements into the countryside should be encouraged through landscaping policies;*
(xxiii) *planting schemes should be associated with access for recreational purposes.*

13.9.5 Policies for Areas of Potential
Within those areas of less intensive demands, it is suggested that :
(xxiv) *policies should be designed to foster increased recreational use by visitors to the region;*
(xxv) *development for recreational purposes should be linked to conservation policies for towns and villages;*
(xxvi) *landscape policies should be instituted in*

parallel with the changes taking place in the landscape.

13.9.6 Movement through the Environment
To take advantage of the opportunities created by the association of recreational trips and facilities at fixed points, it is suggested that :
(xxvii) *a network of recreational and holiday routes across and around the region should be defined;*
(xxviii) *these recreational routes, together with the major rail and road routes, should be associated with the provision of a variety of recreational sites and facilities in both the public and private sectors;*
(xxix) *the recreational routes and facilities should be supported by the preparation of a series of information pamphlets;*
(xxx) *the areas visible from both recreational and major rail and road routes should receive priority in the landscape policies of local authorities;*
(xxxi) *the development of long distance footpaths, particularly along the coasts and the river valleys, should be encouraged;*
(xxxii) *the maintenance of traditional enclosure landscapes and rural crafts as the theme of some recreational sites should be pursued, in association with rural conservation areas referred to above.*

13.9.7 Research and Implementation
(xxxiii) *a programme of research into the changing stock of environmental resources should be mounted to include:*
(a) *the capacity of environments in the region to absorb recreational use;*
(b) *the age and condition of the vegetation cover, and the rate of its replacement;*
(c) *the impact of agricultural techniques on vegetation and wildlife;*
(d) *the identification of archaeological sites and their rate of destruction;*
(e) *the recreation patterns within the region.*
(xxxiv) *more emphasis should be placed on achieving a greater understanding by the public of the significance of different types of environmental resources;*
(xxxv) *the establishment of a regional body concerned with priorities both for recreation and the environment, in association with the joint management committees for specific areas;*
(xxxvi) *consideration should be given to a system of specific grants, to encourage environmental management for a period of ten years and to allow expenditure levels to become established, followed by inclusion in block grants;*
(xxxvii) *consideration should be given to policies which maintain the relationship between the basic value of land and the agricultural production from it.*

Section F   Implementation

In this final section we turn to the question of how the principles and proposals can be put into practice. This is not a straightforward task, as many of the subjects to be covered are themselves under intensive discussion and modification at the present time. We have, therefore, concentrated on the longer term structure of implementation that would seem to be called for, rather than on a set of blueprints of what we would prefer to see, in the knowledge that these could well prove obsolete even in the short term.

The first of the chapters looks at the agencies involved in the region's development, and attempts to assess the implications of the report for them. It goes on to suggest in outline means by which this framework of agencies could be evolved in order to cope with the new tasks that may be required of it. Chapter fifteen turns to the question of financial resources and public expenditure. It explores the current pattern of expenditure, and relates identifiable trends and priorities to the principles adopted elsewhere in the report. This helps to establish the sort of requirements (as regards both scale and priorities) expected of the public expenditure system in the future.

Finally, chapter sixteen looks beyond the content of this report. It looks to the continuing need to take forward work at this level, within both a process of monitoring and a programme of research related to areas where we have found information or understanding inadequate.

Chapter 14

Implementation and Agencies

14.1 Introduction

14.1.1 In this report we are concerned with nothing less than the development of a region and its people in the future. What are the agencies involved in this process, and within what framework will they be working? How are these agencies changing? Are they likely to be sufficiently strong to cope with future demands? Clearly, the answers to these questions will be affected both by the specific circumstances of East Anglia and by the nature of the proposals to modify its future. We consider each of these factors in terms of the types of agency involved in the development of the region. As a final step, we suggest some ways in which this framework of agencies could be strengthened to make it more suited to the tasks required.

14.2 Changing relationships between Agencies

14.2.1 The agencies involved in the development of the region are broadly central and local government, a number of semi-autonomous public bodies, and the private sector. The range of concern of these agencies is very wide. At one extreme, national government concentrates on the creation and distribution of wealth and the achievement of certain national standards of provision. At the other extreme, local government operates more directly in serving people and their needs and with controlling or encouraging development on the ground. Together, central and local government, in a mixed economy, provide a large part of the framework for the activities of the private sector.

14.2.2 The role of these different agencies in the future development of the region can be illustrated by reference to the contents of this report. The examination of the future of the region as a whole in Section B includes the possible effects of national and international developments. It is mainly concerned, therefore, with the activities of central government and other public bodies acting on a national canvas. In Section C, the concern with the broad interactions between population, employment and major transport links, moves into the field where central and local government activities necessarily overlap. Thirdly, the more particular focus of Sections D and E, on the quality of life, and the environment respectively, bring central and local agencies together in a different way. In these fields, the attention of central agencies is mainly on the achievement of national standards and the allocation of resources, whereas local agencies attempt to ensure that the resulting provision meets the particular needs of each locality. In the next chapter of this section the differ-

ent levels and types of financial resources called upon by these agencies are examined.

14.2.3 In practice, the public sector splits up its functions into individual departments which concern themselves with more closely defined areas of operation and objectives. The contents of this report, as described above, are a recognition of the value of bringing together all of these fields of concern, and their policy making, at the regional level. Each level and field of policy impinges on many other levels and fields, so that cooperation and coordination between agencies are the essence of a regional strategy. This can best be explained in three ways. Firstly, the strategic issues and methods of resolving conflicts cross the geographical boundaries of authorities, and may be of greater importance to the region than is recognised at the national level. Secondly, and perhaps more significantly, the strategic issues cross the functional boundaries of particular agencies e.g. education and training, health and welfare, housing, employment and transport. Finally, the existence of a number of levels of policy-making in each field requires those policies to be formed in ways which allow for a degree of discretion in operation, consistent with the overall direction considered necessary.

14.2.4 The current reorganisation of local government and of the administration of several related services such as health and water, may appear in the short-term as isolated and completed events. In a longer term perspective, however, it would be more realistic to view such reorganisation as part of a continuous process of adapting agencies to the increasing pace of change in society, its growing complexity, and the interdependence of its various parts. In this context, three broad pressures appear to be most significant. Firstly, there is a growing interdependence between nations, which increasingly involves central government in the resolution of issues and the formation of policies at an international level; the entry of the United Kingdom into the European Community is just one very important part of this process. Secondly, there is the pressure for increasing efficiency in the use of resources in the public sector. This can be in contrast with the third pressure—for improving the responsiveness of services provided by the public sector to the needs of individuals.

14.2.5 These pressures, and the tensions between them, have been reflected in recent changes in the agencies directly involved in the implementation of the future development of the region. Figure 14.1 illustrates (although by no means comprehensively)

Figure 14.1 Organisational Change affecting Central and Local Government

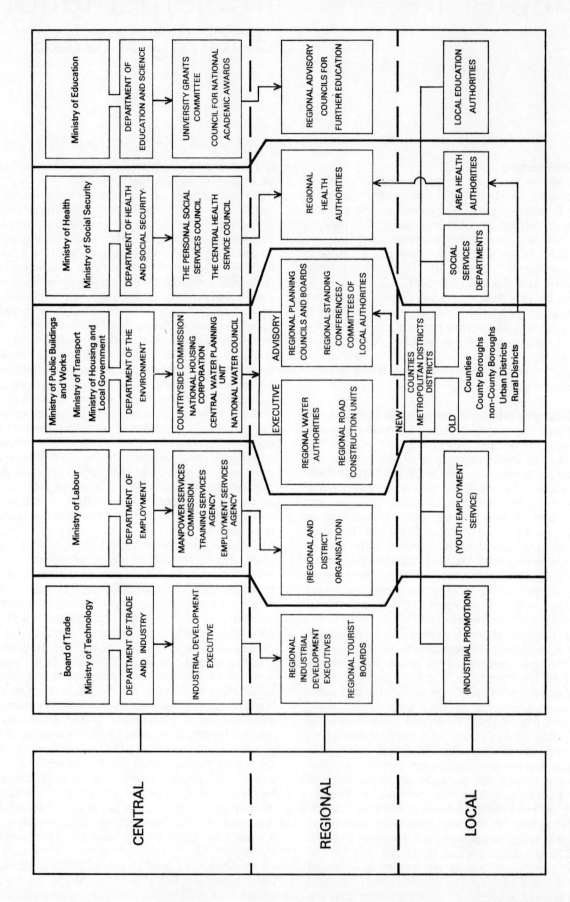

how certain functions are being brought together under larger umbrella organisations, moved from one level in the hierarchy to another, or removed to new, partially independent managements. Thus in 1970 central government departments regrouped into larger units. For example, the separate Ministries of Housing and Local Government, Transport, and Public Buildings and Works, jointly became the Department of the Environment. Most of the central government departments already have, or are creating, their own offshoots, which manage specific functions at national or regional level. The Department of Health and Social Security has, in the recent past, operated many of its health service functions through the Regional Hospital Boards, which have now taken on additional powers as the Regional Health Authorities. Similarly, the Department of the Environment has set up Regional Water Authorities, assuming many functions previously operated at more local levels. The Department of Industry and the Department of Employment are establishing more independent management structures for certain services at national level, involving operational management carried out at lower levels. These are the Industrial Development Executives, and the Training and Employment Services Agencies, respectively. In local government reform itself, a movement towards fewer, but larger, units has been accompanied by considerable shifts in function. In East Anglia 85 authorities—3 county boroughs, 14 non-county boroughs, 27 urban districts and 41 rural districts— within 5 counties have been replaced by 20 new districts, within just 3 counties. Finally, there is considerable uncertainty about those future relationships between central and local government which are of particular relevance to regional planning. The Report of the Commission on the Constitution suggests as one of its majority proposals the establishment of regional councils. Local authority representatives would make up four-fifths of the membership and the councils would command powers in relation to the preparation of strategic plans, and in the determination of public expenditure priorities. These and other proposals in the report, action upon which we cannot anticipate, raise the possibility of substantial changes, which in turn would have major repercussions for the implementation of the principles and proposals contained in this report.

14.2.6 At the present time, almost all of the agencies which are concerned with implementing our strategic proposals at the regional level were originally designed with separate and specific policy-making and executive powers. They have traditionally been backed by the resources and spending powers of central government departments, nationalised industries, and local authorities. As a corollary, there are very few agencies, if any, which have the bridging and coordinating functions required to implement our proposals, together with the necessary backing of executive or spending powers. This can be illustrated most clearly by reference to existing agencies at the regional level. Those agencies which do have executive power at the regional level, for example the Regional Health Authority and the Regional Water Authority, exist to manage relatively narrow fields, and their power devolves essentially from central government. The only regional bodies which do exist and which have much wider horizons are advisory and not executive; the Economic Planning Council addresses its advice mostly towards central government, and within East Anglia the Consultative Committee gives advice to its constituent local authorities. This suggests that there is a need for some strengthening of this type of bridging agency to secure a stronger base for coping with future change, and to increase the effectiveness of policies required in response to that change. This could only be achieved by a combination of approaches. The minimum would appear to be a wider span for these agencies covering the areas of overlapping concern of central and local government, together with reserve or discretionary executive powers to put into operation those functions which cannot be adequately covered by executive agencies.

14.3 The Implications of the Strategic Principles and Proposals

14.3.1 The presentation of the conclusions of the other sections of this report has been in terms of strategic principles, and the more specific proposals which flow from them. In part, this is a recognition of the hierarchical relationships between agencies, but more importantly, it recognises the distinction between the roles of bridging and executive agencies. The strategic principles attempt to define those longer term directions for the future development of the region, which may be lost sight of in the day-to-day execution of policies. In this way, they provide the essential core of the role of bridging agencies, which must influence and intervene where necessary to ensure that these general directions are adhered to. The more specific proposals perform several functions. They illustrate in greater detail the meaning of the principles, which contain some degree of ambiguity because of the more generalised form they take. The proposals also demonstrate clearly how the strategic principles impinge on the operation of executive agencies at all levels. This could be made clear by a listing of the agencies directly or indirectly affected by the strategic principles. It may be sufficient at this point to state that we have found no examples of agencies operating in the region which should not take note of our principles in planning and carrying out their activities. It is no longer possible, for example, to conceive of policies for social services in isolation from their context of communications, shopping, employment, and related health services, or of housing policies solely in housing terms.

14.3.2 The proposals are deliberately framed on a more specific and narrower basis than the principles. The implications of proposals for the future activities of agencies can best be described in terms of a number of examples. In chapter eight, we have proposed the redirection of the planned migration programme to assist in building up a set of secondary centres to serve the central, northern and eastern parts of the region more effectively. The realisation of this proposal would require the active co-operation of central government, particularly the Department of the Environment and the Department of Industry, with the Greater London Council, the source for this programme. Close co-operation with the receiving county and district councils would be vital. A second example arises from the future use of labour resources. Specific proposals for this, made in chapter ten, include the development of training programmes for increasing the overall levels of skills in the workforce. Such a scheme would clearly fall within the responsibilities of the Training Services Agency, and would also involve the Local Education Authorities, unions, and employers in the private sector. At the same time, however, the development of new training programmes would necessitate research and experimentation, designed to extend the existing operations of these agencies. A third example is where we see the need for a third force in the housing field to maintain an adequate rented sector not tied to residential or employment qualifications. In chapter ten, we have made the suggestion that this could be realised by extending the functions of the National Housing Corporation to include the setting up of regional offshoots. These examples serve to demonstrate that the proposals imply a considerable degree of co-ordination between existing agencies at all levels. They also imply that in some specific cases there appear to be grounds for expanding the role of existing agencies to cover related questions. In the concluding part of this chapter, we go on, therefore, to look at two main issues. The first of these is the general question of co-operation between types of agencies. The second is the development of overall bridging functions, where the strategic principles cannot be realised simply by expanding the roles of existing agencies.

14.4 Conclusions

14.4.1 In a mixed economy, a first and all pervasive area of co-operation is between agencies in the public and private sectors. In overall terms, our proposals suggest a more active role for the public sector, particularly in those areas and types of investment where it can, in turn, stimulate a higher level of private investment. As a corollary to this, there are grounds for changing the emphasis of the public sector's role in other areas, where the stimulus to growth through the private sector has already taken place. This is most evident in the planned migration programme. Firstly, the potential of the central, northern and eastern parts of the region has to be underwritten to encourage subsequent investment by the private sector. Secondly, in the areas of more rapid growth in the south and west, the role of the public sector should move away from that of providing a stimulus. Its function in these areas becomes one of ensuring that services and infrastructure keep pace with the demands of the growing population, and that the composition of this growth is reasonably balanced. A major advantage of the long term programme of future development contained in this report is that it has the potential, if accepted, to provide the confidence the private sector requires to undertake major investment in ways which come closer to meeting the objectives for the region.

14.4.2 A second area of co-operation is between local authorities within the region. This takes a number of forms. Firstly, we see considerable scope for further co-operation at the regional level, within the framework provided by the Consultative Committee or any successor body. This has been specifically referred to in chapter nine in terms of the joint use of staff in the development of priorities to be expressed in the transport plans and programmes. Realisation of the development proposed in chapter eight must depend on a recognition by the individual counties of the benefits to be obtained by joint development and implementation of policies, rather than by the separate and isolated preparation of structure plans. Secondly, the change in the functions of counties and districts after local government reorganisation will bring its own questions of co-ordination in train. The powers available to districts will require active co-operation to realise the proposals of the structure plans prepared by the counties, and through these plans some of the proposals in this report at the regional level. This will require the development of much stronger informal links at these levels, equivalent to existing links at the regional level which have made this report possible. We see considerable prospect for this in the encouragement of area structures for services provided at county level, and the establishment of local information offices, where districts and counties can combine to offer a joint point of contact with the people in those areas.

14.4.3 The final area of co-operation is that which most directly affects the whole question of forward planning at the regional level. This is the relationship between central and local government. In this field, there have been considerable changes in the last decade in both formal and informal structures. The Report of the Commission on the Constitution is perhaps the prelude to further substantial changes that could take place in the next few years. It is not possible to anticipate what these changes might be, but it seems useful in the light of our proposals to attempt to state what developments would be most suited to the report's implementation.

14.4.4 The first major factor is the overall uncertainty about changes in the future, whatever strategic policies are adopted. This was considered in chapter five in relation to the region as a whole, and resulted in the identification of the following strategic principle:

B4 regional institutions should be developed, with appropriate powers and resources, to give a firmer basis for the forward planning of capital investment, and to shield the region from major disruptions from external sources.

This principle was exemplified in terms of the planned migration programme, which is the main policy instrument in the public sector for securing a change in the overall locational pattern. This can be illustrated by the fact that no less than a quarter of the new district authorities in the region will inherit town development agreements with the Greater London Council.

14.4.5 The second major factor is the relative absence of ways for adjusting national spending policies to the circumstances of East Anglia. The proportion of the population living in urban areas nationally is much greater than that in East Anglia, and as a consequence national priorities do not always fit the regional situation without adjustment. The possibilities for adjustment to secure a more effective use of scarce resources are limited. There would seem, therefore, to be grounds for developing some form of intermediate mechanism which would allow regional priorities to be more clearly recognised in overall policies.

14.4.6 The third and final factor has already been described earlier in this chapter. This is the relative absence of agencies with the specific role of bridging and co-ordinating the work of a multiplicity of more specialised executive agencies. It takes two forms. Firstly, there is no forum in which these more specialised agencies are required to come together for mutual reconciliation of their objectives and activities. Secondly, there is no agency at present charged with, or given the discretion to deal with, those questions which either lie outside the responsibility of these specialised agencies, or result from changes or events which have not been foreseen. This means not only that the existing structure finds it difficult to give adequate recognition to forward planning in its activities, but also that its response to any new situation may not be as rapid or effective as that situation requires.

14.4.7 These three factors, in combination, indicate that the full realisation of the purpose and content of this report requires some definite changes in the structure of agencies, over and above those related to the specific proposals described above. In trying to state more clearly the form such changes might take, we have avoided the obvious temptation of devising an ideal blueprint. This would be neither realistic in its assumption about the way agencies develop, nor would it be in keeping with the remainder of this report, where the rigidities of fixed and precise patterns have been denied.

14.4.8 The basic requirement appears to be for a growing coalescence of those bodies which serve a bridging function at the regional level. This would be accompanied by the provision of discretionary powers, with appropriate financial resources, to enable these separate or joint bodies to intervene more effectively. We also think that the structure would need to contain representatives of all the public bodies in the region so that it can become an effective forum for reconciling activities. To help ensure that this occurs, there would appear to be a need for some power of sanction over the programmes of these bodies. This is not easy to specify, because powers of intervention on current projects could add a further, and undesirable, delaying factor. A similar objection occurs in respect of powers for the approval of annual budgets. Because the suggested bridging functions are concerned with longer-term directions, any power of sanction should be applied to forward programmes for capital and current expenditure. We, therefore, suggest that executive agencies should be required to submit their forward programmes for approval. The sanction power could be exercised through a percentage precept on the expenditure levels of all public bodies represented at the regional level. The percentage would be varied,

matching the degree to which the forward programme of each body is considered to meet the longer-term requirements of the region, in terms of the objectives or strategic principles. The income that results from this would be part of a regional development fund, to be used in association with the discretionary powers available to regional bodies.

14.4.9 So far we have discussed changes in the agencies concerned with the implementation of the proposals in this report from the standpoint of building on the existing structure. This automatically assumes that this structure, tried and tested by experience, would be strong enough, with a few modifications, to withstand the stresses to which it will be subject and to secure the consistent level of agreement and co-ordination that is required. There must be some reservations about this in practice, as evidenced by the number of substantial changes in agencies recently in response to changing conditions. It is useful, therefore, to take a brief look at what form of agencies would be most likely to achieve the implementation of our proposals. One feature of recent reorganisations has been the increasing separation of bodies responsible for drawing up the main lines of policy, and those responsible for executing that policy. In this perspective, it could be feasible to place the responsibility for reaching agreement on the future direction of policy in East Anglia at the representative level of central and local government. Equivalent to this would be the establishment of agencies for the purpose of its execution. As an example of this, the proposals for secondary centres and selected small towns in chapter eight could be most effectively pursued by an agency with powers resembling those of New Town Corporations. The process of land assembly and servicing to assist the private house builder, and the task of constructing houses for any 'third force' rented sector, as suggested in chapter ten, could be brought into the same framework. Such arrangements need not be derogatory of either local or central government responsibilities, if future policies were carefully delineated and a watching brief was kept over their sensitive application. It is, of course, unlikely that such a suggestion will find favour in present circumstances, particularly in the immediate period after local government reorganisation. It must, however, be seen in the perspective of the likelihood of substantial changes over the next twenty years. It must also be set against the current situation. It has to be admitted that the agency which comes closest to combining the dual functions of a strategic planning body and development agency for East Anglia, through its influence on the planned migration programme, is the Greater London Council. Whatever the benefits that East Anglia gains from this, it is inevitable that the GLC must be primarily concerned with the interests of those who live in London.

14.4.10 On the basis of this chapter, it is considered then that the following strategic principle should be adopted:

Continued overleaf

F1 those agencies, exercising a bridging function between executive bodies, should be strengthened to enable more effective cooperation, and an increased capacity to cope with future situations.

To put this principle into practice, we put forward the following proposals for consideration :
(i) *there should be continued interchange and growing coalescence between those agencies performing a bridging role at regional level for central and local government;*
(ii) *all major executive agencies in the region should be represented within the framework of bridging agencies;*
(iii) *the bridging agencies, either jointly or separately, should be given discretionary powers for action, together with the financial resources required to put those powers into effect;*
(iv) *similarly, the bridging agencies should possess effective powers of sanction over the forward programmes of those agencies, related to the financial resources required for the operation of the bridging role;*
(v) *the possibility should be considered of separating responsibility for defining main lines of policy at representative level, and the execution of that policy by other agencies in the longer term, to secure a more effective means of implementing strategic policies for the region.*

Chapter 15

Financial Resources

15.1 Introduction

15.1.1 The human and environmental resources of East Anglia have been considered in detail in earlier sections of this report. In this chapter, we concentrate on financial resources, in recognition of those regional objectives which seek, where possible, to minimise capital and recurring costs of development. This is in terms of a general assessment of whether or not the resources are likely to be available—both in overall terms and for major segments of what we expect and what we propose. In this way, the problems involved in attempting to cost and compare alternative possibilities, a process open to considerable doubt at this level of planning, have been avoided. As a first step, recent and present expenditure patterns are analysed. This in itself is not straightforward, as expenditure occurs in a number of ways and from different sources, and much of the material is limited in quality and coverage. Many of the conclusions drawn are, therefore, rather more tentative than we would ideally wish. The second step is to project this material forward, taking into account the uncertainty accompanying such forecasts. Finally, we turn to the related questions of the shifts in expenditure priorities implied by the contents of the remainder of the report, and the changes in the mechanics of expenditure which could enable these to be realised more effectively.

15.2 Private and Public Expenditure

15.2.1 In assessing recent expenditure patterns, the first distinction to be made is between public and private sector expenditure. At national level, public expenditure on goods and services as a proportion of the gross national product has increased only marginally over the past twenty years, and now accounts for slightly over 30%. The relative importance of public and private sector expenditures, however, will vary between regions, reflecting the distribution of nationalised industries and the economic potential recognised by investment in the private sector, among other things.

15.2.2 The broad position in East Anglia in this respect can only be indicated in terms of investment, and not the overall extent of expenditure in the regional economy. Thus in the sixties, capital expenditure per head by the public sector was generally comparable to the national average. In the private sector, however, the level of investment per head in the same period was consistently higher than the national average. During the late sixties, as shown in Figure 15.1, it was almost a third higher than the national average, at £45 per head.

Figure 15.1

Private investment in new construction by region, 1968–71

Region (in rank order)	Average annual investment per head of population, (£'s) at 1971 prices
East Anglia	**45·1**
East Midlands	37·7
South West	37·0
South East	35·8
North	35·5
West Midlands	34·4
North West	33·1
Wales	32·5
Yorks and Humberside	31·1
Scotland	28·3
Northern Ireland	26·0
United Kingdom	**34.3**

Source: Abstract of Regional Statistics

This appears to confirm the favourable prospects for the future of East Anglia discussed in Section B. Two important conclusions emerge. Firstly, the private sector has a greater role in overall investment in East Anglia than the public sector. The form which this investment takes is, therefore, of considerable importance to the development of the region, and the achievement of regional objectives. Secondly, the acceleration in the rate of growth of the region reflected in private investment levels has not been matched in the public sector. One possible explanation for this may be that the public sector has not responded as yet to privately financed growth, and may only do so when private sector demands become more explicit. This would only occur as spare capacity in existing infrastructure and services is used up, and implies some growth in the level of public sector investment when this stage is reached.

15.3 Expenditure within the Public Sector

15.3.1 Within the public sector, it is useful to consider first of all the overall national level of expenditure, and its distribution between different programmes and spending agencies. This is shown for 1971/72 in Figure 15.2. About 60% of total public expenditure is accounted for by central government. Only part of this represents a direct claim on resources, with the remainder consisting of transfers between different sectors of the community. Social security payments are an example of this, taking effect through the expenditure of private consumers. Local authority

Figure 15.2 The Pattern of Public Expenditure, 1972–73

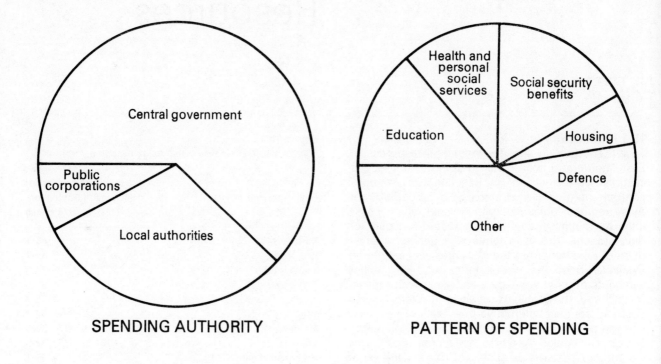

SPENDING AUTHORITY

PATTERN OF SPENDING

expenditure represents about 30% of the total, with one third of this going to capital projects, and the remainder meeting current expenditure, such as staff salaries, maintenance, etc. The balance of public expenditure, 8%, is by public corporations, including nationalised industries, and specialised agencies such as New Town Development Corporations. The expenditure of both local authorities and public corporations, moreover, is subject to considerable control by central government, both in total and in composition.

15.3.2 Attempts to examine the scale and composition of public expenditure in East Anglia are restricted by the quality of the information available. Nevertheless, as shown in Figure 15.3, recent estimates of expenditure flows by regions provide a tentative basis for considering public expenditure levels, and, in particular, current expenditure by central government, where the information is otherwise almost non-existent. They indicate that the region is a net importer of goods and services, as its domestic product per head is fairly low, while its expenditure per head is close to the national average.

15.3.3 At least part of the additional buying power can be explained by public sector transfers between different sectors of the community and which provide a net benefit to the region. Agricultural subsidies and retirement pensions are examples of such transfers, and they are more than likely to counterbalance relatively low levels of payments per head of sickness and unemployment benefits. In other categories of public sector current expenditure, only armed forces and defence are likely to be above the national

Figure 15.3

Gross Domestic Product
and expenditure per head of total population at factor cost
1964 by region

Region	GDP 1964		Expenditure 1964		Net Exports 1964
	(£)	(Index)	(£)	(Index)	(£)
United Kingdom	528	100	532	100	— 4
North	446	85	460	86	—14
E. & W. Ridings	525	99	490	92	+35
North West	515	98	489	93	+26
N. Midlands	515	98	490	92	+25
Midlands	573	109	536	101	+37
S.E. England	599	113	601	113	— 2
(East Anglia) *	(461)	(87)	(538)	(101)	(—77)
South West	463	88	535	101	—72
Wales	459	88	502	94	—43
Scotland	456	86	492	93	—36
N. Ireland	346	66	439	82	—93

*The East Anglian figures, in brackets, are also included in those for South-East England, and are considered to have a greater margin of error associated with them than those given for other regions.

Source:
V. H. Woodward, Regional Social Accounts for the United Kingdom, 1970.
NIESR. Regional Papers No. 1.

average per head. On the information available, expenditure on social services and on central and local government administration is more likely to be below the national average.

15.3.4 On a similar basis, the receipts per head from East Anglia to the current account of the public sector are generally lower than the national average. They are influenced by the lower average levels of earned incomes and a narrow rate base. The underlying factor may be the continuing importance of agriculture in the structure of the regional economy. Taking expenditure and receipts together, a rough balance sheet for the public sector in East Anglia can be drawn up, as illustrated in Figure 15.4. While this excludes items such as defence expenditure which is of indirect benefit to the region, even in these restricted terms the public sector's net receipts from East Anglia amounted to £25·6 per head. This is less than half the national average figure, and is below that of every other region in the United Kingdom, with the exception of Wales and Northern Ireland. In general terms, therefore, there is a presumption that the regional economy gains benefits from public expenditure flows in the national economy.

15.3.5 This general conclusion still leaves a large number of questions unanswered; in particular, those concerned with the levels and effects of current expenditure by central government. We have a general conception of its overall level some years ago. There are, however, no estimates from year to year, and so it is very difficult to even begin to understand what kind of impacts such expenditure has, or how it relates to regional, as opposed to national, objectives, and how it affects different groups of the region's population, and different parts of the region. We consider that efforts should be made to develop regional social accounts, and that research should be mounted to provide a better understanding of the impacts of central government expenditure.

15.3.6 It is now possible to consider those areas of public expenditure in the region where rather better information is available, beginning first with capital expenditure by the public sector as a whole. Figure 15.5 illustrates the general upward trend, both nationally and in East Anglia, in investment in new construction, which represents about 80% of capital expenditure on fixed assets. Both the total and per capita levels of investment in new construction in East Anglia contain items which are more significant nationally than regionally, such as natural gas installations. Such expenditure helps to explain the wider fluctuations at the regional, as compared with the national, level. In the later sixties, the overall level of public investment per head was slightly higher than the national average. Separate consideration of the central and local government

Figure 15.5

Public investment in new construction 1964/5–1971/2, East Anglia and England and Wales
1971 prices

Fiscal Year	England and Wales		East Anglia	
	Total Investment £m	Per head of Population £	Total Investment £m	Per head of Population £
1964/65	1,707·2	36·1	57·4	37·3
1965/66	1,767·8	37·1	56·5	36·2
1966/67	1,995·1	41·5	62·5	39·5
1967/68	2,301·8	47·6	93·5	58·0
1968/69	2,292·6	47·2	78·9	48·1
1969/70	2,241·5	45·9	77·8	46·9
1970/71	2,263·0	46·2	76·8	45·9
1971/72	2,235·2	45·8	77·3	46·0

Source: Abstract of Regional Statistics.

Figure 15.4

Public Sector beneficial expenditure and receipts per head, 1964[1]

	United Kingdom	North	Yorks & H'side	North West	East Midlands	West Midlands	South East	(East Anglia)	South West	Wales	Scot-land	N Ireland
Receipts												
Income tax and Surtax	51·8	34·7	43·0	42·2	41·4	51·1	70·3	(43·4)	47·3	35·9	42·5	26·3
Tax on expenditure	71·7	65·7	66·2	70·6	67·3	77·3	78·1	(65·8)	64·3	64·9	69·2	57·6
Company taxation	13·5	12·3	15·2	16·2	14·4	16·7	14·8	(12·0)	10·3	11·2	12·0	7·5
National insurance and health contributions	25·9	21·5	25·6	24·9	24·1	29·0	30·5	(20·9)	21·1	21·7	21·9	15·8
Rates	20·3	17·1	17·2	18·5	17·5	20·6	26·6	(16·9)	18·6	17·3	21·1	11·2
Total	183·2	151·3	167·2	172·6	164·7	194·7	220·3	(159·0)	161·6	151·0	166·7	118·4
Expenditure												
Current	53·9	51·4	51·5	52·5	48·8	50·2	56·7	(51·0)	53·7	57·8	55·9	49·9
Capital formation	13·6	12·8	12·0	11·7	15·5	13·0	12·8	(18·1)	13·8	16·0	16·4	22·1
Agricultural subsidies	4·5	5·1	3·8	1·7	5·8	3·5	2·9	(14·3)	7·6	5·8	7·4	18·9
Other grants and subsidies	48·7	50·9	50·1	49·6	45·8	43·2	46·7	(50·0)	48·9	54·0	56·9	46·6
Total	120·7	120·2	117·4	115·5	115·9	109·9	119·1	(133·4)	124·0	133·6	136·6	137·5
Receipts less expenditure	+62·5	+31·1	+49·8	+57·1	+48·8	+84·8	+101·2	(+25·6)	+37·6	+17·4	+30·1	—19·1

Source: Woodward, op cit.

(1) Non 'beneficial' expenditure has been excluded from this table i.e. expenditure on defence and most expenditure on central government administration—as this does not confer a direct benefit on the resident population of a particular region.

components of this investment will assist in suggesting reasons for these characteristics.

15.4 Expenditure by Central Government and Public Corporations

15.4.1 The capital expenditure programmes of central government and nationalised industries largely reflect nationally determined programmes. The opportunity at the regional level to influence these expenditure priorities is small, and so the regional pattern of investment reflects only broadly the geographical variations in the incidence of problems being tackled, the quality and quantity of existing capital stock, and changing demands arising from population growth or decline. At the present time, too, the technical basis for assessing priorities for capital expenditure programmes is variable. Some programmes are prepared on the basis of "hard" criteria which measure the economic rate of return on individual projects, e.g. road building, but the majority of programmes cannot be assessed in such terms. For instance, programmes in the health and welfare field rest to a large extent on the pressure of unsatisfied demand.

15.4.2 The average level of regional investment in new construction by central government, nationalised industries and other public corporations, is shown in Figure 15.6 for the period 1967/8 to 1971/2. The distribution of this investment between spending programmes is given in Figure 15.7 for East Anglia and England and Wales. The major capital expenditure programmes undertaken at national level in this period involved central government in the construction of motorways, principal roads, and hospitals, and nationalised industries in investment in transportation and energy projects. The rather low average level of central government expenditure per head—at £6·9 in East Anglia compared with £8·8 for England and Wales—is partially explained by the absence of a major motor-way construction programme. The high level of investment by nationalised industries is accounted for by the once and for all investment in North Sea gas infrastructure. The investment by other public corporations in this period was relatively low, reflecting the early period of the region's new town at Peterborough.

15.5 The Income of Local Authorities

15.5.1 Expenditure by local authorities, both in level and distribution between spending programmes, is influenced by the sources from which incomes are obtained. The day-to-day costs of running local services are financed from three main sources: grants from central government; miscellaneous rents, fees, and charges; and from the proceeds of the rate levy. The grant system is the mechanism by which central government supports the expenditure of local government, and the latter has become increasingly dependent upon grants as the major source of income. The present national grant system is based on central estimates of expenditure, covering all local authority services except housing and trading undertakings (known collectively as 'estimated relevant expenditure'). Central government then decides what proportion of this total sum it will finance—(60% for the year 1973/74)—deducts the estimated amount of grants which will go to providing specific services, and distributes the remainder as the Rate Support Grant. This process is illustrated for 1973/74 and 1974/75 in Figure 15.8. The *needs* element, payable to county councils and county boroughs, is based on various criteria—mostly population characteristics—which measure the variation in need between local authorities. The *resources* element is payable to any rating authority whose rate resources per head of population are below the national average. The *domestic* element, payable to all authorities, is to reduce the call on domestic rate payers.

Figure 15.6

Investment in new construction by Central Government and Public Corporations (1967/8–1971/2) by regions

| Region | Average Annual Expenditure at 1971 prices | | | | | |
| | Central Government | | Nationalised Industries | | Other Public Corporations | |
	£m	per capita £	£m	per capita £	£m	per capita £
North	44·8	13·6	24·4	7·4	9·4	2·8
Yorks and Humberside	35·1	7·3	50·6	10·5	4·9	1·0
East Midlands	20·1	5·9	27·2	8·0	4·5	1·3
EAST ANGLIA	11·5	6·9	19·6	11·7	2·8	1·7
South East	127·7	7·4	140·7	8·2	39·8	2·3
South West	50·0	12·8	26·0	6·7	5·2	1·3
West Midlands	45·9	9·0	33·1	6·5	14·0	2·7
North West	59·2	8·8	38·7	5·7	16·1	2·4
Wales	34·4	12·6	23·4	8·6	7·7	2·8
England & Wales	***428·8***	***8·8***	***383·7***	***7·9***	***104·4***	***2·1***

Source: Abstracts of Regional Statistics, DOE Capital payments, and EARST estimates

Figure 15.7

Central Government and Public Corporation investment by spending programmes (1967/8–1971/2) : East Anglia and England and Wales

Programmes	Average Annual Expenditure at 1971 prices					
	East Anglia			England and Wales		
	£m	%	£ per capita	£m	%	£ per capita
Education	0·3	0·9	0·2	12·4	1·4	0·3
Environment	0·6	1·8	0·4	16·7	1·8	0·3
Housing	2·3	6·8	1·4	81·1	8·8	1·7
Health and Social Services	6·4	18·8	3·8	120·6	13·2	2·5
Protective Services	0·3	0·9	0·2	5·6	0·6	0·1
Highways	2·5	7·4	1·5	206·3	22·5	4·2
Transportation	3·0	8·8	1·8	153·0	16·7	3·1
Fuel and Power	16·6	48·9	9·9	230·8	25·2	4·7
Miscellaneous	2·0	5·9	1·2	90·4	9·8	1·9
Total	***33·9***	***100·0***	***20·2***	***916·9***	***100·0***	***18·8***

Source: Abstracts of Regional Statistics and DOE Capital payments

Figure 15.8

Rate support grant determination : England and Wales

Stages of RSG Determination	1973/74 £m	1974/75 £m
(a) Estimated Relevant Expenditure	5,216	5,671
(b) Aggregate Exchequer Grant	3,130	3,431
(c) Specific Grants	255	355
Needs	*2,299*	*1,907*
Resources	*383*	*723*
Domestic	*193*	*446*
(d) Total Rate Support Grant (b—c) =	2,875	3,076

Source: Department of the Environment

15.5.2 For all local authorities in England and Wales, the proportion of net expenditure financed by grants has increased from about 53% in 1966–67 to 60% in 1973–74. Rateable values generally have not kept pace with the growth of local authority expenditure, resulting both in increases in rate poundage, and more significantly, increased reliance on government grant. The level of dependency, however, varies considerably from one county to another. The proportion of net expenditure met by grants and rates for the former county councils in East Anglia, as compared with the average for all English counties, is shown in Figure 15.9. The region as a whole has an above average dependency on rate support grants, particularly marked in Norfolk and the former East and West Suffolks, where the level of the 'resource' element is high. The former Cambridgeshire and Isle of Ely, and Huntingdonshire and Peterborough counties receive a relatively high level of the 'needs' element, mainly

Figure 15.9

Financing of expenditure by former county councils in East Anglia, 1971/72

Former County Councils	Expenditure met from rates, grants and reimbursements	Proportion financed by				
		Rates and balances	Rate Support Grant			
			Needs	Resources	Other	Total
	£'000	%	%	%	%	%
Norfolk	31,307	25·8	55·7	11·4	7·1	74·2
E. Suffolk	17,394	28·2	51·4	11·7	8·7	71·8
W. Suffolk	11,023	27·3	53·1	13·3	6·3	72·7
Cambridgeshire and Isle of Ely	21,478	38·6	48·4	6·1	6·9	61·4
Huntingdon and Peterborough	15,333	32·8	51·9	8·7	6·7	67·3
All English County Councils (excluding London)	1,970,672	32·1	51·8	7·0	9·1	67·9

Source: Financial and General Statistics, Society of County Treasurers, 1972

because of the growth in the numbers of school children. In contrast, their 'resource' element is relatively low, due to their higher rate income per head of population.

15.5.3 The rate base of former county councils in East Anglia is illustrated in Figure 15.10. The rateable value per head of population in Norfolk and the two former Suffolk counties is particularly low compared with the average for England and Wales, confirming the importance of the resource element of the rate support grant to these counties. The recent revaluation of rateable values in 1973 does not appear to have changed the relative situation substantially. At the regional level, the low rate poundages may

Figure 15.10

Rateable values by former County Councils in East Anglia, 1971/72

County Councils	Home Population (Mid 1971)	Total Rateable Value (April 1972) £'000	Rateable Value per head of population £	Rate call per head
Norfolk	445,490	15,916·6	35·7	25·3
E. Suffolk	262,070	9,529·1	36·4	27·9
W. Suffolk	168,720	5,867·7	34·8	26·8
Cambridgeshire & Isle of Ely	308,140	14,019·0	45·5	36·8
Huntingdon and Peterborough	206,160	8,733·3	42·4	36·4
England and Wales	**27,375,200**	**1,168,483·7**	**42·7**	**33·2**

Source: Rates and Rateable Values, HMSO 1972

reflect the below average income levels, and the greater dependence on agriculture. The rate base of the region has grown faster than that of the country as a whole, and has enabled local authority expenditure to grow without incurring the large increases in rate poundage, or dependency on government grants, that would otherwise have been necessary. This is illustrated in Figure 15.11.

15.5.4 The final source of income for local authorities is their borrowing power. Most of their capital expenditure is financed in this way. Authorities are required to obtain central government loan sanction, i.e. permission to borrow, and under arrangements introduced in 1971, capital expenditure, for control purposes, is divided into four categories:

(i) **key sector** schemes (e.g. housing, education, principal roads, police, personal health and social services);
(ii) the acquisition of land for education, principal roads, housing, etc.;
(iii) housing improvement grants;
(iv) **locally determined** schemes—the remainder of local authority schemes.

Generally speaking, once individual projects within the first three categories have been approved by central government, they also carry the consent to borrow the necessary money. Central government

Figure 15.11

Growth in rateable value per head : East Anglia and England and Wales

Fiscal Year	Rateable Value per head of population			
	East Anglia		England and Wales	
	£	Index	£	Index
1966–67	33·9	100	45·7	100
1967–68	34·9	103	46·7	102
1968–69	36·0	106	47·6	104
1969–70	37·1	109	48·7	107
1970–71	38·4	113	49·8	109
1971–72	39·7	117	51·1	112

Source: Rates and Rateable Values, 1972

can control the overall amount of such borrowing by setting an overall ceiling and dividing this between departments. Thus loan sanction can be refused in the interests of economic policy or of national spending priorities. Within the locally determined sector, local authorities are given a block allocation to borrow money, and within this limit have considerable freedom to determine priorities. The formula which determines, however, the total allocation for a local authority is not based upon any view of future needs, more upon the experience of previous expenditure. Since locally determined schemes include local amenities and environmental improvements (for example, town centre redevelopment, sports and recreation facilities), particular difficulties can be created for fast-growing communities.

15.5.5 Within this system of central control of local government income, there has been a recent shift away from specific grants towards a block grant system. Specific capital grants from central government to local authorities meet some 6% of all capital expenditure. The largest programme which this system has served has been for principal roads. The present transport grant system is to be replaced, however, by a block grant covering the majority of transport services (roads, car parking, public transport, but not rail), and including both revenue and capital expenditure. County councils will have to prepare transport plans and programmes which will be submitted for overall approval to the Department of the Environment. Some of the aid for such expenditure will be absorbed into the Rate Support Grant and special payments in the form of a supplementary grant will be payable to those areas with larger expenditures, if justified by the submitted transport plans and programmes. A similar shift from specific to block grant procedure is being experimented with at present in the education field. Overall, such a trend has three kinds of effect. It softens the rather rigid distinction maintained in the past between current and capital expenditure. It begins to relieve central government of what is, at present, a heavy load of vetting individual projects submitted by local authorities for approval. And, finally, it allows local authorities rather more freedom of action in deciding upon expenditure priorities within broad fields or programmes, as part of a more corporate approach.

15.6 Expenditure by Local Authorities

15.6.1 The level of local authority investment per head is more unstable in East Anglia than in the country as a whole, as is illustrated in Figure 15.12. This may indicate that it is particularly susceptible to national cutbacks in public expenditure. Averaging out these fluctuations for the period 1967/68 to 1971/72, total capital expenditure per head, including land costs, is below the national average. As Figure 15.13 demonstrates, this is largely because of the extremely high costs of land in the South-East, which distort the national picture. In terms of investment in new construction per head alone, the region is very close to the national level. This is somewhat surprising in view of the need to cater for a rapidly growing population. It raises once again the question of whether or not local authority expenditure in East Anglia is lagging behind both the growth of the region and the investment made by the private sector.

15.6.2 The overall level of capital expenditure by local authorities, however, is largely determined by separate programmes, based on standards set at national level by various departments of central government. The distribution of capital expenditure between these programmes, averaged over the same period 1967/8 to 1971/2, is shown in Figure 15.14. This shows that capital expenditure per head is significantly lower than in England and Wales as a whole, for housing, and highways, and marginally lower for health and social services, and education. It is significantly higher for environmental services, which include sewerage and sewage disposal. Comparing the region's changing distribution with that of England and Wales over the period 1966/67 to 1970/71, expenditure on education and highways

Figure 15.12

Local Authorities annual capital expenditure : 1966/67 to 1971/72 : East Anglia and England and Wales

Fiscal Year	East Anglia		England and Wales			
	Land	New Construction	Land		New Construction	
				per capita		per capita
	£m	£m	£m	£	£m	£
1966/67	7·4	44·4	28·1	377·1	1175·8	24·5
1967/68	7·6	50·6	31·3	360·3	1376·1	28·4
1968/69	5·3	46·2	28·2	301·4	1409·1	28·9
1969/70	6·2	42·4	25·6	256·9	1325·5	27·1
1970/71	8·3	45·4	27·1	324·7	1329·6	27·1
1971/72	5·8	49·9	29·7	226·9	1409·1	28·9

Source: Local Authorities' Capital Payments Return, DOE

Figure 15.13

Local authority capital expenditure, by region.
1967/68 to 1971/72 Average Annual Expenditure : 1971 prices

Region	Annual Expenditure			Expenditure per head	
	Land	New Con-struction	Other	New Con-struction	Total Expendi-ture
	£m	£m	£m	£	£
North	14·7	108·2	11·7	32·8	40·8
Yorks and Humberside	20·3	114·9	15·0	23·9	31·2
East Midlands	14·9	76·0	11·3	22·4	30·1
EAST ANGLIA	6·6	46·9	4·8	27·9	34·7
South East	154·7	504·1	66·5	29·4	42·3
South West	14·3	84·4	10·5	21·6	28·0
West Midlands	24·1	142·3	16·0	27·8	35·6
North West	35·9	194·1	22·1	28·8	37·4
Wales	8·5	79·0	7·3	29·0	34·8
England and Wales	**294·0**	**1349·9**	**165·2**	**27·7**	**37·1**

Source: Local Authorities' Capital Payments Returns, DOE

Figure 15.14

Local authority investment in new construction by spending programme, 1967/68–1971/72 : East Anglia and England and Wales
Average Annual Expenditure, 1971 Prices

Programme	East Anglia			England and Wales		
	£m	%	£ per capita	£m	%	£ per capita
Education	6·5	13·9	3·9	196·2	14·5	4·0
Environment	11·6	24·7	6·9	219·8	16·3	4·5
Housing	17·9	38·3	10·6	611·3	45·3	12·5
Health & Social Services	0·9	1·9	0·5	33·3	2·5	0·7
Protective Services	0·8	1·7	0·5	24·3	1·8	0·5
Highways	4·9	10·4	2·9	168·1	12·5	3·4
Miscellaneous	4·2	9·0	2·5	96·9	7·2	2·0
Total	**46·9**	**100·0**	**27·9**	**1,349·9**	**100·0**	**27·7**

Source: Local Authorities' Capital Payments Returns, DOE

has expanded at the expense of housing. Furthermore, educational capital projects in the region increased significantly, contributing a larger than national proportion to the total at the end of the period, compared with a smaller proportion in 1966/67. This higher than average increase can be explained by the rapid growth of the school population, and by reorganisation and some replacement of old schools. In contrast, whilst housing in the region accounted for a smaller than national proportion of the total at the beginning of the period, it also contracted more rapidly. Overall then it can be seen that national priorities are fairly closely reflected in the region.

15.6.3 Finally, we consider local authorities' current expenditure, which is by far the largest of the four main categories of public expenditure that we have been attempting to assess—the capital and current expenditure of both central and local government. Figure 15.15 shows, however, that on a per capita basis, such expenditure is at present lower in East Anglia than in any other region in England and Wales. Although this masks considerable differences between counties within the region, the generally high level of service running costs—especially in education, which accounts for more than half of the total— suggests that local authorities spend much less than

Figure 15.15

Local authority net* rate fund expenditure by region, 1970/71

Region	£ million	per capita £
North	226·5	69
Yorks and Humberside	313·8	65
East Midlands	218·3	65
EAST ANGLIA	106·3	63
South East	1,277·2	75
South West	338·8	67
North West	454·2	68
Wales	197·5	73
England and Wales	**3,384·6**	**69**

*Net expenditure is that met by rates and grants.
Source: DOE, Finance Division

do those in other regions. This is further illustrated by Figure 15.16, which compares regional and national expenditure by programme. In all programmes, except highways, expenditure per head is lower in East Anglia than in England and Wales.

15.7 The Structure of Public Expenditure

15.7.1 The lengthy analysis of expenditure patterns set out above can be summed up in terms of the constraints and opportunities which it contains for the future development of the region. These conclusions are concerned with the overall levels of expenditure by different agencies:

(a) the level of investment by the private sector is high, and has a more important role in East Anglia than in other regions;

(b) the general level of investment by the public sector appears to have lagged behind that of the

Figure 15.16

Local authority net rate fund expenditure by programme, 1970/71 : East Anglia, and England and Wales

Programme	East Anglia			England and Wales		
	£m	%	£ per capita	£m	%	£ per capita
Education	59·8	56·3	35·6	1,913·2	56·5	39·2
Environment	11·4	10·7	6·7	374·7	11·1	7·7
Health and Social Services	9·3	8·7	5·6	322·0	9·5	6·6
Protective Services	6·8	6·4	4·0	232·7	6·9	4·7
Highways	10·0	9·4	5·9	248·7	7·3	5·1
Miscellaneous	9·0	8·5	5·4	293·3	8·7	6·0
Total	**106·3**	**100·0**	**63·2**	**3,384·6**	**100·0**	**69·3**

Source: DOE Finance Division

private sector. This suggests that some growth in public investment may be necessary in the future to ensure that the future capacity of infrastructure and services keeps pace with growth;

(c) central government's current expenditure in East Anglia is probably marginally above the national average per capita level but its changing scale and impacts are largely unknown;

(d) capital expenditure by central government and public corporations in East Anglia is comparable with the national average, although this may be the temporary result of recent major investment in natural gas rather than a permanent feature;

(e) the rate income of local government in East Anglia is lower than average, with a consequently higher level of dependence on central government sources of finance;

(f) the capital expenditure of local government, excluding land costs, is close to the national per capita average, and does not appear to match the rapid growth in population;

(g) the annual level of capital expenditure by local government is more unstable than the national level, with some possibility that the region is vulnerable to the central government's short-term management of the national economy through public expenditure;

(h) the level of current expenditure by local government in East Anglia is, on a per capita basis, lower than that of all other regions in England and Wales.

15.7.2 There are many possible explanations for the conclusions set out in the previous paragraph. One obvious source can be found in the basic characteristics of the region. It has a low population density, without any major concentration of population and employment. This is allied to an accelerating rate of growth, after a long period of stagnation. Both of these factors suggest that the region as a whole has had difficulty in adjusting the level of public expenditure to the increasing demands generated by growth in the private sector. Most capital projects in the public sector are, by their very nature, realised in large units. These require a corresponding level of estimated demand to justify them. The scale of these projects also means that they take a considerable time to prepare and construct. Three important consequences flow from this. Firstly, the levels of demand required to justify such projects are likely to be found in areas of high population densities—areas where demands are concentrated. In these terms East Anglia is unlikely to receive the level of capital investment which would be undertaken in an 'urban' region with a similar population. Secondly, the period required to plan and commission such projects means that they are based on forecasts of future demand rather than current experience. Once again, in areas such as East Anglia where growth has been accelerating there are likely to be considerable lags before the programme of capital expenditure responds to recent experience. Thirdly, those capital projects which are likely to be justified in an area of low population density will probably be smaller than average. This could mean that they are more susceptible to cut backs when national circumstances require restraint on public expenditure, though the evidence for this is not clear. On these counts, therefore, the recent level of capital investment by the public sector in East Anglia is likely to have been lower than expectations. Similarly, levels of current expenditure may in turn be affected, reinforced by the lower expectations of standards of services that have been held by a rural population, and by the importance of agriculture in the regional economy.

15.7.3 With this basis, it is possible to begin the process of considering the likely implications for financial resources of the future development of the region. There are few guidelines or precedents for this task, and for this reason it is useful to explain briefly the approach we have taken. The degree of uncertainty that must exist about the future scale and composition of growth and change in the region makes it impracticable to attempt to place a price on the changes we expect, or our proposals for modifying them. The conclusions presented elsewhere in this report consist of strategic principles, supported by rather more specific proposals. To have gone further—to have produced neatly framed investment projects which can be assessed on current investment criteria—would have required a degree of precision which we could not support. It could, in fact, be positively misleading as an indication of the results which emerge from this work.

15.7.4 In these circumstances, there are a number of questions which it is relevant to ask and for which it is possible to attempt an answer. These are:

(a) will the overall level of financial resources in the future be likely to be sufficient to meet the expected demands upon them?

(b) what qualities are required of the public expenditure system to make it capable of dealing with competing priorities within a region such as East Anglia?

(c) what changes in the present system would help in producing these qualities?

(d) what shifts in public expenditure are implied by the contents of the remainder of this report?

These questions have been reflected in the preceding analysis of recent and present expenditure patterns, where we have been attempting to identify structural or long-run characteristics in this pattern. The analysis provides the basis both for identifying major constraints, and for attempting to sketch the broad outlines of the future position.

15.7.5 The most direct way of answering these questions is by producing long-term forecasts of the overall level and composition of future financial resources. There are considerable difficulties attached to this, the most important of which is the inadequacy of information about past expenditure. In practice, this has meant that our attempt to forecast future levels of financial resources has had to be limited to the local authority sector. It also explains the priority we attach to research in the immediate future on the levels and impacts of expenditure by central government and other public corporations. The second difficulty is the degree of uncertainty which must attend such forecasts. This in itself does not invalidate the principle of making forecasts, but necessitates that our approach should be to identify and narrow, as far as the evidence will support, the bounds of possibility, rather than produce a single figure forecast. Thus the forecasts made here are indicative rather than precise instruments on which future plans can be made with complete assurance. Finally, the approach rests on the interrelationship between different levels of planning activity in the hierarchy. The premise is that this intermediate level of analysis can be beneficial to both central and local government. At this stage of development, however, benefits may lie more in the demonstration of potential from efforts to improve the flow of information rather than the somewhat tentative results gained from the material at present available.

15.8 The Scale of Future Financial Resources

15.8.1 The first question, on the overall scale of future financial resources, can be considered on two levels. Firstly, it can be approached directly by attempts at forecasting, and this is done for the local authority sector in later paragraphs. Prior to this, however, the impossibility of approaching the question as directly for other sectors of public expenditure means that it must be considered in more qualitative terms. Over the period of the preparation of this report, views expressed on the growth of financial resources in the public sector have varied widely, perhaps indicative of a structural change in the situation. On the other hand, the long-run tendencies in the rate of growth of GNP have been reasonably steady. Between 1955 and 1971, GNP increased in real terms by an average of $2\frac{1}{2}\%$ to 3% per annum, and there are indications on a longer timescale that the rate will increase slowly. The results of the context studies, set out in chapter four, tend to confirm this. Similarly, public expenditure as a whole has grown in the post-war period at a faster rate than has GNP, but there are indications that this trend may not continue. The demands for services, provided as a result of public expenditure, may be counterbalanced by the use of the overall level of such expenditure as an instrument of demand management in the national economy. We have, therefore, assumed that the long-run growth rate of public expenditure will be 3% per annum, reflecting actual variations between 2% and 6%, and the continued growth of GNP described above.

15.8.2 The breakdown of public expenditure into its components at national level gives some indication as to future levels in the region. Between 1955 and 1970 these components have grown at different rates. The major growth has been in the field of subsidies, grants, and net lending from the public to the private sector—nearly 6% per annum, on average, compared with 2·3% for expenditure on goods and services. With the increasing concern of government for national and regional standards and equality, and the redistribution of wealth between sectors and areas, a high growth rate may be expected to continue. Public sector capital expenditure has also shown a relatively large long-term increase of nearly $4\frac{1}{2}$% per annum, of which the larger part has been accounted for by central government, with a growth rate of 7·9% per annum compared to local authorities' 4·3% per annum. Given the increasing investment requirement for many public services, public capital expenditure is likely to continue at a fairly high level. Within East Anglia the apparent lag in the level of capital investment by the public sector, in response to the growth of the private sector, could imply that the region will see rather faster growth than the nation as a whole. This growth in capital investment may be subject, however, to rather wide fluctuations in level. This is because, on current procedure, there are difficulties in reaching levels of demand to justify projects.

15.8.3 Public sector current expenditure, compared with capital expenditure, has had a much slower long-term growth rate ($1\frac{1}{2}$% per annum 1955-1970), though it is much larger in absolute terms. It is likely to continue to grow at a slightly lower rate than that of total public expenditure, and whilst partially dependent upon the rate of growth of capital expenditure (because it implies running costs and maintenance), it will generally be less volatile. Much of central government's current expenditure is in the form of transfer payments, and is determined by the characteristics of the population, e.g. unemployed, sick, elderly, etc. Consequently East Anglia can again expect a steadily increasing level of such expenditure, with perhaps the greatest increase resulting from the growing proportion of the elderly in the region's population.

15.8.4 For the overall level of expenditure by local authorities we have been able to construct some indicative forecasts. One of the major explanatory factors in the inter-regional distribution of expenditure by local authorities is the number of people for whom local government is providing services. The rapid growth of the population in the region can be expected to involve at least an equivalent increase in expenditure by the public sector. This is, however, too simple for anything more than an extremely crude forecast, and we have, therefore, attempted to explain, by regression analysis, why the level of per capita expenditure on individual services varies from one region to another. The results obtained on the basis of eight regions pose some problems of interpretation, as the variables used can act as proxies for a variety of components of the regional situation. Generally, however, the degree of explanation is better for revenue than for capital expenditure, as might be expected. The application of the results to the mid-point of the range of the forecasts of the region's future population, given in chapter six, gives the results shown in Figure 15.17. This shows the level of expenditure required to maintain services at the present standard, on the basis of forecast population growth.

Figure 15.17

Estimated annual expenditure levels required to maintain current standards of local authority services in East Anglia

	1971 £m	1981 £m	1991 £m
Capital			
Education	9·1	10·4	11·7
Housing	20·0	22·1	26·9
Environment	12·9	14·2	15·1
Highways	6·4	6·8	8·1
Miscellaneous	10·1	17·7	20·0
Total	**58·5**	**71·2**	**81·8**
Revenue			
Education	59·9	68·5	78·0
Environment	8·8	10·4	12·5
Health and Social Services	9·4	10·9	12·5
Protective	6·7	8·0	9·0
Roads	10·1	11·0	11·0
Miscellaneous	11·5	12·6	15·1
Total	**106·4**	**121·4**	**138·1**
Total (Revenue and Capital)	**164·9**	**192·6**	**219·9**

N.B. programme definitions under capital and current expenditure headings are not synonymous.

Source: East Anglia Regional Strategy Team

15.8.5 The forecasts in Figure 15.17 give an overall growth rate of approximately 1·5% per annum, with capital expenditure growing at a slightly higher rate than that of revenue expenditure. The individual components of the forecasts are more debatable, and are not to be interpreted, in any literal sense, as precise levels for those services in the future. They assume that the standards achieved in each service are uniform between regions, and that the quality of the stock of social capital does not vary. To cope with these difficulties, the cross-sectional data for the eight regions was re-examined to provide maximum and minimum levels of expenditure per capita. These have been applied to the forecast of population growth in the region to produce the range of expenditure set out in Figure 15.18.

15.8.6 As a check on these forecasts, using cross-sectional material from other regions, estimates have been made of the annual level of future local authority expenditure, on the assumptions of long-run growth rates of 2, 3 and 5% per head per year. The estimates which result are shown in Figure 15.19 in comparison with the overall levels of local authority expenditure forecast by the earlier methods. The comparison indicates that an annual rate of growth per head of slightly over 2% at constant prices would enable East Anglia to reach the present maximum levels of expenditure of any other region by 1981. By 1991, the same rate of 2% growth

Figure 15.18
Estimated annual expenditure levels required to achieve regional minimum and maximum standards of local authority services in East Anglia

| | 1981 | | 1991 | |
	Min. £m	Max. £m	Min. £m	Max. £m
Capital				
Education	9·2	12·1	10·3	13·6
Housing	16·3	36·6	18·3	41·2
Environment	8·6	14·8	9·7	16·6
Highways	5·9	12·3	6·7	13·8
Miscellaneous	8·6	15·1	9·7	17·0
Total	*48·6*	*90·9*	*54·7*	*102·2*
Revenue				
Education	68·3	80·0	76·7	89·9
Environment	7·3	12·3	8·2	13·8
Health and Social Services	10·7	14·4	12·1	16·2
Protective	7·1	10·5	8·0	11·9
Roads	8·2	13·2	9·3	14·7
Miscellaneous	12·6	16·1	14·2	18·1
Total	*114·2*	*146·5*	*128·5*	*164·6*
Total (Revenue and Capital)	162·8	237·4	183·2	266·8

Source: East Anglia Regional Strategy Team

would produce an increase of 42% on current levels of expenditure by local authorities in East Anglia. These results suggest that, even with relatively slower rates of growth than those experienced in the past, there are likely to be considerable additional resources available for use by local authorities.

15.8.7 This conclusion has to be modified, however, on a number of grounds. A high proportion of the real costs of providing local government services is

Figure 15.19
Comparison of different forecasts of overall annual levels of local authority expenditure

	1981 £m	1991 £m
Minimum standards (Fig. 15.18)	162·8	183·2
Current standards (Fig. 15.17)	192·6	219·9
Maximum standards (Fig. 15.18)	237·4	266·8
Growth at A) 2%	229·3	314·2
B) 3%	252·7	381·9
C) 5%	306·4	560·9

Source: East Anglia Regional Strategy Team

made up of labour costs. These seem likely to increase faster in relative terms than do other costs, with few opportunities for economies from the substitution of capital for labour. A further reservation is created by the evidence that past expenditure by the public sector has responded only sluggishly to investment by the private sector. There are indications in present programmes of expenditure on highways, and particularly on sewerage to keep pace with housing development, that the region is changing gear in this respect. If this is so, East Anglia may be in the earlier stages of a phase of increased expenditure on infrastructure as a lagged response to earlier private investment. This could mean that past levels of public expenditure will not be typical of future levels, though national circumstances may not permit the region to catch up in this way for some time. On this somewhat conjectural basis, it may be some time—possibly the nineteen eighties—before changes in priorities beyond these requirements for infrastructure can be achieved through the flexibility provided by the increasing level of financial resources available. This makes it even more important to adopt, as quickly as possible, those styles of managing public expenditure which help to ensure that the resources which are available are spent to good effect.

15.9 Future Requirements for Public Expenditure

15.9.1 It is not possible to go further and attempt to draw up any useful estimate of the overall level, and detailed breakdown, of future public expenditure in East Anglia which would be required to support the content of the remainder of this report. Much more detailed information would be required about current levels of expenditure, and there would be many reservations about the necessarily large number of assumptions. In practice, the overall level of financial resources available to the public sector in the region will be mainly determined by the long-term progress of the national economy. Even with the most favourable rate of progress, however, it is impossible to foresee a future situation when financial resources will not be scarce, or apparently inadequate, to meet the potential demands upon them. Present indications are that this scarcity is being reinforced by the tendency for such demands to increase faster than financial resources, as a result both of legislation and the tide of rising public expectations. The consequence is that less emphasis has to be placed on the overall level of resource, and rather more on the priorities to be achieved, within whatever level of financial resources can be made available.

15.9.2. Within this perspective, the priorities suggested in this report can be stated. Before doing so, however, it has to be recognised that this suggested set of priorities is not universal. Circumstances will alter, leading to adjustments to our conclusions. There is more strategic significance, therefore, in ensuring that methods of allocating public expenditure have the required capacity to cope with, and respond to, competing and changing priorities than in seeking only the more straightforward adoption of the set of priorities we suggest. For this reason, the next step is to consider the degree to which the present public expenditure system possesses this kind of capacity.

15.9.3 Both the composition and the level of public expenditure in East Anglia are largely determined at national level by central government. To avoid overlap, this expenditure is organised as a set of separately conceived programmes on a departmental basis. As a result, the overall level of such expenditure in East Anglia is an amalgam of the incidence of these separate programmes rather than a deliberate allocation adjusted to the particular circumstances of the region. There are considerable difficulties in relating these national programmes to a region such as East Anglia. Its low population density and absence of major urban concentrations do not match the national situation, which is coloured by the high proportion of people who live in urban areas. This makes it difficult to reach the specific levels of demand required to justify individual capital projects within particular expenditure programmes. Consequently, the capital expenditure which does occur tends to favour those areas experiencing pressures for growth, and to reinforce those pressures, to the continuing disadvantage of those areas in a more static condition. Similarly, the acceleration in the rate of growth of East Anglia does not seem to have been recognised in the level and type of expenditure. Finally, the increasing use of public expenditure as an instrument in the management of the national economy serves to accentuate, at local level, the apparently arbitrary nature of expenditure programmes.

15.9.4 What qualities are required to make the public expenditure system more capable of dealing with competing priorities in a region such as East Anglia? Perhaps the most obvious, and the most difficult, quality as this report demonstrates, is to make the nature of the competition between priorities more explicit. There is little agreement in many fields of expenditure about the nature of the direct outputs to be gained. This makes it even more difficult to assess the relative contribution which proposed expenditure in any of these fields would make to common goals. It would be unrealistic to imagine that these difficulties of securing some objective measures of cost-effectiveness can be overcome even in the long-term. Efforts in this direction through the adoption of more corporate styles of managing public expenditure would assist, but are unlikely to provide more than a partial answer.

15.9.5 A different approach to this question may be through a recognition that competing priorities make themselves evident at different levels—national, regional and local. This is a feature we have come to respect in this report, as we have been in contact with both the national and local levels, and it has been a strong influence on the expression of our conclusions. In the absence, and perhaps the impossibility, therefore, of any totally objective and foolproof methods of resolving competing demands, we would place the emphasis on giving each of these levels a role in this process. By establishing bodies at each level charged with recognising competing priorities, and formally making adjustments to public expenditure, the matching of financial resources to regional and local priorities could be made more effective. A by-product

would be the stimulus to better flows of information. At national level, there should be benefits from the attention given to competing priorities for financial resources rather than to claims for increasing their amount, and to improved understanding of the effects to be gained from their use in different circumstances. It could also make the process of absorbing periodic cutbacks in public expenditure less harmful, without necessarily adding to the delay before they take effect.

15.9.6 The adoption of such a system would also assist in providing some measure of the flexibility which is required in the public expenditure system. Not only must there be uncertainty about future demands for financial resources, but the use of public expenditure as an economic regulator has produced more uncertainty about the short-term supply of these resources. This indicates that the system has to have the capacity for rapid adjustment to changes both in supply and demand. What does this imply? Firstly, a greater degree of potential adjustment and interchange between capital and current expenditure, and between spending programmes at a more local level, would be an advantage. Secondly, a reserve capacity, at regional level, could help to ensure that the region, or more local areas, were shielded from major dislocations in external sources of expenditure. Finally, a capacity to undertake experimental or innovatory programmes of expenditure, to gauge their effects, would assist in matching resources more closely to needs.

15.9.7 On this basis, it is possible to indicate some broad strategic principles for developing methods of allocating financial resources to and within East Anglia:

F2 the public expenditure system should have a capacity for recognising and resolving competing priorities, within whatever level of financial resources can be made available;

F3 the adoption of more corporate styles of management of public expenditure at regional and local levels should be encouraged;

F4 both regional and local levels should be given more formal roles in the recognition of competing priorities and in making consequent adjustments to the allocation of public expenditure;

F5 further flexibility in the public expenditure system should be encouraged by greater capacity for interchange between capital and current expenditure, and between spending programmes, for reserve funds, and for experimental programmes.

15.10 The Mechanics of Public Expenditure

15.10.1 At this point it is useful to illustrate these broad strategic principles in terms of the present mechanisms employed to allocate public expenditure. This appears to present a difficult choice. At first sight, it would seem most valuable to attempt to establish what short-term and relatively marginal changes to the present system would be feasible in order to move it in the directions indicated by the principles. It is evident, however, that at the present time a large number of such changes are either taking place or under consideration, and this approach would invite quick obsolescence. We consider it more important, therefore, to look at the long-term structure, and attempt to identify those changes which would be more significant to the strategic perspective adopted for this report. Even so, we have limited this attempt by assuming that no new local sources of income will be introduced to markedly affect the financial dependence of local government upon central government. In this way, it may be possible to establish some markers from the East Anglian situation, to be taken into consideration at those times when the system comes under review.

15.10.2 The first set of mechanisms to be considered are those that determine the level and composition of capital expenditure by the public sector. We have noted above several important consequences of these mechanisms. The level of capital expenditure per head in East Anglia is likely to continue to be lower than the region's rate of growth would appear to imply. Its basic nature will reduce the likelihood that individual projects will reach the levels of expected demand required to justify them. This does not necessarily mean, in turn, that there should be some compensating adjustment so that a regional share of national capital expenditure is achieved. This would be unlikely to lead to the effective use of scarce financial resources. It does seem to indicate, however, that capital expenditure is relatively less important in a rural region like East Anglia, and current expenditure relatively more important. There are some grounds, therefore, for considering methods of compensating the long-run disadvantages of East Anglia in capital expenditure terms, by appropriate upward adjustments to the level of current expenditure. This will be returned to later when local government current expenditure is considered.

15.10.3 A second feature of the mechanics of capital expenditure determination is the nature of the appraisal methods used within each spending programme to decide whether or not individual projects will receive priority for expenditure. Not only do these methods vary widely in the 'hardness' or 'softness' of the criteria they apply, but in most cases the criteria are orientated only to the individual spending programme, with little reference to their wider and secondary effects on more fundamental social goals. This makes it impossible to make objective comparisons of the relative priorities given to projects in different spending programmes, or to assess the social and long-run costs inherent within them. We do not think that this can be fully resolved by attempts to widen the criteria used, and partial efforts to do so could obscure the clarity of spending programmes set up for specific action, directed towards, for example, transport objectives or educational objectives. The case for bridging agencies to reconcile the operations of such executive agencies was discussed in chapter fourteen. The conclusion reached there was that such agencies should be given some formal power of adjudication, and sanction, on the question of the wider social and long-run costs of spending programmes of executive agencies.

15.10.4 Turning to the question of current expenditure, it is possible to consider only the local government side. This requires consideration, firstly of the rate support grant, and the rating system itself. Each of the three elements making up the rate support grant has a discriminatory or redistributive function between different areas or different occupiers of property, which at present is largely determined by central government. The national criteria used in this determination are unlikely to reflect East Anglian priorities, because of its very different circumstances. This suggests that some intermediate level of determination might be considered. To see how this might operate it is useful to consider more closely the attributes of each element.

15.10.5 The 'needs' and 'resources' elements discriminate between areas on the basis of clearly defined criteria. The 'needs' element is clearly the more flexible of the two in the way in which it combines both attributes of the population, and weighting factors to those attributes which attempt to recognise their potential calls on public expenditure. The weighting factors used are based, however, on past experience of public expenditure rather than on decisions about the future priorities to be represented in expenditure. The attributes, themselves, have been expressed in terms of absolute quantities rather than as differences from the national average. Areas with either higher or lower population densities than the national average are likely to experience greater costs, and the same would be true of disproportionate numbers of elderly or school children in the population.

15.10.6 The 'resources' element is also redistributive between areas, but it is calculated from the rateable value per head of population. This has the disadvantage that rateable values are only reviewed periodically, and is, therefore, a base which does not take account of inflation or rapid changes in values. More significant, however, may be the indications that the redistribution which is brought about is fairly insensitive. The analysis presented earlier in the chapter showed that the 'resources' element favoured the eastern half of the region, and detailed evidence suggests that it favours rural, rather than urban, authorities within East Anglia. In these terms, therefore, the 'resources' element appears to achieve some of the redistribution of financial resources implied by the conclusions of Sections C and D. This may be counterbalanced, however, by the failure we experienced in attempting to correlate the general levels of rateable value per head in different parts of the region with other characteristics of the population or building stock. Our reluctant conclusion is that rateable values are a much more useful measure of variations locally than they are at regional or national level. For this reason, their use as an instrument for the redistribution of financial resources on any scale must be blunt and of limited effectiveness.

15.10.7 The final element in the rate support grant is the 'domestic' element, which discriminates in favour of residential occupiers. The converse of this is that the discretion of local authorities is limited to deciding what overall level of rate to fix each year, without any similar power to discriminate between types of users of property or between areas. Thus the 'domestic' element is, in principle, a national tax on different types of property. This has a differential effect on regions and on areas within regions because of the varying mix of types of property and the absence of rating on agriculture, one of East Anglia's main industries.

15.10.8 There is considerable scope in the longer-term for modifying the rate support grant system in the direction of the principles set out earlier in this chapter. The first possibility takes up the point made earlier, on the potential for adjusting levels of current expenditure to compensate for disadvantages in the level of capital expenditure that can be realised. It would be possible to subdivide the global total allocated at national level to the rate support grant, on a regional basis. This would give scope, at the regional level itself, for bridging agencies, including local government participants, to allocate the regional total in accordance with regional priorities. The second possibility comes from the application of the three elements to make the allocation closer to regional and local priorities. The present division into three elements is both cumbersome and not clearly understood at large. We consider that the resource element is both inflexible and arbitrary in redistributing resources. There are better comparative indices available of the condition of building stock and infrastructure. Use of such indices would allow the needs element to be expanded to cover both human and physical needs. The essential addition to this is that the relative weightings of all the attributes adopted as needs should be based on a view of relative priorities to be achieved. We consider it much more likely that this can be done at regional level than at national level, where it has been necessary to rely largely on past experience. Finally, the domestic element could be reconsidered. In effect, as a tax on different categories of property, it could be a useful support to strategic planning policies if its level of determination was devolved to regional level. There may be more awareness at this level of the benefits to be gained than appears, at present, in the apparent national discrimination against those sectors of the economy providing employment. Promotion of industry and commerce, and the favouring of more concentrated forms of development associated with public transport systems in rural areas, could be encouraged by these means.

15.10.9 We have referred both in this chapter and in chapter fourteen to the concept of a regional development fund. This has been discussed in terms of a mechanism which would reflect the social costs of expenditure programmes, where they were unable to take full account of the longer-term strategic implications of that expenditure. This presumes that appropriate mechanisms could be made available to allow the resulting income to be transferred to other spending programmes. It would also allow the region to possess a reserve capacity to mitigate the full effect of changes from outside, for example if the Greater London Council or central government withdrew support from the town expansion programme. Experimental projects or programmes would also be an element, either by direct funding or by specific grants and subsidies to other agencies. What may be difficult, however, in practice, would be

to ensure that the operation of the fund is linked to a wide discretion in its use. In present circumstances, the 'ultra vires' rule requires that public bodies can only act in ways in which they are empowered to do so by statute, and it is also not usual for a body to have powers to act in fields where other public bodies are already empowered. Realisation of the bridging, and discretionary, nature of the fund and agency operating it, could only be achieved if one or both of these conditions were relaxed. We have not attempted, therefore, to produce a blueprint or exhaustive list of provisions for such a fund, as we are not satisfied that to do so would help the system of public expenditure to meet the requirements set out above. The real requirement is for further experiments with regional institutions that combine the accountability of public bodies, and some of the freedom of action available to the private sector.

15.11 Shifts in Regional Expenditure Priorities

15.11.1 In this part of the chapter we return to the priorities for public expenditure which are indicated by the remainder of the report. We do so in the difficult condition of being unsure of what overall level of financial resources is likely to be appropriate in the future. East Anglia may be faced with a period of much heavier public investment on infrastructure, perhaps for the next decade, in response to the rapid growth it has already experienced, and which is expected to continue. How quickly national circumstances will allow this investment to be realised is uncertain, and restraints on the overall growth of public expenditure may make it difficult to realise other shifts in priorities. The result could be that much greater efforts may be required even to maintain current standards in services provided by the public sector.

15.11.2 This outlook makes it difficult to establish a firm yardstick on which to base the priorities we suggest. It seems unlikely that any type of expenditure will decrease significantly in real terms if the expected growth in the population is to be supported. We are, therefore, attempting to identify those types of expenditure which are likely to claim higher or lower proportions of overall expenditure in the future. Yet if investment in infrastructure does show a major increase, it could well be that other spending programmes will not maintain their current proportions. In this perspective, three general types of shifts in expenditure can be considered. The first is the question of changing priorities between different areas of the region. A second is the changes in priorities given to different expenditure programmes and within programmes. The third is the extent to which these priorities will change over time.

15.11.3 The first set of possible shifts in priorities can be illustrated by considering the conclusions of Section C. They indicated that the south and west of the region, together with the main urban centres, would continue to grow faster than the region as a whole. The main thrust of the strategic principles for the location of development is to redress, in part, the increase in disparities that would result from this. This means, in effect, the selection of policies which favour growth to the north and east, and in the centre of the region, along with the development of secondary centres to assist the rural areas. In expenditure terms, the corresponding conclusions are complex. Firstly, we expect the south and west of the region, together with the main centres, to claim an increasing proportion of the region's overall financial resources, simply to keep pace with the growth which will take place in these areas under any circumstances. There are indications, however, that the per capita incidence of public expenditure in these areas is considerably higher than that in the remainder of the region, as suggested in Section D. On this basis, the outcome of the strategic principles for the location of development is that in the north, east and centre of the region, and particularly in the rural areas, the per capita level of public expenditure should grow faster than in other areas, both in absolute and in proportional, terms. This type of measure will be an important part of the kind of monitoring process discussed in the next chapter, as an indicator of whether or not the strategic principles are being applied, though it will not, of course, indicate whether that experience is effective.

15.11.4 The second arena for shifts in expenditure priorities is that between and within spending programmes. There are particular difficulties in this field, both in attempting to adjudicate between programmes and in determining in some cases the role to be played by the public sector. The latter point can be exemplified by housing expenditure. In the last decade East Anglia has mirrored national trends, and the public sector has been responsible for a decreasing number of completed homes, with the proportion of financial resources given to the housing programme declining even faster than the national average. The actual circumstances of East Anglia would indicate the need for some reversal of these trends. The proportion of local authority housing is much lower than the national situation, and it has a housing market in which the difficulties of new households in obtaining a house are frequently much greater than they are nationally. On these grounds, we are led to conclude that the housing pressures within the region are likely to dictate that the proportion of public expenditure claimed by housing will increase in the future. If this does happen, other benefits could accrue. It could help to redirect additional resources towards the north and east, and assist in realising the economies to be gained from more concentrated forms of development in secondary centres and selected small towns, in association with public transport.

15.11.5 Some further shifts in expenditure priorities are likely to arise from what we have been able to deduce about changes in the age structure of the region's population. These can be most clearly illustrated for children under fifteen and people over sixty-five, with most effect respectively on expenditure on education and on the health and social services. Population growth in recent years has led to an increase in the proportion of children in the population, and this seems likely to continue during the seventies as growth accelerates. During the eighties, the proportion of children is expected to stabilise, as the earlier migrants reach older age groups. In the next decade, therefore, we expect to see both capital and current expenditure on school

provision concentrated in and around the major centres and the areas of planned migration. For this reason, we have put forward for consideration a system of supplementary grants designed to assist those areas unlikely to experience substantial population growth, and whose buildings are most in need of replacement. Nevertheless, major opportunities for the transfer of resources in this way will come only when the proportion of school-children stabilises. In the future, some economies could be sought in these heavy expenditure claims by meeting changing and uncertain needs through the use of more flexible forms of provision.

15.11.6 The proportion of the region's population which is over sixty-five is expected to be at its highest in the eighties. This will add to the increasingly heavy demands for expenditure on services for the elderly. At present, the demands on the social services are increasing rapidly, and we expect this to continue, with no clear indication of what the saturation level could be. On this basis, we think that expenditure on these services could grow faster than the norm, merely to maintain present levels of service. Above that level there will continue to be pressures to meet more of the unsatisfied demand. This will place more emphasis on deciding priorities and on attempts to alleviate these demands by attention to preventive measures in other fields, such as housing.

15.11.7 A further area of choice between programmes comes in transportation. We came to the conclusion in chapters eight and nine that the priority given to public transport should be increased. This undoubtedly means that its claims on public expenditure would rise substantially. At the same time, as explained earlier, the present programme of expenditure on improvements to strategic roads would seem to be justified as part of the infrastructure investment required to catch up with earlier investment in the private sector. There will, however, be some scope for extending this programme over a longer timescale. This could assist both in giving added support for public transport, and for introducing, somewhat earlier, the shift we propose towards routes distributing traffic within the region. This part of the region's infrastructure will come under increasing pressure, and routes designed more closely to the needs of industrial and recreational traffic will need to be prepared. In the longer term, the achievement of a strengthened public transport system, and an overall network of routes to a reasonable standard across the region, could allow transport expenditure to be stabilised, and perhaps reduced, as a proportion of total public expenditure.

15.11.8 Finally, in chapter thirteen, from our examination of the environmental resources of East Anglia, we concluded that there were no grounds for complacency in this field of expenditure. The rapid growth of the region, and the speed at which change is occurring, means that many of those assets which make the region attractive and which bring economic benefits could be swept away. For the future prosperity and quality of life in East Anglia, therefore, much more positive management of environmental resources will be required. This applies not only to the urban areas, where conservation

141

policies have had some success, but also to the rural areas, landscape and ecology. Much of this management can be achieved through the private sector, though it will require the public sector to take a leading role. This, too, will make a claim for additional financial resources, and one which we consider to be justified, if just for the significance of East Anglia's environment in attracting firms and workers in the post-war period.

15.11.9 The results of this examination of changing priorities for public expenditure tends to confirm the earlier diagnosis. The rapid rate of growth of the region appears likely to be producing, and to require, a change in gear in the level of public expenditure which accompanies and supports it. We have found it difficult to identify expenditure programmes which will not make additional claims on resources. Some marginal economies are possible, for example, in the costly provision of sewerage to rural areas, but these are unlikely to be significant. Part of the problem arises from the absence of methods to compare the effectiveness of expenditure in different programmes. Is more investment in housing to be preferred to more investment in hospitals, or roads, or in the environment? If we are forced to make such choices, it must inevitably be on subjective grounds and acknowledged to be such. Our view of the dynamics of the East Anglian situation suggests that we would hold back, to some degree, on capital investment into infrastructure likely to take place in response to previous private investment. This capital investment not only caters for existing demands, but also creates additional spare capacity attracting further private investment. By this process, the advantages of the areas growing rapidly are reinforced, to the disadvantage of those which are less favoured. A degree of caution, therefore, in the rush to cope with frustrated demand in the favoured areas should enable growth to be achieved more steadily, and spread more equitably, across the region. A more measured approach of this nature could ensure that East Anglia remains a pleasant place in which to live and work, even during a period of growth faster than it has experienced before.

15.12 Conclusions

15.12.1 In the two previous parts of this chapter we have attempted to consider the ways in which the strategic principles set out in paragraph 15.9.7 could be translated into practical form. All that remains for this concluding part of the chapter, therefore, is to express the results as a more formal set of proposals.

15.12.2 On the basis set out in 15.10, we put forward the following possibilities for consideration at those times when the mechanics of the public expenditure system is under review:

(vi) *the provision to an appropriate regional agency, of formal powers of adjudication and corresponding financial sanctions, recognising the wider social and long run costs involved in the spending programmes designed to meet the more specific objectives of executive agencies;*

(vii) *the introduction of a two-tier system determining the distribution of the rate support grant, i.e.*

(a) *an initial determination of the regional distribution which recognises the differential claims of regions on capital and current expenditure;*

(b) *a second level of determination of its distribution within regions by an appropriate regional agency to secure improved recognition of regional and local priorities;*

(viii) *within the rate support grant itself, the progressive elimination of the resource element in favour of the needs element, extended to cover building stock and based on priorities to be achieved in the future;*

(ix) *the reconsideration of the domestic element, to transform it into a variable property tax to support strategic planning policies at the regional level.*

15.12.3 More particularly, we have considered in 15.11 those shifts in public expenditure priorities which would reflect the strategic principles and proposals set out in the remainder of the report. These shifts have to be seen, and understood, within the general context of the changing priorities resulting from developments that are largely outside the influence of strategic policies. They are further compounded by the inherent difficulties in comparing the benefits obtained by different types of expenditure. On this basis, the following shifts in priorities seem to be indicated:

(x) *a faster rate of growth of public expenditure per head in the north, east, and centre of the region, and particularly in the rural areas, than in the south and west, and around the major centres;*

(xi) *an increase in the proportion of public expenditure allocated to housing programmes;*

(xii) *a gradual shift in emphasis in education expenditure towards those areas unlikely to experience substantial population growth, and with the most urgent need for replacement of existing buildings, possibly aided by supplementary grants and more flexible forms of provision;*

(xiii) *a shift within expenditure on health and social services towards more preventive measures, together with improved methods of establishing priorities;*

(xiv) *an increase in priority for expenditure on public transport, together with a shift towards expenditure on the internal road network of the region in the longer term;*

(xv) *the growth of expenditure to support the positive management of the environmental resources of the region, particularly in the rural areas;*

(xvi) *the exercise of some degree of restraint on capital expenditure on infrastructure in areas of rapid growth, with corresponding favouring of investment and current expenditure in the remaining areas of the region.*

Chapter 16

The Continuous Planning Process

16.1 Introduction

16.1.1 The conclusions we have reached about the future of East Anglia are set out in the earlier chapters of this report. At each step, we have attempted to present the main lines of reasoning that lie behind these conclusions. In part this approach has had to be taken, because in present circumstances forward planning at the regional level achieves its main effects by persuasion. The degree to which the basis of our conclusions is both understood and taken into account by those taking decisions about the region in the future, could be much more significant than the formal acceptance of these conclusions.

16.1.2 There is another reason, however, for taking this approach. No report such as this is ever totally complete. The information which is available about the past and the present is patchy and varies in quality. Further information about the region and its context constantly becomes available. Even where it is to hand, and of good quality, there are often several possible explanations of the bare statistics, making the projection of the future a hazardous operation. In any event, the future rarely turns out in practice to be a straightforward extension of past experience. Even the most stable trends can be undermined by such uncertainty. Past projections of car ownership, for example, now look very doubtful. Population projections change every year. The more subjective aspects of the work are equally problematical. The objectives listed in chapter two have been used at each stage to assist in coming to conclusions. The value judgments we have used in placing emphasis on objectives may or may not approximate to either present or future values held in the region.

16.1.3 These reservations in themselves do not constitute a valid argument against the principle of strategic planning at this, or any other level. They do, however, have at least two strong implications for the form it should take. The first of these is that uncertainty about the future means that the temptation to produce precise blueprints has to be avoided. This goes against the common image of a plan, expressed as apparently cut-and-dried population levels, numbers of houses and jobs required, etc. In this report we have attempted to recognise uncertainty by expressing forecasts in terms of ranges, and expressing conclusions as strategic principles and proposals. By so doing, it is hoped that the principles will retain their relevance to decision-making into the longer-term, with the proposals stimulating the tactical execution of these principles in the shorter-term.

16.1.4 The second implication for the form of forward planning is that a report like this has to be viewed as part of a stream of continuing planning activity. The process includes not only further work at the regional level, but also a continuous dialogue with equivalent work at national and local levels. In this way, further information, the results of research, and changing circumstances at other levels, can be drawn into the work to best effect.

16.2 Monitoring

16.2.1 The recognition that this report is only part of a continuous planning process does not necessarily mean that an equivalent amount of detailed work must follow. The momentum established can be taken forward by a period spent monitoring results. The concern of this monitoring process is with the question, 'is the future development of the region on course?' The answer requires the determination of whether or not the objectives for the region are being achieved in terms of the strategic principles and proposals. In turn, this concern can be broken down into several more specific questions:

(a) have decisions about the future of the region followed the principles set out?

(b) have the policies and proposals been more or less effective than was expected?

(c) have any unexpected factors influenced the situation?

(d) have the assumptions made about external factors proved to be valid?

and

(e) what improvements can be made to either the conclusions or the methods of monitoring?

16.2.2 These questions help to define both the work and the organisation required for monitoring. The first question requires knowledge of the major decisions concerning the future of the region. For the answers to be of use, the monitoring process must be closely associated with a body providing a bridge between the major executive and decision-taking agencies in the region. This suggests that it should be part of the secretariat or intelligence unit attached to the form of agency proposed in the conclusions of chapter fourteen. In this position, commentaries on this question could be effectively prepared, perhaps in the form of annual reports.

16.2.3 The second question may be more taxing in terms of the work required. For the effectiveness of policies and proposals to be assessed, a series of performance measures directly related to the objectives will be required. The difficulties of achieving this are demonstrated in earlier sections of the report. Even where formal evaluation processes have been attempted, they have had to be carried out largely in general terms. This is firstly because the relationships between policies and objectives are only imperfectly understood, and secondly because both indices and methods of forecasting are open to considerable doubt, which could invalidate the use of more precise methods. This means that a considerable effort in the initial stages has to be put into developing methods of assessing the effectiveness of policies in realising regional objectives.

16.2.4 The third question, concerning unexpected factors, is closely related to a fourth. It is fairly straightforward to forecast and anticipate changes which result from what is known to be happening at present. The real difficulties, and much of the real opportunity to influence the future of the region, lie in anticipating those changes which are not rooted in current experience. In the preparation of this report the use of the Delphi Principle (described in chapter four) was an acknowledgement of this. We think that this, and allied approaches, could be taken forward as part of the monitoring process, in association with similar work at national and local levels.

16.2.5 The final question looks at the improvements that could be made. It is, perhaps, the most difficult to explain. It requires the continued injection of fresh thinking into the ideas and methods used for forward planning, and also presumes a willingness for the results to be applied to the future of the region. This will not be easy to achieve. Where the results present a challenge to established methods and routines, the possibility of too facile a rejection must always exist. Much will, therefore, depend on both the presentation of new thoughts and ideas, and the further growth of that general climate of goodwill and readiness to listen which we have found in the preparation of this report.

16.2.6 The translation of this approach to monitoring to the practical circumstances of the region needs to be considered. The resources will be small, both in manpower and finance. The effect of local government reorganisation is to produce only three county planning authorities, which can be expected to be preoccupied with internal questions in their early years. In the terms presented here, the most practical solution could lie in the joint appointment by central and local government of a small nucleus of staff, augmented by secondment for limited periods. In this way, a degree of continuity would be assured, together with an input of fresh thinking. The same system could also serve to widen the mutual understanding of local and central government personnel through the emphasis placed on their working together.

16.2.7 Local government reorganisation will also have the effect of reducing the statistical basis of monitoring. The present sub-divisional breakdown of the economic planning region tends to mask many of the important relationships within the region, because each sector is centred on one of the four main towns. This excludes separate consideration of the urban-rural differences. In this report we have adopted a breakdown into thirteen areas, some of

which extend across the boundaries of existing and future counties. In fact, our attempt to reform these areas into the new pattern of districts, when this became known, was unsuccessful. Either suburban areas would have been detached from the towns they look to, or more remote rural areas could not be separately distinguished. It is our view, therefore, that effective forward planning at the regional level, and also at the county level, will require a set of statistical areas defined separately and distinct from the new district authorities, and that discussion to this effect should be put in hand between central and local government.

16.2.8 Finally, the process of monitoring must draw on the results of planning work at other levels. Such results are often difficult to reconcile because of the different approaches used. Each structure plan seems likely to use a process of evaluation against objectives. There could be substantial differences between the objectives adopted in each plan and those used in this report. There are also likely to be considerable variations in the criteria used in cost-benefit analyses to support major investment projects. This suggests that a reconcilation of the priorities proposed in forward planning may be difficult to achieve. It would be unfortunate if reconciliation were to rely on an examination of whether or not the population forecasts are compatible. We consider, therefore, that in the preparation of forward plans, every effort should be made to use objectives and criteria which are explicitly related to the objectives for the region proposed in this report.

16.3 Further Research

16.3.1 In the course of preparing this report there have been many instances where better information, or a clearer understanding of the forces represented by that information, would have been a great advantage. It is clearly impossible to prepare an exhaustive list of all the points where improvement could or should occur. We have taken the view, however, that a brief statement of the more important points would benefit both our successors and those in related fields.

16.3.2 The areas of further research that we have suggested below have been identified to satisfy the following requirements:

(a) to contribute towards a better understanding of the region and the way it is changing;

(b) to assist in formulating future policy for the development of the region;

(c) to assist in the future process of reconsidering the conclusions presented in this report.

16.3.3 Serious difficulties have been experienced in the field of **incomes,** concerning information on both types of individual earners and household incomes in different areas of the region. The difficulty here lies in reconciling a respect for confidentiality and obtaining data in an aggregate form, so that the current situation and the reasons for it can be more clearly understood. The New Earnings Survey has gone some way towards this, but it has also demonstrated that a greater spatial break-down, with a larger sample, would be of value. The material available to us suggests a considerable stability in the overall pattern both within the region and between the region and the rest of the country—a situation which corresponds with the surfaces of employment opportunity presented in chapter seven. This relationship needs to be explored in an examination of the social and economic forces producing spatial patterns of income in the region.

16.3.4 The major element of population growth in East Anglia is likely to be **in-migration.** At any one point of time this tends to concentrate in relatively few areas. The conditions which need to be satisfied before an area attracts voluntary migration on any scale must be better understood. As a corollary to this, the effects of such concentrated growth also need to be examined. This research will require separate consideration of the incidence of different migration streams, e.g. retirement migrants, young married couples with children etc.

16.3.5 The stimulus of growth in any locality resulting from a programme of **planned migration** can have many effects extending into the second generation. Sufficient is known about the likely repercussions of this growth to repay anticipatory research into the problems which could arise. A second facet of such research would be into the capacity of towns to absorb newcomers. At present, the planned rate of growth of such schemes is largely based on the speed at which physical constraints can be overcome. We consider that more emphasis should be given to the speed at which the more diffuse process of social absorption can take place.

16.3.6 Over the next decade the region will experience the impact resulting from the completion of a number of **major road projects,** including the M11, the M1/A1 link, and the improvement of the A45 to the Haven Ports. We have concluded that these schemes will increase developmental pressures on the south and west of the region. A research project which followed through the development of one or all of these schemes could assist in helping to establish the precise nature of these impacts. The results could be used to guide future policy, and could assist in identifying what additional traffic has been generated.

16.3.7 Allied to the effects of major road projects, it is considered that insufficient is known about the origin and destination of **traffic carrying goods to and from the ports.** With the expansion of the ports in the future, this port traffic could be of increasing importance in determining priorities for transport investment.

16.3.8 The difficulties of identifying standards of need in various **public services** in the longer term places more emphasis on the constraints imposed by buildings and manpower on the ability of those services to adapt to changing ideas. We consider that it should be possible to identify, by detailed investigation, those areas of East Anglia where the constraints of older buildings and relatively low levels of professional staff create particular disadvantages. This could be coupled with an investigation of the degree to which population growth could serve to loosen such resource constraints.

16.3.9 A rapid rate of growth of short distance and duration **recreation** from adjoining regions is ex-

pected. This type of recreation will impose considerable burdens upon the roads of the region. We suggest that research is required to identify policies which will allow this growth to contribute to the economy of the region.

16.3.10 Several areas of the region are under pressure from **intensive recreation,** some of which could be diverted to other parts of the region. There is a need for more quantified measures of the capacity of the environments of different areas to absorb pressures of demand.

16.3.11 The important role which **agriculture** plays in the life of the region is not reflected in the understanding of its effects. We think there is scope for research on two aspects of this. Firstly, the future of the agricultural labour force needs careful examination as the decline begins to level off. Secondly, there are many potential side effects of new agricultural techniques on the environment. These effects have to be clearly understood if conflicts are to be resolved in the best interests of both agriculture and the environment.

16.3.12 Substantial changes in the **vegetation cover** of the region are taking place, and more needs to be known about the ageing and removal process, and the dynamics of replacement. Research could include a regular census of trees and hedgerows, possibly by the Forestry Commission, allied to research into rates and the economics of replacement.

16.3.13 The continuation of urban growth, redevelopment, road building and deep-ploughing in agriculture can damage and destroy unexplored **archaeological remains.** We consider that there is an urgent need to establish priorities of areas and sites to be protected by a programme of mapping.

16.3.14 There are considerable difficulties in establishing the pattern and effects of **public expenditure** within the region, particularly in respect of current expenditure by central government. We consider that, as a priority, regional social accounts should be developed as rapidly as possible covering all aspects of public expenditure.

16.3.15 With the establishment of regional social accounts, it becomes increasingly practical to research into the **impacts of expenditure.** Firstly, the degree to which different kinds of public expenditure stimulate the growth of private investment needs to be more clearly understood. Secondly, we need to know more about the relationship between different types of public expenditure and their respective demands for future recurrent expenditure.

16.3.16 The list of possible research areas above does not cover some of the suggestions for study contained in the report. These include the review of the town expansion programme in the south-west of the region, and a special study of the Great Yarmouth-Lowestoft area. In addition, we have not included here any proposals for research into the effectiveness of the policies proposed in the report. These items will require priority in themselves.

Continued overleaf

16.4 Conclusions

16.4.1 On the argument presented in this chapter, it is considered that the following strategic principle is appropriate:

F6 the strategic planning of the future of East Anglia should be recognised as a continuous process, supported by effective monitoring, and a programme of research;

To put this principle into effect, we make the following proposals:

(xvii) *a process of monitoring should be established, using joint staff, in association with the strengthening of bridging agencies between central and local government, as soon as possible after the completion of this report;*

(xviii) *priority in the monitoring process should be given to methods of establishing the effectiveness of policies in respect of the regional objectives;*

(xix) *a system of statistical areas should be defined, distinct from the areas of the new district authorities: discussions to this effect should be put in hand immediately;*

(xx) *objectives and criteria adopted for forward planning of any kind should have an explicit relationship with the objectives proposed for the region in this report;*

(xxi) *the programme of research as set out should be adopted as a basis for selecting and encouraging projects sponsored both by government agencies and separately through various research bodies.*

Section G
Summary and Conclusions

This concluding section is not strictly part of the main body of the report. It exists to acquaint the reader with the general drift of the argument in the preceding sections, and to present him with the more formal principles and proposals as a consistent interpretation of strategic choice as it affects East Anglia.

Chapter seventeen, then, is in two parts. The first provides the summary, whilst the second lays out the formal statements of our conclusions found at the end of each of the earlier sections. Here, the important distinction between strategic principles and individual policy proposals is maintained, expressing our own view as to how the conclusions can best be interpreted.

Chapter 17
Summary and Conclusions

17.1 Introduction

17.1.1 What does the future hold for East Anglia? We began the report with this question, and we end by summarising the answers we have found for it. We do so in two ways. In the first of these, we present the main points which emerge from the content of the rest of the report. In the second, we restate, in the more formal terms which are necessary, the strategic principles and proposals we are recommending for consideration as the basis for making decisions about the future of East Anglia.

17.2 Summary

17.2.1 How will East Anglia change in the future? All the indications are that the pace of change will continue to accelerate. The amount of change that will occur, and its nature, must remain uncertain, as it will be heavily influenced by factors outside the region. The most potent of these factors will be the fortunes of the national economy. Even so, we expect that, in the remainder of the century, the population of the region will continue to grow at a much greater rate than that of the country as a whole. Over the next ten years, the volume of growth will be larger than the region has ever experienced in the past.

17.2.2 What kind of change will this be? We know that much of the growth in the future will come from people moving here from choice. They are looking for jobs in the industries and offices also moving into East Anglia, and for the benefits of living in an attractive environment. Others will come as a result of planned movement into Peterborough New Town and the town expansion schemes. As growth speeds up, however, it will bring its own consequences. Towns will increase in size; traffic will grow in intensity and in congestion; services will be stretched to keep up with the demands made upon them. The East Anglia we know today will inevitably become more like the rest of the country, as its environment absorbs and adjusts to these pressures. Growth itself will bring vulnerability to outside factors. There will be a greater possibility that the numbers of people and jobs will be out of balance in particular localities. The risk that has to be faced is that rapid growth will be unsteady, and move forward in jerks, with marked yearly fluctuations.

17.2.3 Can this change be influenced to better effect? The answer to this question is not wholly straightforward, as it must depend on what view is taken of the likely results of the changes. It is our view that many of the changes which can be expected will go a considerable way towards resolving many of the present problems of East Anglia. It is evident, for example, that job opportunities and improved income levels should result from the expected growth. It would be too simple, however, to assume that efforts to stimulate further growth in the region would necessarily lead to the earlier resolution of the remaining problems. In national terms, such efforts are unlikely to receive priority over other regions with less favourable long-term prospects. Indeed, the expected growth will pose some difficulties in its absorption, and in countering the imbalances it will create, and even faster growth would only accentuate this. This is evident in the environments of the region, which will require much more conscious management to retain their attractiveness. In our view, this indicates that policies directed towards the pursuit of growth in purely numerical terms should be subordinated to policies which are deliberately selective in the composition and location of growth. The nature and location of growth and change is likely to be much more significant than the actual volume, in determining the extent to which East Anglia is able to make the best use of the opportunities which its favourable prospects offer for the future.

17.2.4 Where is this growth likely to occur, and who will benefit from it? A number of factors are important in answering these two questions. The continuing outward spread of the influence of the London metropolitan area will bring more pressure on the south and west of East Anglia. The four major towns of Norwich,

149

Ipswich, Cambridge and Peterborough will continue to attract jobs, particularly in offices and services for the areas around them. Peterborough, in particular, will emerge as a much more important centre for an area extending well beyond the boundaries of the region, as the New Town is developed. Similarly, the town expansion schemes should show increased vigour in the employment and services which they can offer to people living in and around them. Highway construction outside the region, and across it to the ports, will bring traffic, both industrial and recreational, and more pressure for development. It is probable that only a small minority of people living in the region will suffer major disruption from the direct effects of these changes. Many more will regret that the places they grew up in will change dramatically over the years. For others, the possibility of a variety of jobs, particularly for school-leavers, and services of a higher standard, will be important. Indeed, in these terms, we expect that almost all of the region will benefit. What has to be recognised, however, is that these benefits will not be equally spread. Those areas with the most opportunities at present stand to gain most from the changes which can be expected, with fewer benefits going to those areas which at present are at a disadvantage.

17.2.5 What changes to this expected pattern of growth would be possible, and prove to be beneficial? Again our answer to this question is conditioned by the view we take of the effects which we expect. We are concerned that the disparities in opportunities enjoyed by people living in the south and west of the region, as compared to those in the centre, north and east, will increase rather than decrease. Similarly, the gulf between the opportunities available to those with easy access to the four main towns, and those who are too remote or isolated, will widen. We do not foresee that the continued expansion of the areas within the direct influence of these four towns will be sufficient to overcome this situation. In contrast to this, those areas which will experience most rapid growth will have difficulties in providing services and in keeping some sense of individuality and character. In these circumstances, we see most sense in policies designed to even out growth and change between different parts of the region. Allied to this, however, we would associate policies designed to strengthen the framework of towns in the region, so that in the longer term all parts of East Anglia are within reasonable access of an urban area offering a variety of jobs and services. To these ends, we favour the adoption of policies which encourage a measure of growth above that which is otherwise likely in the north, east, and centre of the region, and a corresponding degree of restraint on growth in the south and west. Within this pattern, we think that there is much to be gained from concentrating some of this growth into a limited number of secondary centres and small towns. This could provide a better range of jobs and services to those people living in the rural areas, where jobs in agriculture have been declining. We also think it could assist in securing a system of public transport more in keeping with the nature of East Anglia.

17.2.6 What other changes could have a substantial effect on the way in which people live in East Anglia? Looking back over the postwar period, perhaps the two most dramatic changes in the way people live have come from the more widespread use of the private car, and the introduction of television. Both of these changes have enriched people's lives, by extending their interests and the activities they can enjoy. It is no coincidence that they are both in communications—one concerned with how people move from place to place, and the other with the instant trans- mission of visual information. We expect that communications will continue to contribute fairly dramatic changes, though with a somewhat different emphasis. One of these could come from the recognition that, for various reasons, a substantial proportion of people will not have use of a private car to move from place to place, and that public transport will have to be remodelled to cope with their needs. This in itself will require a period of experiment and innovation to find appropriate solutions. In addition to this, more stress is likely on means of bringing information of all kinds to people, even in areas which are remote at present. We think the technology and the need exist, and what remains is for a concerted effort in the public sector to produce a network of telecommunications which would be as important to the region of the future as the railways and waterways were in the past, and as its roads are at present.

17.2.7 Are there any other activities of the public sector which should be considered? We have indicated above that in the building of roads, in the provision of public transport, and in the construction of any telecommunications network, the de- cisions taken by public bodies will tend to dictate the course and nature of what happens. The same pattern is found in other fields. Education, health, and social services are largely the province of public bodies, and decisions taken by those elected or nominated on behalf of the community will have a large effect on the services which are provided, and the extent to which future needs are satisfied. In the housing field, the private sector, particularly through owner-occupation, is more important. The public sector still has a major role to play, not only in meeting the needs of those who are at a disadvantage, through low incomes or other reasons, but also in ensuring the stability of the financial structure which supports the private sector. Even in shopping and employment, which fall largely to the private sector, the public sector has a supporting role in guiding new shopping developments, and in promoting industrial and office development to provide jobs locally.

17.2.8 How can the public sector use the influence it has to the best effect? This is not the place in which to try to identify the nature of the best educational or housing or shopping policies for East Anglia for the remainder of the century. The only certainty is that ideas in these and other fields will continue to change and develop. We have, therefore, to approach the answer to this question from other directions. If ideas on the best policies will change, we have to consider what policies on buildings and staffing will allow different approaches to be introduced. We have also to consider how the particular circumstances of East Anglia will require national policies to be modified in practice. Finally, and perhaps most importantly, we have to recognise that each of these services cannot be considered in isolation, but much more in terms of their joint contribution to the fabric of people's lives.

17.2.9 What conclusions have we reached? First of all, we see a need for services to become much more integrated, both in the locations they choose for investment, and in the way they carry out complementary functions. This applies particularly in the circumstances of East Anglia, where a high proportion of the people do not live in towns, and where access to specialist facilities, such as hospitals or polytechnics, is much more difficult. The same argument leads also to the conclusion that national policies in these fields have to be adjusted to the needs of rural areas. Heavy investment in large units of provision will reach a smaller proportion of the people than the same expenditure in smaller units and in mobile facilities. We also take the view that heavy investment in big units tends to reinforce, and to commit resources to, those areas already experiencing rapid growth, and that the more static areas will tend to fall further behind, unable to adapt readily to current ideas on how services should be provided. In each of these ways, we think that the major influence which the public sector exercises over people's lives could be used to good effect by imaginative and constructive policy making.

17.2.10 Will East Anglia continue to be an attractive place to live in? We are aware that for many people this is an important question about the future. Many of the newcomers to the region have moved here because they like the charm of its towns, the coasts, and the countryside, and many of those who arrive in the future will do so for the same reasons. We know, however, that the change and the growth which they represent will make East Anglia more like other places. For some, this will mean that growth should be resisted, and the opportunities which it brings should be forgone. Whether or not we sympathise with this point of view, we do not think it is practicable. Much of the change and growth that is coming cannot be prevented by any of the means likely to be available. The only realistic approach is to recognise this, and take firm, positive steps to maintain and even enhance the environment of the region, using the extra resources that growth will bring. We think this is justified, since a considerable part of the growth is attracted by the pleasant environment, and it is precisely that growth which poses a major hazard.

17.2.11 What can be done to keep East Anglia as attractive as possible? The general answer to this question is that the environmental resources have to be managed much more positively and effectively. Part of this falls to public bodies, in being prepared to spend more money in investing in the environment, and by ensuring that in their other activities, the environment is treated sensitively. But much will depend upon individual people in the region. The farmer, in his everyday work, shapes and moulds the landscape as he seeks to produce the food we need. The drivers of cars, through impatience and lack of thought, can spoil carefully planted areas for a few moments pleasure. Everyone can take much more care to understand the places they live in, why they are as they are, and the forces that are changing them. With this deeper knowledge, not only should it be possible to adapt the environment more successfully, but it will be seen with a fresh and more sympathetic eye.

17.2.12 How can all these things be done? The real answer to this lies in having the bodies and the money to put them into effect. Whether or not these exist, or are brought about, very much depends upon the will of the people living in the region to see things happen. Several obstacles have to be overcome. It is much easier to understand and obtain money for an agency which is only concerned, for example, with building roads or planting trees. Where authorities should, as county councils, for example, combine a wide range of responsibilities, it is much more difficult to understand the processes by which they have decided priorities and spent money. As a result, we see a tendency for there to be a lot of separate bodies, each doing a specific thing very well. What is less clear, however, is whether there are effective arrangements for pulling all these different activities together, to ensure that they are consistent and are generally understood. We think that the strengthening of this type of arrangement will assist in getting priorities clearer, and help to establish whether or not the will exists for doing the kinds of things which we consider to be important for the future of East Anglia.

17.2.13 What comes next? We know that the job we have done is unfinished, and must remain so. It is impossible to gain perfect knowledge of the future, or to know what values people will want to see presented in the future of the region. We regard this report, therefore, as a platform, or foundation, on which our successors will build, just as we have built on the work that others did before us. We want the work that we have done to be scrutinised, both for its validity at present and for its continued relevance as the future rolls forward. To do this, there has to be careful monitoring, with people charged to take that responsibility, and the gathering of further information and understanding of the way in which the region works. Above all, we recognise the problem of uncertainty: next year, or the year after, could well bring the unexpected to confound even the best-laid strategy. Without a capacity to adapt and to adjust, even within the broad limits to which we have worked, it will be possible to pursue outdated policies. Even so, we trust we have carried out the task we were set. We must now leave those who have the responsibility for taking the practical decisions which could put it into effect, to judge how well we have done so by their actions.

17.3 Strategic Principles

17.3.1 As far as possible, the conclusions arising from this report have been set out, firstly, as broad strategic principles, and secondly, as policies which seem most appropriate to carry out those principles. This division recognises the need to define principles which can have longer-term validity, and that many different policies may be possible to put those principles into effect. This means that we place more emphasis on adherence to the principles. The proposals, therefore, are meant to be partly illustrative of the principles, and partly to stimulate discussion of how to put those principles into practice. This carries with it, however, the reservation that any alternative approach should be demonstrably an improvement in applying the principles, and ultimately the regional objectives.

17.3.2 Principles for the Future of the Region

Para 5.4.2.

B1 policies should be designed to maintain the diversity, and the sense of continuity with the past, that make East Anglia recognisably different;

Para 5.4.3

B2 policies should be designed to be selective both in the composition and location of growth encouraged in East Anglia;

Para 5.4.4

B3 policies should be designed to be adaptable, with emphasis on smaller units of provision, to minimise the risk associated with a large degree of uncertainty;

Para 5.4.5

B4 regional institutions should be developed, with appropriate powers and resources, to give a firmer basis for the forward planning of capital investment, and to shield the region from major disruptions from external sources;

Para 5.4.6

B5 policies should be designed to build up internal structures in the region which are likely to be resilient to change, by a greater emphasis on securing longer term potential and assets, rather than on realising the totality of short-term growth prospects.

17.3.3 Principles for the Pattern of Development

Para 7.10.2

C1 the encouragement of a rate of growth above projected levels in the centre, north and east of the region, with an equivalent exercise of restraint on the rate of growth in the south and west of the region;

Para 7.10.3/.4

C2 the development of a set of secondary centres, with associated growth in small towns, within those areas likely to remain outside the direct influence of the main centres of Cambridge, Ipswich, Norwich and Peterborough ;

Para 7.10.6

C3 as and when appropriate, the redirection of the planned migration programme within the region away from the south and west to support the development of secondary centres in the central, northern and eastern parts of the region ;

Para 7.10.2/.4

C4 as and when appropriate, the gradual reorientation of the programme of road investment to support the improvement of major routes to the north and east, and across the centre of the region, and to provide a network of routes of good standard between the main and secondary centres ;

Para 7.10.4/.5

C5 the encouragement of more concentrated forms of development to reduce the dependence of the region on the private car, to give more support to public transport, and to improve economies in the provision of a wider range of services to the rural areas ;

Para 7.10.4

C6 the selection of secondary centres and small towns for concentrated growth should be related to their locations at major intersections on the rail and road networks, the size and quality of the employment and services they offer at present, and their ability, in social and environmental terms, to absorb the required rate of development.

17.3.4 Principles for the Forward Provision of Services
Communications

Para 9.2.9

D1 the public transport system in the region, particularly in the rural areas, should be rethought to provide an alternative to the private car, to match local requirements as closely as possible, and to provide a consistent basis for financial support ;

Para 9.3.1

D2 the flow of information between services and the public should be improved, to allow services to gain more understanding of the public's needs, and to improve the access of the public to available services ;

Para 9.4.1

D3 preparations for a telecommunications infrastructure should be put in hand, harnessing the opportunities presented by technological development to reduce the remoteness of rural areas ;

General Welfare Services

Para 10.2.8

D4 policies should be designed to strengthen the range of facilities available at secondary centres and selected small towns, so as to provide a structure resilient to short-term change, and a base on which to develop supporting activities ;

Para 10.2.9

D5 policies should be designed to develop organisational structures at different levels, encouraging the integration of, and substitution between, services, so as to allow the most effective use of resources ;

Para 10.2.10

D6 policies should be designed to give priority to recognising and anticipating the needs of those likely to require support, and to the diffusion of information ;

Para 10.2.11

D7 policies should be designed to be flexible in their use of adaptable units of provision, and in meeting variations in needs, so as to be more responsive to local circumstances, and to uncertainty over future demands.

Housing

Paras 10.3.1 to 10.3.13

D8 policies should be designed, within the context of present national housing policies, to maintain the existing emphasis given to home ownership ; to encourage a specific rented sector not tied to residential or employment qualifications ; and to also direct public sector housing to the needs of those households excluded for various reasons from owner-occupation.

Employment

Paras 10.4.1 to 10.4.9

D9 policies should be designed to improve employment opportunities, particularly in those parts of the region outside the areas of dependence on the four main centres, and to improve the overall level of labour skills in the working population by appropriate training and educational programmes.

Education

Paras 10.5.1. to 10.5.10

D10 policies should be designed to extend the ability of schools and colleges to respond to new developments in educational methods ; to increase the range of opportunities to those unable to benefit fully from existing provision, particularly those living in rural areas, and those unaccustomed to learning by reason of age or background ; to develop closer integration with other areas of service provision, especially training and leisure activities ; to recognise the opportunities for educational provision in the proposed pattern of development.

Health Services

Paras 10.6.1 to 10.6.6

D11 policies should be designed to encourage more flexible and smaller units of care, as part of a general move to integrate the working of health services with other welfare services.

Social Services

Para 10.7.1 to 10.7.6

D12 policies should be designed to encourage more flexible forms of provision, based upon priorities agreed between related services, and having regard for the variety of local circumstances.

Shopping

Paras 10.8.1 to 10.8.7

D13 policies should be designed to encourage a wide range and variety of shopping choice, both in goods and in location.

17.3.5 Principles for the Management of Environmental Resources

Para 12.5.1

E1 policies should be designed to enable the progressive strengthening and remodelling of the environment and landscape of the region in relation to changes in land management ;

Paras 11.2.3/.4

E2 policies should be based on a general commitment to the conservation of all indigenous species of animal and plant life, together with habitats for migratory species ;

Paras 12.2.7 to 12.2.9

E3 policies should be designed to identify and retain sites and buildings of archaeological, historic and architectural interest or significance ;

Para 12.5.3

E4 policies in areas subject to intensive recreation should be designed to keep such pressures within the environmental capacities of these areas ;

Para 12.5.3

E5 policies in areas subject to competing demands from intensive arable farming and local population pressures should be designed to reconcile the conflicts that occur ;

Para 12.5.4

E6 policies in areas not subject to intensive demands should be designed to improve the stock of resources and to allow the diversion of recreational demands from other areas ;

Para 12.5.4

E7 policies for the development of recreational uses in the future should be associated with the pattern of movement of holidaymakers and recreational traffic across the region ;

Para 11.5.1

E8 policies should be designed to secure effective co-operation between responsible agencies, in association with programmes of education and research, and the achievement of levels of funding which are appropriate.

17.3.6 Principles for Implementation

Paras 14.4.1 and 14.4.9

F1 those agencies, exercising a bridging function between executive bodies, should be strengthened to enable more effective cooperation, and an increased capacity to cope with future situations ;

Para 15.9.2

F2 the public expenditure system should have a capacity for recognising and resolving competing priorities, within whatever level of financial resources can be made available ;

Para 15.9.4

F3 the adoption of more corporate styles of management of public expenditure at regional and local levels should be encouraged ;

Para 15.9.5

F4 both regional and local levels should be given more formal roles in the recognition of competing priorities and in making consequent adjustments to the allocation of public expenditure ;

Para 15.9.6

F5 further flexibility in the public expenditure system should be encouraged by greater capacity for interchange between spending programmes, for reserve funds, and for experimental programmes ;

Paras 16.1.4, 16.2.1 and 16.3.1

F6 the strategic planning of the future of East Anglia should be recognised as a continuous process, supported by effective monitoring, and a programme of research.

17.4 Policy Proposals

17.4.1 The proposals that follow are put forward for consideration by central and local government, and by other agencies involved in the future of East Anglia. They intend to illustrate our view of the strategic principles in practice, and in the different areas of concern to the strategy.

17.4.2 The Future Pattern of Development

Para 8.3.1

C (i) the continuation of the present programme of development of Peterborough New Town, with more emphasis given to its function as a major employment and service centre for the surrounding area ;

Para 8.3.2

C (ii) the encouragement of further growth in the area within the direct influence of Norwich, with emphasis on the location of future office and industrial development outside the central area towards the south and west ;

Para 8.3.3

C (iii) a review in depth of the employment structure of the Great Yarmouth and Lowestoft areas, in relation to future prospects of the holiday industry and the environmental qualities of the surrounding areas ;

Para 8.3.4

C (iv) to implement the development of a set of strengthened secondary employment and service centres :

Para 8.3.5

(a) the development of a growth zone in West Norfolk, extending existing town development agreements, focused on King's Lynn and including other areas to the south and east ;

Para 8.3.6

(b) the further extension of the present town expansion scheme at Thetford ;

Para 8.3.7

(c) the continuation of Bury St Edmunds' present function as a secondary centre ;

Para 8.3.8

(d) the commissioning of a preparatory study to establish a secondary centre at Diss and Eye, including the possibility of a town expansion scheme ;

Para 8.3.9

C (v) the selection of a number of small towns to act as growth points in association with the development of secondary centres ;

Para 8.3.8

C (vi) in any further extension of the planned migration programme, priority should be given to :

(a) Diss-Eye as a new location for town expansion ;

Paras 8.3.5./.6

(b) King's Lynn and Thetford for extensions to existing scehmes ;

Para 8.3.12

C (vii) to assist in bringing forward the development of these secondary centres, a review of the future of the town expansion schemes in the south-west of the region, to include the following factors :

(a) the peaking of future demands for services ;

(b) future employment needs of the second generation ;

(c) the impetus given by the schemes to migration above the levels set by the housing targets ;

(d) the possibility of increasing the contribution of the private sector ;

(e) the level of advanced public investment committed in these schemes ;

Para 8.3.10

C (viii) the exercise of some restraint of growth in the Cambridge area consistent with maintaining the special character of the city centre ;

Para 8.3.11

C (ix) the exercise of some restraint of growth in the Ipswich area, with development away from Ipswich itself encouraged to the north and north-west ;

Para 8.3.14

C (x) the continuation of the general policy of restraint in the coastal areas, and in equivalent inland areas having environmentally sensitive qualities ;

Para 8.3.15

C (xi) a shift in the priorities in the programme of transport investment towards :

(a) public transport ;

(b) the development of routes in the north and east of the region ;

(c) improved connections between main and secondary centres ;

(d) road routes where no alternative rail service is practicable ;

Para 8.3.15

C (xii) consideration should be given to the improvement of a strategic route connecting the Haven Ports with the Kings Lynn-Peterborough areas.

17.4.3 The Forward Provision of Services
Communications

Para 9.2.10

D (i) financial support to public transport should be used to promote a comprehensive system of connecting services on a limited-stop basis, linking the major and secondary centres of the region with each other and with selected small towns, at regular and agreed intervals ;

Para 9.2.11

D (ii) the choice of financial support between rail and bus services should be related to the amount of support required in either case, and to existing travel conditions ;

Para 9.2.11

D (iii) the provision of public transport services focusing on the small towns should be defined on the basis of local needs, with communities, encouraged by an appropriate grant system, taking responsibility for the scope and continuity of the local services ;

Para 9.2.13

D (iv) to support the preparation of transport plans, and the selection of transport priorities, local authorities should consider the joint use of staff on a regional basis, using the framework offered by the Consultative Committee, or any successor body ;

Para 9.3.2

D (v) local information offices should be established to provide an improved point of contact between people and services ;

Para 9.3.2

D (vi) these offices should be recognised in the area structure of services to increase informal contact between fieldworkers ;

Para 9.3.2

D (vii) priority should be given to locating these offices in secondary centres and smaller towns, with mobile facilities developed for areas of scattered population ;

Para 9.4.2

D (viii) in the longer term a telecommunications network should be set up, initially confined to the public services, but capable of extension to the private sector at a later date ;

Para 9.4.3

D(ix) such a network should be capable of the rapid two-way transmission of complex information, in sound and picture, and linking all major, secondary and smaller centres in the region;

Para 9.4.4

D(x) in the shorter term, experimental projects should be considered using the skills already available to the region through the local electronics industry, and through the GPO research headquarters at Ipswich.

Housing

Paras 10.3.7/.8

D(xi) the development of means of shielding the construction industry from short-term fluctuations in demand for houses, both through improvements in the capital structure supporting the industry, and in ensuring a stable supply of materials and labour;

Para 10.3.8

D(xii) as an extension to (xi), local planning authorities should ensure an 8–10 years supply of serviced building land for housing, and carry out regular audits to this end in conjunction with the building industry in areas which form identifiable housing markets;

Para 10.3.11

D(xiii) the more widespread adoption by local authorities of means whereby newer households could be encouraged to obtain the benefits of owner-occupation, possibly by savings schemes, and joint schemes with private developers;

Para 10.3.12

D(xiv) the provision of a rented sector not tied to employment or residential qualifications, through either public or private enterprise, and possibly by the regionalisation of the National Housing Corporation, with appropriate powers and finance;

Para 10.3.13

D(xv) local authorities should attempt to identify and to meet the needs of those likely to be at some disadvantage in local housing markets, as a consequence of the marked concentration of groups of the population in certain areas, e.g. the elderly, retired migrants, young single workers, etc.

Para 10.3.10

D(xvi) an increased programme of local authority homes for rent, particularly in the rural areas, with emphasis given to secondary centres and selected small towns, located on public transport routes, and possibly given support through a regional development fund.

Employment

Para 10.4.3

D(xvii) the promotion of industrial development should be encouraged on a more concerted basis amongst local authorities, drawing on the experience of the town expansion programme;

Para 10.4.3

D(xviii) advice should be made available from national and regional bodies, concerned with industrial and commercial development, on a formal basis to local authorities, to enable them to assess their future potential;

Para 10.4.3

D(xix) local authorities and central government should have the joint responsibility for advising firms moving into the region, or from the larger centres, on local employment and social conditions;

Para 10.4.4

D(xx) part of the locally determined sector funds of local government could be specifically allocated for industrial promotion on the basis of priorities established at regional level and in structure plans;

Para 10.4.4

D(xxi) local authorities should consider means of securing the movement of small firms, and of particular functions, to secondary centres and small towns from the major regional centres;

Para 10.4.7/.8

D(xxii) training programmes in basic industrial and commercial skills should be developed, capable of refinement by existing training measures, and placing particular emphasis on mobile training methods, flexible in timing and content, and on co-operation with adult education projects;

Para 10.4.9

D(xxiii) an experimental project on these lines could be established within East Anglia, sponsored by the Training Services Agency in consultation with employers, unions, local education authorities, and local industrial promotion bodies.

Education

Para 10.5.5

D(xxiv) upper and secondary schools should be developed in association with the proposed pattern of urban centres and communications;

Para 10.5.5

D(xxv) school building programmes should examine the use of small, adaptable, and temporary, units, particularly in the field of nursery and primary education;

Para 10.5.5

D(xxvi) support for teachers in rural areas should be given special priority;

Para 10.5.6

D(xxvii) a system of block grants covering both capital and revenue financing should be introduced, along with a supplementary grant for use in areas experiencing slow population growth, as part of the development of an educational planning procedure;

Para 10.5.8

D(xviii) more advanced courses should be made available, preferably within a federal polytechnic structure, based on the main centres of the region;

Para 10.5.9

D(xxix) local further education colleges should jointly prepare a long-term programme to make course material readily available in the home and at work, perhaps on the lines pioneered by the Open University;

Para 10.5.10

D(xxx) the Regional Advisory Council for Further Education might assist in the promotion of education policies within the overall framework of development in East Anglia by their representation on regional bodies concerned with forward planning;

Para 10.5.9

D(xxxi) in providing educational facilities, in both school and further education sectors, the needs of other services such as training, social services, and public transport, should be actively considered, possibly through the joint use of buildings and the development of common programmes.

Health Services

Para 10.6.4

D(xxxii) a review of the district general hospital programme, to include the possibility of using smaller functional units around the main centres, and of releasing resources to allow the more rapid development of community care in areas away from the main centres;

Para 10.6.5

D(xxxiii) an increase in the priority given to the development of the community hospital and health centre programme;

Para 10.6.5

D(xxxiv) the location of fixed capital projects of health provision at the main and secondary centres, and at selected small towns lying on the proposed communications network, so as to gain the maximum benefits of an integrated pattern of development and transport for the region;

Para 10.6.6

D(xxxv) the establishment of mechanisms at regional and local levels for closer and more integrated working with other welfare services, and associated flexibility in the use of resources on a continuing basis.

Social Services

Para 10.7.3

D(xxxvi) the greater use of small and flexible units of provision, in both residential and other forms of care, to allow scope for adaptation to changing ideas on methods of providing the service;

Para 10.7.4

D(xxxvii) the acceptance of greater use of voluntary effort in local communities and its encouragement by appropriate programmes of training;

Para 10.7.3
D(xxxviii) the location of capital projects at the main and secondary centres, and selected small towns, to gain the advantages of an integrated pattern of development and transport;
Para 10.7.5
D(xxxix) a greater emphasis on using intelligence gained about local conditions as a general source for deriving priorities and improving effectiveness in all welfare services;
Para 10.7.6
D(xl) the development of the area structure as the focus for a number of related services, in association with an enlarged degree of discretion and flexibility in the use of resources.

Shopping
Para 10.8.5
D(xli) the main centres of the region should continue to be regarded as providing the main opportunity to select from a wide range of goods;
Para 10.8.5
D(xlii) effective alternatives to the main centres should be encouraged by the building up of secondary centres and selected small towns;
Para 10.8.6
D(xliii) small centres should be encouraged to compete for trade advantages by developing non-shopping attractions, and by making adequate provision for car parking, whilst maintaining the essential character of their central areas;
Para 10.8.7
D(xliv) major out-of-town developments should be considered in circumstances where population growth is likely to outstrip the capacity of existing centres to absorb it, and for a period of time likely to justify the investment;
Para 10.8.7
D(xlv) consideration of the siting of these developments should include the availability of public transport, access to an adequate route network with the capacity for the traffic to be generated, and the potential for alternative use if and when commercial conditions and shopping habits change.

17.4.4 The Management of Environmental Resources
Policies to strengthen and conserve Environmental Resources
Para 11.4.4
E(i) the emphasis in future landscape policies should be on blocks of woodlands, copses, and hedgerows separating large fields;
Para 11.4.4
E(ii) the more widespread use of tree preservation orders, extended to cover hedgerows;
Para 13.3.1
E(iii) the designation of rural conservation areas on similar principles to those applied to built up areas;
Para 13.3.2
E(iv) the retention of a lattice of linear habitats, including belts of deciduous trees and older hedgerows, with a variety of species of historic significance;
Para 13.3.2
E(v) the development of road verges as habitats for plant life;
Para 13.3.3
E(vi) the sensitive control of the siting, form, materials and screening of agricultural buildings by appropriate modifications to present planning procedures;
Para 13.3.4
E(vii) the restoration of derelict land, and future sand and gravel sites in river valleys, for recreation purposes;
Para 13.3.4
E(viii) the more active application of clean air legislation in urban areas, and the inclusion in local authority by-laws of current codes of practice for stubble burning;
Para 13.3.5
E(ix) the reappraisal of current lists of buildings of architectural and historic merit, together with powers to inspect and record structures above a specified age prior to any proposed demolition;
Para 13.3.6
E(x) the designation of 'areas of historic significance' within towns recognised to be

of historic importance, and within these areas:

(a) powers to allow the prior notification and approval of the demolition of buildings;

Para 13.3.6

(b) proposals for deep foundations to constitute reasons for the refusal of planning permission, without corresponding provision for exploring the possibility of significant archaeological material;

(c) a general presumption against major redevelopment extending beyond the frontages and heights of existing sites and buildings;

Para 13.3.7

E(xi) provision for access for systematic observation of major construction projects for archaeological purposes to be included in contracts by public bodies and as a condition on planning permission;

Para 13.3.8

E(xii) a programme of identification and recording of significant archaeological sites, with consideration given to designation as Historic Monuments;

Para 13.3.9

E(xiii) an increase in the numbers of full-time archaeological staff;

Para 13.3.10

E(xiv) land management schemes covering the future development of farm holdings should be encouraged on a tripartite basis between farmers, the Ministry of Agriculture, Fisheries and Food, and local authorities.

Policies for Areas of Intensive Recreation

Para 13.4.2

E(xv) the establishment of joint management committees for the North Norfolk and East Suffolk coasts, the Broadland, the Breckland and the Great Ouse river system;

Para 13.4.2

E(xvi) the leading role in the formation and activities of these committees should be taken by the appropriate county and district authorities, except in the Broads and the Great Ouse river system, where the Regional Water Authority would be most appropriate;

Para 13.4.2

E(xvii) in each case, the committee should include all major public and private interests in each area;

Para 13.4.3

E(xviii) active steps should be taken by the committee to estimate the environmental capacity of an area to absorb visitors and, where necessary, divert visitors elsewhere and harden the environments to accept increased use;

Para 13.4.3

E(xix) consideration should be given to the development of the Southern Broads for recreational use;

Para 13.4.4

E(xx) in the Great Ouse river system policies should be designed to promote recreation, through additional moorings, off-water facilities, and planting schemes.

Policies for Areas of Competing Demands

Para 13.5.2

E(xxi) a long-term programme should be developed to reshape the environment and landscape;

Para 13.5.2

E(xxii) the closer integration of settlements into the countryside should be encouraged through landscaping policies;

Para 13.5.2

E(xxiii) planting schemes should be associated with access for recreational purposes.

Policies for Areas of Potential

Para 13.6.1

E(xxiv) policies should be designed to foster increased recreational use by visitors to the region;

Para 13.6.1

E(xxv) development for recreational purposes should be linked to conservation policies for towns and villages;

Para 13.6.2

E(xxxvi) landscape policies should be instituted in parallel with the changes taking place in the landscape.

160

Movement through the Environment
Para 13.7.1

E(xxvii) a network of recreational and holiday routes across and around the region should be defined;

Para 13.7.2

E(xxviii) these recreational routes, together with the major rail and road routes, should be associated with provision of a variety of recreational sites and facilities in both the public and private sectors;

Para 13.7.2

E(xxix) the recreational routes and facilities should be supported by the preparation of a series of information pamphlets;

Para 13.7.2

E(xxx) the areas visible from both recreational and major rail and road routes should receive priority in the landscape policies of local authorities;

Para 13.7.3

E(xxxi) the development of long distance footpaths, particularly along the coasts and the river valleys, should be encouraged;

Para 13.7.3

E(xxxii) Traditional enclosure landscapes and rural crafts should be maintained as the theme of some recreational sites, in association with rural conservation areas referred to above.

Research and Implementation
Para 13.8.1

E(xxxiii) a programme of research into the changing stock of environmental resources should be mounted to include:

(a) the capacity of environments in the region to absorb recreational use;

(b) the age and condition of the vegetation cover, and the rate of its replacement;

(c) the impact of agricultural techniques on vegetation and wildlife;

(d) the identification of archaeological sites and their rate of destruction;

(e) the recreation patterns within the region.

Para 13.8.2

E(xxxiv) more emphasis should be placed on achieving a greater understanding by the public of the significance of different types of environmental resources;

Para 13.8.3

E(xxxv) the establishment of a regional body concerned with priorities both for recreation and the environment, in association with the joint management committees for specific areas;

Para 13.8.5

E(xxxvi) consideration should be given to a system of specific grants to encourage environmental management for a period of ten years to allow expenditure levels to become established, followed by inclusion in block grants;

Para 13.8.6

E(xxxvii) consideration should be given to policies which maintain the relationship between the basic value of land and the agricultural production from it.

17.4.5 Implementation
Agencies
Para 14.4.8

F(i) there should be continued interchange and growing coalescence between those agencies performing a bridging role at regional level for central and local government;

Para 14.4.8

F(ii) all major executive agencies in the region should be represented within the framework of bridging agencies;

Para 14.4.8

F(iii) the bridging agencies, either jointly or separately, should be given discretionary powers for action, together with the financial resources required to put those powers into effect;

Para 14.4.8

F(iv) similarly, the bridging agencies should possess effective powers of sanction over the forward programmes of those agencies, related to the financial resources required for the operation of the bridging role;

Para 14.4.8

F(v) the possibility of separating responsibility for defining main lines of policy at representative level, and the execution of that policy by other agencies in the longer term, to secure a more effective means of implementing strategic policies for the region.

Public Expenditure

Paras 15.9.4/.5 and 15.10.9

F(vi) the provision to an appropriate regional agency of formal powers of adjudication and corresponding financial sanctions, recognising the wider social and long run costs involved in the spending programmes designed to meet the more specific objectives of executive agencies;

Para 15.10.8

F(vii) the introduction of a two-tier system for determining the distribution of the rate support grant, i.e.

(a) an initial determination of the regional distribution which recognises the differential claims of regions on capital and current expenditure;

(b) a second level of determination of its distribution within regions by an appropriate regional agency to secure improved recognition of regional and local priorities;

Para 15.10.8

F(viii) within the rate support grant itself, the progressive elimination of the resource element in favour of the needs element, extended to cover building stock and based on priorities to be achieved in the future;

Para 15.10.8

F(ix) the reconsideration of the domestic element, to transform it into a variable property tax to support strategic planning policies at the regional level;

Para 15.11.3

F(x) a faster rate of growth of public expenditure per head in the north, east, and centre of the region, and particularly in the rural areas, than in the south and west, and around the major centres;

Para 15.11.4

F(xi) an increase in the proportion of public expenditure allocated to housing programmes;

Para 15.11.5

F(xii) a gradual shift in emphasis in education expenditure towards those areas unlikely to experience substantial population growth, and with the most urgent need for replacement of existing buildings, possibly aided by supplementary grants and more flexible forms of provision;

Para 15.11.6

F(xiii) a shift within expenditure on health and social services towards more preventive measures, together with improved methods of establishing priorities;

Para 15.11.7

F(xiv) an increase in priority for expenditure on public transport, together with a shift towards expenditure on the internal road network of the region in the longer term;

Para 15.11.8

F(xv) the growth of expenditure to support the positive management of the environmental resources of the region, particularly in the rural areas;

Para 15.11.9

F(xvi) the exercise of some degree of restraint on capital expenditure on infrastructure in areas of rapid growth, with corresponding favouring of investment and current expenditure in the remaining areas of the region.

Monitoring and Research

Para 16.2.2

F(xvii) a process of monitoring should be established, using joint staff, in association with the strengthening of bridging agencies between central and local government, as soon as possible after the completion of this report;

Para 16.2.3

F(xviii) priority in the monitoring process should be given to methods of establishing the effectiveness of policies in respect of the regional objectives;

Para 16.2.7

F(xix) a system of statistical areas should be defined, distinct from the areas of the new district authorities: discussions to this effect should be put in hand immediately;

Para 16.2.8

F(xx) objectives and criteria adopted for forward planning of any kind should have an explicit relationship with the objectives proposed for the region in this report;

Paras 16.3.1 to 16.3.15

F(xxi) the programme of research as set out should be adopted as a basis for selecting and encouraging projects sponsored both by government agencies and separately through various research bodies.

Appendix A

Composition of Accessibility Model Zones

Notes:
(i) the following zones are shown on the accompanying map
(ii) all zones are either single local authority areas or amalgamations of these
(iii) zones numbered 1, 2 and 43 to 48 (inclusive) are external to the region and more particularly are either in the South East or East Midlands economic planning regions
(iv) it follows that internal zones are numbered 3 to 42 (inclusive)
(v) the second column in the lists denotes which of the thirteen areas the internal zones are a part of

Zone No.	Included in Area	Local Authorities included
1	External	Lincoln CB
		Lincolnshire (Parts of Holland)
		Lincolnshire (Parts of Kesteven)
2	External	Rutland (County)
		Northamptonshire (County)
		Leicester CB
		Leicestershire (parts of)
3	A	Cambridge MB
		Chesterton RD
4	A	South Cambridgeshire RD
5	B	Wisbech MB
		Wisbech RD
6	B	Ely UD
		Ely RD
7	B	March UD
		North Witchford RD
		Chatteris UD
8	C	Peterborough MB
		Old Fletton UD
9	C	Barnack RD
		Peterborough RD
		Thorney RD
		Whittlesey UD
		Norman Cross RD
10	D	Huntingdon and Godmanchester MB
		Huntingdon RD
11	D	St Neots UD
		St Neots RD
12	D	St Ives RD
		St Ives MB
		Ramsey UD
13	L	Great Yarmouth CB
14	E	King's Lynn MB
		Freebridge Lynn RD
15	M	St Faiths and Aylsham RD
16	K	Diss UD
		Depwade RD
17	G	Mitford and Launditch RD
		East Dereham UD
18	E	Downham Market UD
		Downham RD
		Marshland RD
19	L	Blofield and Flegg RD
		Loddon RD
20	H	Thetford MB
21	J	Ipswich CB
22	L	Lowestoft MB
		Lothingland RD
23	J	Stowmarket UD
		Gipping RD
24	K	Eye MB
		Hartismere RD
25	J	Felixstowe UD
26	J	Woodbridge UD
		Deben RD
27	J	Samford RD
28	H	Thingoe RD
		Thedwastre RD
		Bury St Edmunds MB

Zone No.	Included in Area	Local Authorities included
29	I	Haverhill UD Clare RD
30	H	Newmarket UD Newmarket RD
31	I	Melford RD Cosford RD Hadleigh UD Sudbury MB
32	H	Mildenhall RD
33	M	Norwich CB
34	F	Smallburgh RD North Walsham UD
35	G	Wayland RD
36	F	Sheringham UD Cromer UD Erpingham RD
37	F	Walsingham RD Wells UD
38	F	Docking RD Hunstanton UD
39	G	Swaffham UD Swaffham RD
40	M	Wymondham UD Forehoe and Henstead RD
41	L	Wainford RD Bungay UD Beccles MB
42	K	Southwold MB Halesworth UD Saxmundham UD Leiston UD Aldeburgh MB Blyth RD
43	External	Bedfordshire (northern parts of) Buckinghamshire (northern parts of)
44	External	Essex (south-eastern parts of) Southend-on-Sea CB
45	External	Bedfordshire (southern parts of) Hertfordshire (most of) Luton CB Buckinghamshire (eastern parts of)
46	External	Essex (north-eastern parts of)
47	External	Essex (western parts of) Hertfordshire (eastern parts of)
48	External	Greater London

Note:
Zone 43 includes Milton Keynes
Zone 44 includes Maplin
Zone 47 includes M11

Map A Accessibility Model Zonal System
(*All zones are either single local authority areas or amalgamations of these*)

Select Bibliography

1. General Reference

Belbin, E. and Belbin, R. M. 'Problems of Adult Retraining'. Heinemann (1972).

Bielckus, C. L., Rogers, A. W., and Wibberley, G. P. 'Second Homes in England and Wales'. Countryside Planning Unit, School of Rural Economics and Related Studies, Wye College (University of London) (1972).

Birley, D. 'Planning and Education'. Routledge and Kegan Paul (1972).

Brech, R. 'Britain 1984: Unilever's Forecast'. Unilever (1963).

Brown, A. J. 'The Framework of Regional Economics in the United Kingdom'. Cambridge University Press (1972).

Burlon, T. L. and Wibberley, G. P. 'Outdoor Recreation in the British Countryside'. Countryside Planning Unit School of Rural Economics and Related Studies Wye College (University of London) (1965).

Carritt, E. F. 'The Theory of Beauty'. Methuen (1962).

Chisholm, M. (Ed.) 'Regional Forecasting'. Colston Papers No. 22. Butterworths (1971).

Chisholm, M. and Manners, G. (Eds.) 'Spatial Policy Problems of the British Economy' Cambridge University Press (1971).

Clark, C., Witson, F., and Bradley, J. 'Industrial Location and Economic Potential in Western Europe' Regional Studies Vol. 3 No. 2 (1969).

Coates, B. E. and Rawstron, E. M. 'Regional Variations in Britain' Batsford (1971).

Council for British Archaeology. C. M. Heighway (Ed.) 'The Erosion of History'. Council for British Archaeology (1972).

Countryside Commission. 'Second Homes in England and Wales'. An appraisal prepared by Downing, P. and Dower, M. HMSO (1973).

Dalkey, N. C. et al. 'Studies in the Quality of Life: Delphi and Decision Making'. Levington (1972).

Davies, B. 'Social Needs and Resources in Local Services'. Joseph (1968).

Despicht, N. 'The Transport Policy of the European Communities'. PEP (1969).

Donaldson, J. G. S. and F. 'Farming in Britain Today'. Penguin (1972).

Fairbrother, N. 'New Lives, New Landscapes'. Penguin (1971).

Friedmann, J. 'Regional Development Policy'. MIT Press (1970).

Friend, J. K. and Jessop, W. N. 'Local Government and Strategic Choice'. Tavistock (1969).

Ewald, W. R. (Ed.) 'Environment and Change: The Next Fifty Years'. American Institute of Planners (1968).

Godley, W. and Rhodes, J. 'The Rate Support Grant System'. University of Cambridge. Department of Applied Economics (1973).

Haggett, P. 'Locational Analysis in Human Geography'. Arnold (1965).

Isard, W. 'Methods of Regional Analysis: an introduction to Regional Science'. MIT and Wiley (1960).

Jantsch, E. 'Technological Forecasting in Perspective', OECD (1967).

Jones, K. (Ed.) 'The Year Book of Social Policy in Britain'. Routledge and Kegan Paul (1971 & 72).

McChrone, G. 'Regional Policy in Britain'. Allen and Unwin (1969).

Mack, R. P. 'Planning on Uncertainty'. Wylie, N. Y. (1971).

Marsh, J. and Ritson, C. 'Agricultural Policy and the Common Market'. PEP (1971).

Moseley, M. J. 'Growth Centres in Spatial Planning'. Pergammon (1974).

Orr, S. C. and Cullingworth, J. B. 'Regional and Urban Studies'. Allen & Unwin (1969).

Richardson, H. W. 'Regional Economics'. Weidenfeld and Nicolson (1969).

Self, P. and Stoning, H. J. 'The State and the Farmer'. Allen & Unwin (1962).

Vickers, G. 'Value Systems and Social Processes'. Penguin (1968).

Willmot, D. 'Some Social Trends'. Urban Studies, Vol. 6. No. 3 (1969).

Wills, G. et al. 'Technological Forecasting'. Penguin (1972).

Woodward, V. H. 'Regional Social Accounts for the United Kingdom'. In National Institute of Economic and Social Research, Regional Papers 1. Cambridge University Press (1970).

Young, M. (Ed.) 'Forecasting and the Social Sciences'. Heinemann (1968).

2. Official Publications

(a) Government Departments

Department of Education and Science. 'Adult Education: a plan for development'. HMSO (1973).

Department of Education and Science. 'Education: a framework for expansion'. Cmnd 5174 HMSO (1972).

Department of Employment. 'Employment and Training: government proposals'. Cmnd 5250 HMSO (1973).

Department of the Environment. 'Report of the Working Party on Local Authority/Private Enterprise Partnership Schemes'. HMSO (1972).

Department of the Environment. 'The Future Management of Water in England and Wales'. A report by the Central Advisory Water Committee. HMSO (1971).

Department of the Environment. 'The Future Shape of Local Government Finance'. Cmnd 4171. HMSO (1971).

Department of the Environment. 'Strategic Plan for the South East'. South East Joint Planning Team. HMSO (1971).

Department of the Environment. 'Strategic Plan for the North West'. North West Joint Planning Team. HMSO (1974).

Department of Health and Social Security. 'National Health Service Reorganisation: England'. Cmnd 5055. HMSO (1972).

Department of Health and Social Security. 'Management Arrangements for the Reorganised National Health Service'. HMSO (1972).

Prime Minister's Office. 'The United Kingdom and the European Communities'. Cmnd 4715. HMSO (1972).

Expenditure Committee of the House of Commons. 'Relationship of Expenditure to Needs'. 2nd Report Session, 1971/72. HMSO (1972).

Royal Commission on the Constitution. '(a) Report (b) Memorandum of Dissent (c) Research papers 9 and 10'. HMSO (1973).

(b) Others

National Economic Development Council. 'Agricultural Manpower in England and Wales'. Agriculture Economic Development Council. HMSO (1972).

National Economic Development Council. 'Future Pattern of Shopping'. Distributive Trades Economic Development Council. HMSO (1971).

Greater London Council. 'Greater London Development Plan'. GLC (1969).

Department of the Environment. 'Report of the Panel of Inquiry: Greater London Development Plan'. Vols. 1 and 2. HMSO (1973).

(c) Regional bodies

East Anglia Consultative Committee. 'East Anglia: A Regional Survey'. EACC (1968).

East Anglia Consultative Committee. 'East Anglia: A Regional Appraisal'. EACC (1969).

East Anglia Consultative Committee. 'East Anglia Regional Strategy: A Preparatory Report'. EACC (1971).

East Anglia Consultative Committee and East Anglia Economic Planning Council. 'Small Towns Study'. EACC and EAEPC (1972).

East Anglia Economic Planning Council. 'East Anglia: A Study'. HMSO (1968).

East Anglia Economic Planning Council. 'Regional Economic Review'. EPC (biannually 1970–74).

Broads Consortium. 'Broadland Study and Plan'. Norfolk County Council (1969).

Countryside Commission. 'The Coasts of East Anglia'. HMSO (1967).

Department of the Environment. 'The Problems and Future of East Anglia Archaeology'. Report of the Scole Committee. DOE (1973).

Water Resources Board. 'The Wash: Estuary Storage'. HMSO (1970).

Water Resources Board. 'Review of Water Resources in South East England'. WRB (1971).

Water Resources Board. 'Wash Feasibility Study.' Interim Report. (1974).

Department of the Environment. 'A Study of the Cambridge Sub-Region. Pts. 1 and 2'. HMSO (1974).

East Suffolk County Council and Ipswich County Borough Council. 'The Strategy Report'. ESCC and ICBC (1973).

Huntingdon and Peterborough County Council. 'Peterborough. Sub-Regional Study'. H&PCC (1968).

Norfolk Joint Structure Plan Steering Committee. 'A Survey' and 'Issues and Possibilities'. Norfolk County Council (1974).

Norfolk County Council. 'Norfolk Recreation Survey'. NCC (1972).

Peterborough Development Corporation. 'Greater Peterborough. Master Plan'. PDC (1967).

3. Regional Background

Astbury, A. K. 'The Black Fens'. Golden, Cambridge (1958).

Blythe, R. 'Akenfield'. Allen Lane (1969).

Clarke, R. R. 'East Anglia'. Thames & Hudson (1960).

Evans, G. E. 'The Pattern Under the Plough' et al. Faber (various/1970).

Scarfe, N. 'The Suffolk Landscape'. Hodder and Stoughton (1972).

Seymour, J. 'The Companion Guide to East Anglia'. Collins (1970).

Taylor, C. 'The Cambridgeshire Landscape'. Hodder and Stoughton (1973).

Printed for Her Majesty's Stationery Office
by The Hillingdon Press, Uxbridge, Middx.
Dd 288308 K40 5/74